A
WOMAN OF VISION

A Life of
Marion Phillips, MP

Marian Goronwy-Roberts

bRidge
books
Wrexham

A Woman of Vision
First published in Wales in 2000
by
BRIDGE BOOKS
61 Park Avenue, Wrexham
LL12 7AW

ISBN 1-872424-84-9

Printed and bound by
MFP, Stretford, Manchester

To the Memory of
My Mother

Contents

Introduction

The political impact of Marion Phillips (1881–1932) on the lives of working women and their families, in the second and third decades of the 20th century was immeasurable. Her powerful intellect, personality, and energetic organising skills found expression mainly in her capacity as Chief Woman Officer of the Labour Party and briefly as Member of Parliament for Sunderland (1929–31). Her crusade to free wives and mothers from drudgery and to educate them to become independently-minded individuals, capable of participating in social and political reforms resulted in a sustained country-wide campaign that brought a quarter of a million housewives into the Labour Party in a comparatively short period of time — a feat described by Beverley Kingston as 'The largest mass movement of working women that had yet been seen'. Consequently, when Labour for the first time formed a government in 1923, Lord Younger was prompted to say that it was the women who were mainly responsible for the defeat of the Conservative Party — and one might add, that the victory had been achieved in spite of a limited female franchise, granted a mere five years previously.

A forceful and eloquent public speaker, her condemnation of injustice and preventive suffering was always apparent, but Phillips was no demagogue, and just as the simple, lucid prose of her writings carefully sign-posted the way ahead, so, on platforms up and down the country, her oratory sought to inspire rather than to inflame. Her mission was always to inform and explain in clear, straightforward terms, how steady progress could be made to change legislation. In this way, a new confidence and hope for the future, flooded into her audiences.

Framed photographs of 'Dr Marion' — of a cheerful, determined-looking, bespectacled woman with dark bobbed hair, began to appear on mantelpieces in houses across the land especially in the industrial areas. Women admired her, trusted her and held her in deep affection that lasted throughout her life.

With her formidable intellect — 'the best brains of the whole lot' according to a senior civil servant of that era, and following her training as an economist, she was naturally drawn towards monetary matters and international finance. However, in her comparatively short life, she chose to concentrate on social reform and the relief of suffering among the deprived sections of the population, first as Secretary of the Women's Labour League. Her appointment in 1918 as Chief Woman Officer of the Labour Party gave her so much power and influence in the Party hierarchy that after her death no other woman was appointed to replace her.

Though remaining unmarried herself, maternity and baby care were always of abiding concern to her. In conjunction with Dr Ethel Bentham and others, she set up the first baby clinic in the country. The welfare of school children too, with emphasis on regular school medical inspections, followed immediately by treatment if necessary, and the provision of open-air schools and facilities, claimed much of her attention at this time.

Housing and town planning, she saw as being closely allied with the health of the family, not least that of the overworked mother. All sub-standard, insanitary dwellings should be replaced by decent homes with basic requirements like bathrooms and fitted too, with labour-saving devices. To enact such sweeping changes however, she saw the need for the co-operation and thrust of working women themselves. Non-stop education therefore was the key, and she sought with might and main to provide for them the knowledge needed for their advance. In her own plans for new houses for the working-class family, she included a room set aside for mothers for the purpose of reading and studying. On the same lines, she advocated at the Women's Section meetings that a book box should always accompany a visiting speaker for distribution among the members.

During those early days, before the First World War, Phillips and Dr Bentham became members of Kensington Borough Council, where they sought to press hard for adequate housing and reforms.

Meanwhile, her mission to educate women continued. During the passage of Lloyd George's Insurance Bills through Parliament, she and Mary Macarthur set up the Industrial Women's Insurance Advisory Board, and in *The Labour Woman*, sought to supply information and answer questions about the implications so that women would be qualified to sit on Advisory Committees, Insurance Committees or Committees of approved societies on a central and local level.

In 1914, she was one of the speakers at a mass rally in Trafalgar Square to protest against the coming war, but once the declaration of hostilities had been made, she threw herself into the task of protecting women and children against the inevitable consequences. Her drafting talents rendered her services invaluable to various bodies, acting, for instance, as Secretary to the Standing Joint Committee of Industrial Women's Organisations from its inception in 1916 until her death, and serving on a number of important committees like the Prime Minister's War Reconstruction Committee. In 1919, she gave evidence before the Royal Commission on Income Tax, and in the following year gave evidence before the Departmental Committee on the Employment of Women and Young Persons on the Two Shift System. Her valuable contribution to the work of the Consumer Council included her sustained campaign for free milk for school children.

A steady flow of pamphlets relating to these and other matters ensued, while at the same time, she continued to edit *The Labour Woman* in a crisp and lively manner.

Other publications also appeared. At the end of the war, her long standing interest in housing and town planning led to the publication of *The Working Woman's House*, in collaboration with A. Sanderson Furniss, in which she advocated the continuation of the war-time National Kitchens and the establishment of take-away restaurants, as well as launderettes, and made a plea for a system of municipally-run home helps to lighten the housewife's burden. This was nearly eighty years ago!

In 1918, she was inevitably appointed Chief Woman Officer of the Labour Party since, in the words of Maureen Callcott, 'she was probably the most important and most talented [woman] in the Party'.

For her, the Twenties were more years of unremitting toil: organising the regions, and writing and campaigning on a national and international level. In 1926, responding immediately to an urgent request to organise the relief of distress in the coalfields during the miners' dispute, a major campaign swung into action. She described the event in *Women and the Miners' Lock-out*, written a year later. The sum raised within a few months was equal in value to £6,000,000 today.

The following year, the Durham Labour women persuaded her to accept the nomination as Parliamentary candidate for Sunderland, and in 1929, despite acute local difficulties, she won the seat and held it until the National Government's landslide victory of 1932 swept out most of the Labour M.P.s including all the women.

During her two active years in the House, speaking frequently and serving on various committees — one of which was the Ullswater Committee on Electoral Reform, and still attending assiduously to her duties as Chief Woman Officer of her party, she had doubtlessly over-stretched even her great physical resources in her dual role. As late as mid-December 1931 she was planning a new campaign to bring more women members into the Labour Party and still pressing on with her efforts to secure a 'Domestic Workers' Charter' She entered hospital a few days before Christmas and died one month later after an operation. She was just fifty years of age.

The tributes paid to her at home and abroad indicated an overwhelming sense of loss. The woman dedicated to reforming old wrongs, whose clarity of thought and expression, and ability to 'get things done' had indeed left her mark on the lives of so many. She had chosen a life of relentless hard work, with scant remuneration as the stated amount in her will revealed. She left no diary or personal papers that might have shed light on what Dr Johnson called 'domestic privacies'. The beneficiary of her small estate was a close friend, Charles Wye Kendall, a barrister who had himself stood unsuccessfully for Parliament as a Labour candidate. Mrs Deacon, her devoted housekeeper for fifteen years, commented that her way of life was simple. That is all the information that has come to light.

After her death, there was much speculation among her colleagues about wha' she might have achieved as a prominent — if not most prominent member of some future Labour administration. However, it might be more useful to attempt to establish why she chose such a vocation in preference to a more lucrative one that her talent and training would surely have commanded.

First and foremost, there was her strong rejection of injustice and preventable suffering in all its forms. This trait was already apparent in her family's philanthropic background. Her Conservative father — a successful lawyer, looked after all the members of his extended family when need arose, while her brother, M. M. Phillips, also a lawyer with a distinguished record of public service, was a long-standing member of the Australian Natives' Association and Chief President 1913–16. Her nephew A. A. Phillips, the literary critic, said of Marion '… she was just the sort of person you would expect to emerge from that family at that time'.

Secondly, there was the harrowing experience of assembling information for the report presented by Beatrice Webb to the Commission of Inquiry on the Working of the Poor Laws. This stayed with her all her life, and one of her last speeches in the House in 1931 contained a passionate condemnation of the treatment of sick old men in Poor Law Institutions. Then of course, children deprived of the basic necessities of life always affected her deeply, as she compared their lives with her own 'protected and prolonged childhood'.

Finally, there can be little doubt that the influence of the I.L.P. and Fabian Society, which she joined during the first decade of the century, and the friendship of lively figures like Shaw and Wells, Graham Wallas and the Webbs would surely have convinced her of her mission in life.

Her appeal to the women in the regions was predictable and profound, especially in the north of England and the Welsh valleys, where the duty of 'being of service' to the oppressed and least fortunate in life was a strong strand in the fabric of their Nonconformist upbringing. On Sundays, children collected the 'Weekly Offering' contributions to the work of the missionary societies, returning them with their collecting cards to their Sunday School teachers.

Phillips's emphasis on education was likewise readily embraced by their mothers. Chapel literary and debating societies and dicussions in the adult Sunday Schools had already sharpened their minds. Many read books as rapidly as oratorio scores. Her positive, practical message — shorn of empty rhetoric — that steady progress through political education and involvement in local government was the only way ahead. In matters of health — she predicted, one day, an enlightened society would be bound to produce a national health service.

The enthusiasm of her audience was understandable. Years later, the late George Thomas, the former Speaker of the House of Commons (afterwards Lord Tonypandy), recalled how his mother had cherished her memory, and always given her photograph pride of place in their house. Similarly, my own mother —

a shrewd judge of character and capacity regarded Phillips as 'outstanding'. Many baby daughters, who are probably grandmothers by this time, were given her name, which therefore still survives here and there (even when wrongly spelt as in my own case by the local Registrar of Births, to my mother's intense irritation). For many years too, in many areas, an annual public speaking competition, the winner of which was awarded 'The Marion Phillips Shield', became a notable event.

However, as the depressed Thirties lurched into the Second World War, the memory of Marion Phillips and her contemporaries faded, as the long struggle for the survival of the nation was waged. Then came the resurgence of hope and jubilation after the 1945 General Election as gifted men and women — as Phillips had done, joyfully abandoned all thought of financial reward and security, for the privilege of helping to create, as they saw it, a new civilised society. Within three years and in spite of all the post-war difficulties, the long battle of the Webbs and Beveridge, of Phillips and her colleagues to secure health care for all, was finally over, with the creation of the National Health Service in 1948. In other spheres too, there has been progress since Phillips's premature death in 1932, though much of her far-sighted vision of the future still remains to be realised. In her introduction to the book *Women and the Labour Party*, published in 1918, she declared her political philosophy in the following words:

> The Labour Party will fail to be a People's Party if it leaves its thinking to a few. It must not become a caucus of superior persons but must in truth be broad-based upon the people's will. Essentially it deals with the simple, primary needs of life — desire for home and shelter, security and sufficiency of material needs, control over the framework of life, in order that mobility of action and thought, joy, beauty and the gift of service may be the rule for all. Love of the cheery humanity of common things makes the background of its political work.

The word 'cheery' constantly recurred in her writings and her faith in the experience of ordinary people who provided the 'common facts' for others to 'interpret and transform', always shone undimmed throughout her life.

Acknowledgements

I am greatly indebted to the following for help and inspiration in the preparation of this book. First and foremost, to Professor Beverley Kingston of the University of New South Wales, for permission to quote from her masterly thesis *Yours Very Truely, Marion Phillips*, in the *Women at Work* series, Sydney, 1975. Her entries on Phillips in the *National Dictionary of Labour Biography* and in *The Australian Dictionary of Biography*, have also been valuable sources of information. Also to Maureen Callcott for permission to quote from her article on Marion Phillips in the *Bulletin of the North East Labour History Society*.

I wish to acknowledge too, the National Museum of Labour History, Manchester, for allowing me the use of its facilities and especially to the Archivist, Stephen Bird, for his untiring help and sound advice throughout the years. Similarly, I am indebted for the use, in former times, of the Labour Party Library in Walworth Road, London and for the encouragement and guidance in the early stages of my research of Pat Francis, the Librarian. To both I extend my warmest thanks. My gratitude is also due to the House of Lords Record Office and the Public Record Office at Kew and to their unfailing courteous staff.

I must acknowledge also the kindness of the late Margaret Gibb, former Labour Women's Regional Organiser, for her reminiscences in personal correspondence. More recently, Mrs Sarah Forster and Cllr Mary Smith and Mr Peter Hedley of Sunderland have written to me with anecdotes and sent me photographs and local newspaper cuttings, for which they are warmly thanked

Also to the family of Marion Phillips — they deserve my lasting gratitude for their assistance in the preparation of this book. My debt to Marion's niece, Catherine Jacobs of London, for her consistent help and great good humour, is beyond measure. Through her I have been able to correspond with Dr A. S. Ellis (Perth, Australia) and with Len Fox (Sydney) whom I would like to thank for permission to quote from his delightful book *E. Phillips Fox and His Family*. Through the good offices of Catherine, too, the late Frances Levy, another niece who was closer to Marion Phillips than any other relative living in London at that time, was kind enough to write to me, as did her late brother, Roger Levy.

I am also indebted to my own family, to my son Dafydd for many constructive suggestions, and to my daughter Ann who readily agreed to research certain aspects of the book on my behalf.

I must express my gratitude to Joy Evans who typed the manuscript with care and patience.

Finally, it is my great pleasure to thank Alister Williams of Bridge Books for his valuable advice and commitment to the publication of this book.

Any shortcomings or errors that may remain in the text are my responsibility.

Marian Goronwy-Roberts
Pwllheli, 2000

Chapter 1: The Family

Marion Phillips, born in Melbourne, Australia on 29th October 1881, came from an illustrious Anglo-Jewish family who over the years brought great distinction to the fabric of Australian life in law and letters, in art and medicine, in education and the public service.

One of the founding fathers of their great clan was Solomon Phillips who, with his wife Caroline, emigrated from London as free settlers on *The Enchantress* on the 4th December 1832 and set up business in Sydney and later in Melbourne. Described by one of his descendants — the journalist Len Fox, as a 'pious and kindly man', he was greatly respected and admired for his welfare work among the Jewish Communities of both cities.[1] Early photographs of him reveal a sensitive face and twinkling eyes. In Meg Chapman's book, *The Humanist Jew*,[2] L. M. Goldman explains that though he was referred to as the Reverend Solomon Phillips, 'he was not a Minister of Religion, but because of his profound learning and previous positions held, had the right to act in a clergyman's capacity'. A kindly tolerant man, he participated in all the social, cultural and democratic aspects of community life. His philanthropy and compassion were proverbial.

Twelve of the fourteen children of Solomon and Caroline Phillips survived infancy, and from their respective marriages emerged the Phillips, Ellis, Fox and Jacob dynasties.

One of these families produced the most prominent Australian artist between 1890 and his death at fifty in 1915 — Emanuel Phillips Fox, Marion's first cousin. He studied in France, painted in Brittany with the Impressionists and many of his landscapes bear the same sun-dappled lyricism of Monet and Gaugain. He painted too, at various periods at St. Ives. Len Fox, in his book *E. Phillips Fox and his Family*[3] points out that there may have been a strong connection with Monet, as six of Fox's landscapes exhibited in Australia in 1892 had been painted in Giverny where Monet lived and painted from 1883. Len Fox also refers to Bernard Smith who, writing in *Australian Painting*,[4] comments, 'He (Emanuel Phillips Fox) is an Australian artist who in his best work came closest to the Impressionist love of sunlight, colour and the good life'. Many of his paintings noted for their grace and elegance now hang in the major art galleries of Australia. The enchanting 'Green Parasol' is at the National Gallery in Canberra, while 'The Arbour' hangs in the National Gallery of Victoria. Among his most famous paintings is 'The Bathing Hour', chosen as the cover illustration of Geoffrey Dutton's book *Sun, Sea, Surf and Sand — the Myth of the Beach*. In all of his portraits, especially of children, there is a moving tenderness.

Phillips Fox exhibited regularly at the Royal Academy and his painting 'Reverie' was exhibited there in 1904 and at the Paris Salon des Beaux Arts. Sir Lionel Lindsay in *Art in Australia*,[5] described this as his masterpiece. It is now in the collection of the Luxembourg in Paris. However, the best-known of his paintings and indeed of all Australian paintings, is the landing of Captain Cook in Botany Bay in 1770. It was commissioned in 1901. In 1970, the bi-centenary of Cook's landing, the painting was copied on government notices, postage stamps, magazine covers, wrappers and advertisements. Alan Villiers, in his book, *The Seamen's Seaman*,[6] reveals that this painting had been a strong influence on his life. He talked of a 'benevolent Captain Cook ... restraining some of his men from firing at a handful of Aborigines ... I liked the look of Captain Cook', said Villiers. Cook was depicted as a humanitarian by an artist who was, according to his relatives, himself a humanitarian, always showing great kindliness and warmth towards his art students and to friends and acquaintances — a family quality shared by his cousin Marion. Like him too, she loved light, sunshine and the open air, tirelessly seeking to substitute for the shadowed drabness of working-class homes and schools, brightness, sanity and space.

Closely knit to the Phillips family was the vast Ellis clan. In *The Humanist Jew*, Meg Chapman traces the descendants of Elias and Rebecca Ellis, early Anglo-Jewish migrants to Australia. It is a fascinating account, complete with a genealogical table that is almost a yard long, and a hundred and sixty nine family photographs spanning five generations. Many members cut across tradition and married non-Jewish spouses. This independence of mind is found in an interesting entry in the book about one Esther Miller (née Ellis)[7] born in 1844. It states that she and one of her sisters 'seem to have been restless' and 'although they were surrounded by family ... seem to have determinedly set out to live their own lives. On her wedding certificate, Esther gave her occupation as 'Private Individual'; there seems to have been something of a women's Liberationist in her attitude. Both girls dropped eight years from their ages, a fact that Esther's husband never seems to have discovered. The age he gives on her death certificate reveals this'. Much later, Marion too (though she never bothered to conceal her age) left her happy, close-knit family for ever and crossed the oceans to campaign for women's rights.

Another Ellis relative was Dr. Constance Ellis, one of the first women to qualify in Australia as a medical doctor. She helped to establish the Queen Victoria Hospital in Melbourne and to set up Baby Health Clinics — as Phillips was to do in London. 'Dr. Con' was also much in demand as a concert violinist.

Dr. Isabella Phillips became the first Registrar of the Melbourne Hospital, while Dr. A. S. Ellis of Perth, at one time President of the Australia and New Zealand College of Psychiatrists, was until his retirement the Director of Mental Health Services in Western Australia. He tells the story of the development of those services between 1830 and 1975 in his book, *Eloquent Testimony*.

Another relative prominent in Australian life was Sir Roland Jacobs who became Lord Mayor of Adelaide.

Marion's brother, Morris ('M.M.' in the family) was a distinguished lawyer, practising first in the firm founded by his father, before becoming Taxing Master of the Supreme Court of Victoria and its Chief Clerk, and publishing works on the function of both offices. In 1923 he was appointed Master in Equity and having campaigned for along time for the establishment of a Public Trustee Office, he became the first Public Trustee in 1939. He supported the League of Nations Union and was a member and later, President of the Australian Natives' Association. He held a number of important offices in connection with Melbourne University where he had graduated and from 1924–34 was Warden of Convocation. Like his sister Marion he was non-religious and was President of the Rationalist Association of Melbourne. He succeeded his father as President of the Melbourne Shakespeare Society and was an authority on Bridge, publishing three books on Contract Bridge and becoming President of the Australian Bridge Council.

Morris's wife, Ray, was a philanthropist and writer. One of their two sons, Philip David, known to his relatives as 'Young P.D.' but better known as Sir Philip Phillips QC, directed many important inquiries and commissions. From 1960–66 he was the Chairman of the Commonwealth Grants Commission. His brother, A. A. Phillips was a highly regarded literary critic, lecturer and educationalist. He was the editor of Meanjin and author of The Australian Tradition. It was he who coined the much-quoted phrase 'The Cultural Cringe'.[8] It is still being used, though its author in 1983 believed that 'the cringe scarcely exists in Australia today'. He went on to make a most penetrating observation: that he was advocating 'not the strut, but a relaxed erectness of carriage', adding, 'an over-conscious nationalism can only be destructive or limiting'. He was a wise, far-seeing man, a gentle, perceptive scholar. When questioned once about his upbringing, he talked about the books and constant discussions that formed his background and of the happy atmosphere in the home that owed much to his father's 'dry wit' and his mother's 'unquenchable sense of fun.'

Indeed a happy home life of this kind seems to have been the lot of most of the members of this great clan that surely contained all the elements of an Australian Forsyte Saga.

Marion Phillips was the youngest of seven children born to the eldest son of Solomon Phillips — Philip David Phillips and his wife Rose Asher of Sydney. After his grandson, 'Young P.D.', was born, Marion's father was henceforth known in the family as 'Old P.D.'

At twenty four, after the death of his father, Solomon Phillips, Old P.D. assumed responsibility for the large extended family as well as his own. A man of many talents, he was by profession a highly successful lawyer who founded the Melbourne firm of Phillips, Fox and Masel, where he was eventually succeeded by Morris, his son, who like his father, added lustre to the legal, social and cultural life of the city.

Old P.D. was well-known as a literary figure in Melbourne. He had a deep, abiding love of English literature that was almost an obsession. George Eliot was one of his loves. He was too, a considerable Shakespearean scholar and became the President of the Melbourne Shakespeare Society. He frequently conducted readings and produced Shakespeare plays at his grand house, 'Raveloe'. There, the numerous cousins would assemble to take part in the acting and production of the plays. Everyone took part; some provided music, others provided costumes and scenery. Everyone joined in.

He was too, in frequent demand as lecturer at various literary clubs in the City. The literary flair that was to make A. A. Phillips so respected as a critic, may have been inherited from his grandfather, though only in some small measure since his carefully balanced judgements differed considerably from Old P.D.'s rather extreme pronouncements as he lay about him. Nevertheless, his ebullient approach and forthright comments and generally independent opinions made him a stimulating performer. No one was spared. A. A. Phillips thought his grandfather was 'a highly dogmatic and very testy person.'[9]

An instance of his directness appeared in the *Melbourne Review* of January 1880. Old P.D.'s contribution was a review of Anthony Trollope's book, *English Men of Letters: Thackeray*, in which he expressed his disappointment and emphasising certain inaccuracies. He ended his review with the words, that he was left 'in wonder that it should have been possible to say so little to the purpose and so much beside the purpose, to exhibit so small a modicum of Thackeray as against so intolerable a quantity of Trollope'.

This tendency to be acerbic on occasion was not confined to Old P.D. It was, according to Catherine Jacobs, Marion's niece, a family trait described by members of the clan themselves as 'being phillipsy'. Marion was known to have made the odd 'biting' remark!

But irascible or not, Old P.D. had a certain greatness about him. It was not only that he had as as young man of twenty four, shouldered the responsibility for a large extended family and that throughout his life had shown compassion for the less fortunate in society, as his father had done before him, but there was something else. He was a man of vision.

In the Melbourne La Trobe Library, there is a copy of an address which P. D. Phillips gave in 1888 to the Melbourne Jewish Literary Society, bearing the title, *The Jew in English Literature*.[10] After a wide-ranging historical account, including a host of quotations — one from Macaulay — he exhorts the younger generation present 'to continue to deserve esteem from the people among whom we are scattered'. This comment, one feels is quiet, thoughtful and restrained in view of the immeasurable contribution of the Jewish race to the sum of culture, truth and beauty in the world.

His concluding remarks are pertinent to the contribution of his own family to the welfare of mankind on two continents, and especially to the life-long service of his youngest daughter, Marion, who translated the following words into deeds: 'Let us be able to say to the future: we will continue to cultivate ... those sciences, those arts which are the best products, the crowning flowers of civilisation. We will assist in the making of just laws, in the promotion of charity, in the amelioration of social conditions. We will aid you to elevate to beautify, to refine existence.'

Marion was born in a house called 'Tyrryngsholme' in St. Kilda — a fashionable suburb of Melbourne. It was a fine, attractive, airy house built in the colonial style, with a balcony running along the whole of the first floor. When she was a young child however, the family moved to 'Raveloe' — a more spacious house, built to accommodate the needs of a growing family. The new house contained a ball-room where the plays were performed. It was quite near their former home because one of Marion's sisters — Addie (Adele) told her daughter — Catherine Jacobs, that the children — three sons and four daughters, were allowed to help in the removals by carrying ornaments from one house to the other. The Phillips home was always the centre of jollification and bustling activity. Apart from music and play-acting, outdoor pursuits too were organised on a grand scale. Bicycling weekends would be arranged with hordes of cousins from all directions descending on the scene. There is a faded photograph in Meg Chapman's book of fifteen bicycling enthusiasts gathered together with their machines in Rose Phillips's garden. Marion's mother, believed that her four daughters — Charlotte, Rosetta, Adele and Marion should be given the same educational opportunities as their brothers. Although in those days, there was some form of state primary education, it was the churches that provided the more substantial opportunities and Victoria at that time was a strong Presbyterian State. So Marion and her older sisters were sent to the Presbyterian Ladies College. (It is interesting that Disraeli who came from a similarly literary background in which religion played little part and whose father, like Marion's was a well-to-do Conservative, also went to a Nonconformist school which was of course, Higham Hall, where the Headmaster was a Unitarian Minister — the Rev. Eli Cogan.)

From The Ladies College, Marion went to Melbourne University, which had been founded in 1853, and covered herself in glory. She was the first student to win the Wyselaski Scholarship in Political Economy when she graduated in 1903. She was also the Wyselaski scholar in History, obtaining First Class Honours in that subject. In addition, she was the winner of exhibitions in Logic, Philosophy and History and was the Cobden Prize Medalist of her year. In 1904 she won a Special Scholarship in Economics and History at the London School of Economics. That was to prove the turning point of her life.

In her time, Melbourne was already a thriving, progressive city and when the Australian states became a Federation and the Commonwealth of Australia came into existence in 1901, Melbourne became the Federal Capital and remained so until 1927 when it was replaced by Canberra. It had a strong cultural life and was the centre of vigorous political debate. Since mid century, trade unions had grown apace in Australia and the Labour Party had been formed, making marked headway in Queensland and New South Wales. It held power intermittently between 1904 and 1915. Old Age Pensions were introduced in 1908 and Maternity Grants in 1912. Women's Suffrage too, had come into being as early as 1894. British women would have to wait for another thirty five years before full rights would be accorded to them. South Australia was the home of Catherine Helen Spence who became active in political and social movements but is better known for her novel, *Clara Morison*. Then there was Vida Goldstein who was brought up in Phillips's own district of St. Kilda in Melbourne, went to the same school and became the first woman to stand for Parliament in Australia.

So, when Marion Phillips set sail for England in 1904, she left behind her a country well on the way to an egalitarian society of opportunity and optimism in which a brilliant young scholar like herself could look ahead buoyantly to a rewarding future in any number of fields of her choice. There was too the reassuring security of a progressive city like Melbourne and the support of a large and loving family. It was indeed for her a 'glad confident morning', but it is idle to conjecture as to what her intentions were at the moment of departure. There is no evidence that she was in the least way inclined to follow Vida Goldstein into politics. Did she intend to return, after completing her studies in London?

Actually she did return on a visit of uncertain length in 1911. I am indebted to Dr. A. M. Ellis of Perth, Western Australia, for drawing my attention to the fact that she was a speaker at the Old Collegians' Congress of 1911 (the Congress of the Presbyterian Ladies College) which was organised by Vida Goldstein and convened by Dr. Constance Ellis, Marion's cousin. The reference occurs in a volume of *The Ladies came to Stay* — *the History of the Presbyterian Ladies College*, by M. O. Reid.[11] According to Dr. Ellis, there is also a picture of her in a group entitled 'The 98 Brigade' in the same volume.

Photographs of her taken in the early years of the century show her to be a slender and lovely woman. The eyes though reflective, gaze steadily out of the picture. There is some determination in the set of the lips and already a hint of defiance is discernible in the fine features. One is oddly reminded of Esther Miller's 'Private Individual'.

Later on, in maturity, Marion put on much weight and her face became more rounded, but the hint of defiance — even of pugnacity — always remained in her handsome features. It is the later picture — of a cheerful confident, fearless fighter that became one of the best-known photographs in Labour Politics in Britain after the First World War.

Two conflicting aspects of her personality were already apparent. From information supplied by Len Fox. It is clear that from her graduate days, many went in awe of this aloof, clever young woman. Later too, on first acquaintance, intelligent, experienced people found Marion rather formidable because of her razor-sharp mind and the cold logic of her arguments. On the other hand, there stands the testimony of a host of ordinary folk who found her warm, compassionate and understanding. Later, that she had a heart as well as a mind soon became apparent to Violet Markham, Chairman of the Central Committee on Women's Training and Employment, set up during the First World War to deal with the problem of unemployment among women. In the March 1932 Memorial Issue of *The Labour Woman* she wrote of her impressions of Marion as a Committee member:[12]

> At first, I was alarmed by my new colleague, but a small incident connected with one of the many tragedies of the War revealed her real depth of feeling and put our relations on a friendly footing where they remained for seventeen years ... Marion Phillips had strong views and held them strongly. Her clear, ruthless analysis of a proposal from which she dissented often made me think as I listened, of Huxley's remark about the mind trained to forge the anchor, or spin the gossamers of the brain. Her concern for the unemployed women made her intolerant of compromise where their interests were at stake, and I learnt very early in our acquaintance, in how warm a soil of human sympathy, the roots of her being lay embedded — to value not only her great intellectual powers but her courage and passionate love of the underdog. Marion Phillips had a horror of sob stuff and sentimentality in all its forms. But in more intimate surroundings she allowed the other side of her powerful personality to come to the surface.

Len Fox would agree. His simple tale is easily told: 'Whenever my mother mentioned Marion's name her face softened.' He talked of the time when both his mother and Marion were in their early twenties, sharing a love of books and theatres and a sense of fun. Then his mother lost an infant daughter and was plunged into total darkness. It was then, said Fox, that Marion coming to play at the adjacent golf course, would spend time talking and trying to comfort his mother and finally persuading her to come out and walk with her. During these walks together, he said Marion helped her 'to find her way back to happiness again. It is a picture that has always appealed to me — the university graduate and the housewife walking across the rolling green paddocks that were beginning to turn yellow with the cape-weed flowers of early Spring, and my mother finding something in the green and the gold and the blue of the Dadenongs and the closeness of her companion that re-kindled the flame in her that had been burning so low. Soon afterwards,' he concluded, 'Marion left for England and we didn't see her again.'[13]

Chapter 2: London: Attractions and Influences

On her arrival in London in 1905, Phillips entered The London School of Economics as Research Scholar (1905–06) and under the supervision of Graham Wallas, prepared her thesis — 'A Colonial Autocracy: New South Wales under Governor Macquarie 1810–21'. This earned her a Doctorate in Economics and the Hutchinson Medal. Her thesis, written in a pithy, forthright style was later published as N° 16 in the *Studies in Economics and Politics Series*, 1909. During her time at the London School of Economics, she had come under the spell of Wallas, a distinguished Fabian and a fine speaker. He was deeply concerned with education and had been a leading member of the London School Board. Marion's regard for him is apparent in a letter dated July 1905 to a friend, B. A. Levinson. She writes, 'He is such a mental shower-bath. His intellect is always balanced by his knowledge of and love for humanity'.

The same letter makes it clear that she was already taking a great interest in politics and spending some time in the gallery of the House of Commons. She comments on some of the political figures of the time: 'I have been watching Crooks[1] making his parliamentary position stronger. He speaks vigorously, free from aitches and pedanticism, often shouts and yet hardly ever fails to carry his point'. She thought that the future boded well for him. She is contemptuous of Balfour and his Cabinet — 'Not one able man left in it.' The Liberal Party in 1905 also received short shrift from her. She pronounces them to be mere 'Whigs and milk and water individualists' — sweeping statements indeed from a young woman who had just arrived on the political scene, from Australia.

Through Wallas, Phillips became friendly with Sidney and Beatrice Webb and in 1906 she started work under Mrs. Webb on an inquiry into the condition of the children of widows in Derby, as part of the Royal Commission of Enquiry into the working of the Poor Laws. The following year, when it was decided to widen the field, the general supervision of the research was taken over by Dr. Ethel Williams, a feminist who was in charge of a medical practice in the north of England. Dr. Williams had trained at the London School of Medicine at the same time as another Ethel — Dr. Ethel Bentham, a descendant of Jeremy Bentham. Dr. Bentham had joined Dr. Williams in her practice in Newcastle but in 1909 she too returned to London, to work with the Fabian Society and the Women's Labour League. Another researcher on the Inquiry was Mary Longman, working first in Paddington and then like Phillips, reported on children in England and Wales, and later, on children in Scotland. Their investigations exposed the evils of the Poor Law System and an overwhelming case for its abolition was made by

Beatrice Webb in her Minority Report to the Royal Commission on the Poor Law which was published in 1909.

Phillips, after her arrival in London had lived for some time at the home of one of her married sisters — Charlotte (Lottie) Levy, but according to her niece, Frances, she soon found the Conservative politics of the household irksome and took her departure. Later, under her influence, Frances, to her parents' dismay, became an active Socialist. Frances's younger brother, Roger Levy, referring to his aunt, told me, 'I saw very little of her. My parents were perhaps ... mildly horrified at Marion's ascendancy over my sister and determined it shouldn't happen to me, so my aunt and I met seldom'.

It appears too, that Marion's father, back in Australia was never made aware of her adoption of the Socialist faith. Yet the compassion and philanthropy inherent in the family history surely helped to pave the way she decided to take. Another of her nephews, A. A. Phillips tended to bear this out. He once said, 'Her father was a Conservative, but she was just the sort of person you would expect to emerge from that family at that time.'[2] Be that as it may, Phillips, young and impatient, packed her bags and left her sister's home to live elsewhere in London.

When Dr. Bentham returned to London, she let a part of her commodious house — 74 Lansdowne Road, Holland Park to Marion and Mary Longman, and here they remained until the war years when Dr. Bentham moved to another part of London, and they found another flat in the same road until after the hostilities. During those years 74 Lansdowne Road was the centre of humming industry, as projects to implement Socialism, in particular as it affected the lives of women and children, were successfully launched.

What converted Marion Phillips so totally to Socialism? There was of course the undisputable attraction of Graham Wallas, followed by the revelations of the Inquiry into the working of the Poor Law, but there is little doubt that it was her decision in 1907 to join the Independent Labour Party that shaped the rest of her life.

The buoyant tide that swept Phillips into the Independent Labour Party in London was already in full surge throughout the country, particularly in the industrial areas of the north of England (where it had been founded — in Bradford — in 1893), in Scotland and in the valleys of South Wales. Given the Liberal Nonconformist traditions of these areas: the Sunday schools, their literary and debating societies and consequent extensive reading, it was inevitable that discontent with economic and social conditions would be channelled into a movement with such a strong moral appeal.

In 1900, the prophet and founder of the new crusade, James Keir Hardie, became the Member of Parliament for Merthyr and Aberdare, where his warm humanity, his sincerity and total uncorruptability kindled a life-long love and devotion among his followers. A branch of the Independent Labour Party was formed in Aberdare in 1904 by men and women fired by his vision of a new world and it was typical of other branches throughout the land. They were of course, concerned with economic problems: with the need to secure employment with wages and conditions that provided dignity and self-respect. They were equally concerned with spiritual and intellectual needs. For them, Socialism pointed the way to a better life as well as a better livelihood. Education was of paramount importance. They read books on history, economics, literature, politics and philosophy, sharing Hardie's vision of a new world where people would live with 'the light of knowledge in their eyes'. Naturally then, they always looked upwards — as one miner once put it 'a reaching for the stars', with never a reference to that mythical second-rater 'the man in the street'. Their upbringing had planted within them respect for the individual and a reverence for life.

Harnessed to their preoccupation with learning was their concern for the health and social welfare of the nation. Early on — forty years before the creation of the National Health Service, they saw the necessity for state-run hospitals and state-run doctors and other services. It was intolerable, they felt, that matters of life and death should depend on charity and voluntary effort. They advocated a more informed approach to all health matters, backed by adequate housing and social amenities. Believing in the importance of preventive medicine, they themselves took courses in keep-fit exercises, walked for miles and many — possibly inspired by George Bernard Shaw, became vegetarians. They were serious, deeply committed Socialists, fully aware of the urgent need for reforms, but faith in the future, supported by a warm fellowship, made them confident and happy. Although, economically, it was 'the worst of times', it was also 'the best of times' — certainly in the history of the grassroots of the Labour Party. Before the formation of the Independent Labour Party, if there was one particular need in their lives, it may have been the need to laugh. And now laughter came. Sometimes in gales.

It came mainly through the writings of the inimitable Robert Blatchford and his merry men. Blatchford, already a successful journalist in the north of England, became one of the most effective political propagandists of all time. His superb, simple style and his uproarious humour endeared him to his readers and affected them deeply. He wrote with a Dickensian gusto. Chesterton in his magical book on Dickens, points out that it was by making the public laugh at the monstrous Squeers and Bumble that he helped to destroy them and the obscene institutions they represented. Blatchford likewise, devastatingly attacked the social iniquities of his time with boisterous fun. He and his colourful, gifted team — Alex Thompson, Edward Francis Fay and Robert's brother, Montague — with very little money, started a new Socialist weekly, *The Clarion*, and in 1894 Blatchford started to write a series called *Merrie England*. Blatchford was later to describe its presentation thus: 'We had a splashy, jolly, colloquial style, an intimate style, which the strictly proper journals considered bad form.'[3]

The articles were an immediate success, were reprinted in book form and their sale was phenomenal at home and abroad. They were translated into a great number of foreign languages, winning acclaim around the world. Blatchford's Socialism was simple, human and non-Marxist. He wanted people to hate poverty, injustice and cruelty and at the same time he wanted them to be happy. Dogma, he found depressing, preferring to concentrate on improving the lives of the 'jolly nobodies'. The 'Clarion Fellowship' came into being and 'Clarionettes' arranged all kinds of activities up and down the country, organising meetings and outings and distributing literature. Their gaiety invaded the Independent Labour Party as its members struggled to create a brave new world. People of all professions and occupations joined their local branches: doctors and dentists, miners and musicians, teachers and caretakers, shop assistants and labourers, many of them adopting nicknames in the style of *The Clarion's*, 'Nunquam', 'The Bounder', 'Dangle', and 'Mong Blong'. They trudged cheerfully through snow and slush and in bitter winds to distribute leaflets and to spread the faith. Neither distance nor darkness was a deterrent. They attended packed meetings to listen to Hardie and MacDonald and Snowden. They sang their favourite hymns, often turning political gatherings into revivalist festivals.

It was just as well that joyful and sometimes bizarre elements were present to leaven the serious dedication of these early pioneers to the tasks that lay ahead. Nor should anyone believe that the deeply-committed Keir Hardie was devoid of humour. On the contrary, he would often sing and dance at social gatherings of the Independent Labour Party in his constituency. He knew well enough what the good book says about the merry heart and understood better than anyone that it is laughter that lends grace to conviction and rescues faith from fanaticism.

The Independent Labour Party had a special appeal for women. Indeed it was a luminous lantern on the dark and rocky road, leading to equal rights for them. The journey had already taken a long time — a century in fact — since the brave lone voice of Mary Wollstonecraft had been heard in the land. The silence that followed her pronouncements had been deafening, but one by one, a few intrepid travellers had set out along the road. Elizabeth Fry had shocked her contemporaries by working publicly for prison reform. Elizabeth Garrett Anderson in 1865 became the first woman licensed to practise medicine in Britain. Across the Channel — since prejudice knows no bounds, it was as late as 1903 that a Doctorate of Science was awarded to a woman, for the first time in Europe, when a frail but iron-willed Pole, Maria Slodowska — better known as Marie Curie — dressed in a simple black dress, entered the great hall of the Sorbonne to receive her award. She too, had been totally deprived of the education available to her brothers but had battled on alone and triumphed in spite of indescribable obstacles. In Britain during the last century support for their cause was gradually growing. It came from men like John Bright, John

Stuart Mill, Disraeli; from movements like the Social Science Society, as well as from the women themselves. Millicent Fawcett, sister of Elizabeth Garrett Anderson waged a long campaign for votes for women. There were the Educationists — Emily Davies, Bessie Raynor Parkes and others, while Josephine Butler and Florence Nightingale fought their own separate valiant battles. Florence Nightingale was infuriated that women's latent abilities should be wasted in the Victorian home. At the same time it should be remembered that the women with whom she was concerned, lived comfortably enough, entirely relieved from toil by servants who had no choice other than to work as domestics or as mill and factory hands — often in scandalous conditions, always for a pittance.

The nineteenth century reformers, then, were radical members of the middle class concerned with women of that class and it was left to the formidable Annie Besant, Suffragist and Fabian to turn her attention to the desperate plight of women and children in the sweated industries. She is perhaps best remembered for having successfully organised a strike of the match girls at the East End factories of Bryant and May and winning victory for them. Her articles in her journal *The Link*, as well as the publication of Charles Booth's survey, *Labour and Life of the People* (1889–91), describing the industrial and domestic squalor among the working class, did much to stir the conscience of the nation.

From then on, with the growth of the Socialist Societies, coupled with the growth of the unskilled unions and their affiliation to the earlier craft unions, the emphasis was moving rapidly on the lives of working women.

This change of focus was heralded on the fly-leaf of the Independent Labour Party Report of the Manchester Conference in the Lesser Free Trade Hall, February 2nd–3rd, 1894 just one year after the formation of the Independent Labour Party. *To the Women of the Independent Labour Party.*

Of all the victims of our present industrial system, none are so brutally enslaved as these wives and mothers who are compelled to go to the mills and factories because their husbands can't earn sufficient to keep their families in necessaries. For a wife and mother to work all day in the mill and then to be called upon to do her housework at night is sufficient to drive one to revolting point. All Labour women and men should be determined opponents of this low standard and should find, in the work necessary for its removal, a strong incentive to vigorous and determined action. Women must — themselves study the Labour problem according to their opportunities, and all branches of the Independent Labour Party should try to secure the necessary opportunities to get an intellectual grip of the big problem now before the world. Such women will find a pleasure in helping their children to understand, so that as we disappear, the work shall continue. Seize the opportunity; Labour women join with the men in raising Labour's standard, that real life shall become possible. Do not wait 'till it shall become more fashionable to endorse Labour politics; but right away embrace the Labour gospel and work for Social Redemption.

Social Redemption! The challenge was indeed taken up by women. On 27th February 1900 in the Memorial Hall, Faringdon Street, London, the Labour Party was born — an amalgam of the Socialist Societies and the Trade Unions. It was first known as the Labour Representative Committee and its prime purpose was to seek the election of Members of Parliament that would represent the interest of the working class. The only woman present at that historic meeting was Isabella Ford, a union delegate, but the first years of the new century would see the burgeoning of Socialist women's movements urgently concerned with tackling problems affecting women in industry and in the home. Chief among these would be matters relating to health, housing, maternity and child care education, industrial conditions and wages and equal rights as citizens of the realm. Certainly they were idealists but there was no time for theorising. Reforms were long overdue and they were a generation of practical women concerned with the needs of everyday life.

Women from all walks of life joined the Independent Labour Party: housewives, teachers, trade unionists, nurses and a large number of graduates, some of them straight from university. Among the early members were Enid Stacey, a Bristol socialist, who like Isabella Ford, worked with Women Trade Unions; Caroline Martin; Katharine St. John Conway — later Mrs. Bruce Glasier who became the editor of *The Labour Leader* after her husband's death, and of course, Margaret MacDonald and Mary Macpherson, the founders of the Women's Labour League.

Already in existence was the Railway Women's Guild and though the Co-operative Women's Guild was not aligned to any political party, under the guidance of its remarkable general secretary for over thirty years — Margaret Llewelyn Davies — it campaigned tirelessly for reforms in all matters affecting the lives of working women.

There can be little doubt that all these women moved by conscience and an innate sense of justice, would in different ways have campaigned for social and political reform in the early years of this century, even if the Independent Labour Party had not existed. Equally, there can be little doubt that it was the moral thrust of Hardie's crusade that kindled a new awakening. This was the *zeitgeist* that inspired not only a bright vision of the future but also the will to turn it into fact.

For Marion Phillips, the appeal was irresistible.

In the same year as Marion Phillips found a joyous home in the Independent Labour Party, she joined the Fabian Society. This was a predictable move because of her connection with Graham Wallas and the Webbs.

The Fabians were a collection of brilliant young men and women. Founded in 1883 by E. R. Pease and Frank Podmore, the Society had immediately attracted Sidney Webb, Wallas, Annie Besant, Sydney Olivier, Bernard Shaw, Stewart

Headlam, Herbert Bland and to add further lustre to the company, Beatrice Webb. Others — H. G. Wells among them, soon followed. Before her marriage to Sidney Webb, Beatrice Potter, interested in the problems of poverty, had published in 1891 *The Co-operative Movement in Great Britain*. Then, with her husband, she produced two other works: *The History of Trade Unionism* and *Industrial Democracy*, before the end of the old century.

The Fabian Society was named after the Roman general, Quintus Fabius Maximus Cunctator, who, during the war against Hannibal, declared his strategy of waiting and waiting until the right moment came to attack the enemy, and when the moment came, to attack hard. Non-Marxist in theory and practice, the belief of the Fabians was in 'inevitability through gradualness'. They published innumerable 'Tracts' and 'Essays' on social legislation and reform. Sidney Webb was the most prolific writer of all. Profound meticulous research into conditions would be followed by detailed logical proposals. It was intended that these 'blueprints' should be accessible to all parties and classes and that their ideas should permeate the minds of thinking people everywhere and fructify therein. Indeed, Beatrice Webb's Minority Report to the Royal Commission on the Poor Law, delivered by Beatrice and written by Sidney, drew attention to the social security measures put forward in the Report. It was the National Committee for the Prevention of Destitution which conducted the campaign for the Report which may be regarded as the basis for the Beveridge Report and the Welfare State.

The writings of the Fabians, apart from giving confidence and support to Labour Party policies, were also a basis for economic and philosophical discussions at meetings and W. E. A. classes throughout the land. Max Beer in his *History of British Socialism* called the Fabian Society 'An Institute of Social Engineering.' What was the role of George Bernard Shaw in such a Society? Francis Williams, in his *Fifty Years March — The Rise of the Labour Party* captures much of Shaw's sparkle in the following passage:

> Shaw's contribution was to destroy with enormous verve ... the Victorian myths ... and to clear the ways for new ideas and attitudes. He broke down the prison walls of Victorian social morality and let in fresh air. He took the social conceptions that Victorian capitalism had established in its defence, stood them on their heads and pelted them with fireworks.[4]

How Marion Phillips must have enjoyed the 'fireworks', and the company of so many congenial souls. Nevertheless, there were inevitable arguments and divisions. She herself was involved in one of them. 'The Fabian Reform Committee' was set up by H. H. Schloesser (later Sir Henry Slesser) and Marion Phillips, which presented a report recommending that Fabian electoral support should be confined to candidates who were members of the Labour Party. This report was opposed vigorously by Mrs. Webb and eventually, the recommendation dissolved and peace was again restored.

Phillips herself seems to have been rather amused at the amount of feuding that went on among the distinguished band of Fabians. In a letter to a friend dated around this time she wrote:

> There has been trouble in the Fabian camp. About two years ago H.G. Wells joined and went pretty quickly to the position of a leader. He was eager to do many things which he could do well, but he got swelled head, a rather bad attack and began lecturing the Society on the 'faults of the Fabian', about whom, after all, he knew but little. Then, he managed to have a special committee appointed of which he was chairman and which presented a report suggesting all sorts of alterations in basis, organisation, objects. Then came trouble between Wells and the Executive. Wells, who is thoroughly muddle-headed in practical affairs, had drawn up a thoroughly impractical scheme ... Then came a series of meetings at which the scheme was discussed. The great night was when Wells moved a First Reading of his Report and Shaw replied for the Executive. There had been a great fight in the Executive itself. On one occasion, Sidney Webb and Shaw had talked three hours over one question, ending in Shaw's capitulation. But this time, Shaw, always the chief spokesman on grand occasions, completely outdid himself and overwhelmed Wells.
>
> But the discussion has left two parties in the Society. You are either a member of the 'old gang' or a 'new ganger'. I am an 'old ganger'.
>
> The next election was a score for the old gang, Sidney Webb, Pease and George Bernard Shaw topping the poll and Wells next. All is outwardly at peace but old Fabians are rather bitter against Wells who took the matter badly. He did not show well in the fight. Last week a Fabian Dinner was given to Sydney Olivier who is going to Jamaica as Governor. Shaw presided and Webb proposed his health as Chairman, a funny episode after the letters he has been writing to the *Fabian News* about 'Shaw'![6]

Sydney Olivier, later Lord Olivier, Labour's first Secretary for India, was a shining light in the Fabian Society and a description of him wearing a velvet jacket and looking like 'a dignified Spanish hidalgo' in the Fabian setting is provided by W. Stephen Sanders in *The Book of the Labour Party*.[5] The venue of the meetings varied. Sometimes they were held in the opulent

> Willis's Rooms, King Street, St. James's ... in aristocratic surroundings, in which Sydney Olivier's personality fitted perfectly, after 'the Fabians' had been turned out of dingy quarters in Anderton's Hotel, Fleet Street. In Willis's Rooms, the Fabian Essays were delivered as lectures. If the proprietors of the premises could have foreseen that out of these addresses and the discussions which followed them, a creative revival of Socialist thought would arise, culminating in the birth of a new democratic governing party in the State, they doubtless would have decided that a body too revolutionary for a City inn was not a suitable tenant for a West End institution.

The 'tenants' were certainly gifted, colourful and occasionally mischievous. Sanders continues, 'Before the calibre of the society became noised abroad, it was sometimes possible to lure well-known individualists to the Fabian forum in order to oppose or criticise Socialist doctrines. The result was that the unsuspecting guests were, dialectically speaking, 'butchered to make a Fabian holiday'. One such victim was R. B. Haldane, M.P., later Lord Haldane, who addressed the society in 1888 on 'Radical Remedies for Economic Evils', to his great ensuing discomfiture.

Poor Haldane! Phillips in a letter dated in 1907 to B. A. Levinson tells a rather ludicrous story about him after he had been promoted to Minister for War. As a Liberal he would, one assumes, have been fair game! Her tale unfolds:

A clerk was asked how the new chief had impressed the officials. 'Oh, old Schopenhauer's all right. He thinks we are remarkably well-read. The first day he went to the Office, he went to one of the rooms and found the man there deep in Kant's ,Critique of Pure Reason,. Next day he visited another and found him studying the same great work. In the afternoon, he found the same intellectual pursuit followed by others. It made a great impression. All done with the same book too'.

Marion was clearly enjoying life in London. She had become an enthusiastic part of the two societies which together would draft the new constitution of the Labour Party in 1918. The Independent Labour Party provided passion, incentive, drive and political organisation. The Fabians provided the means of turning aims into reality. Stone by stone, they laid down firm foundations for reform through research, analysis and scrupulous planning.

At the same time, too, the foundations of Marion Phillips's personal future were firmly — if unwittingly — being set in place.

Chapter 3: The League, the Vote and the Unions

In 1908, while she was still working on the Report for the Poor Law Commission, Marion Phillips, predictably, joined the Women's Labour League.

The Labour Representative Committee, founded in 1900 by the Socialist societies and trade union representatives, in order to obtain the return to Parliament of 'men of character' to represent the interests of working people, was renamed 'The Labour Party' in 1906. Its political position was tenuous and to implement any measure of reform, it was necessary to co-operate with the Liberals. There were no women on its executive committee and seemingly little enthusiasm for becoming involved with women's issues at a doubtless difficult stage in its development.

In 1904, an Independent Labour Party delegate, Isabella Ford, deplored the absence of women in its deliberations, but to no avail. Then Mary Fenton Macpherson, a linguist, took up the cudgels. Mary Macpherson wrote a Women's Column in *The Railway Review*, — the organ of the Amalgamated Society of Railway Servants. The Society had its own women's organisation, The Railway Women's Guild, membership of which was available to the womenfolk of railway workers, with the clear advantage of political education. Christine Collette shows that by analogy, Mary Macpherson envisaged a similar organisation that could become the female counterpart of the Labour Representation Committee, incorporating not only members of trade unions and Socialist societies but also others who were outside both. She wrote to Ramsay MacDonald in 1904. The response was unenthusiastic but she persisted. Finally an inaugural meeting of the Women's Labour League was held at the home of Ramsay and Margaret MacDonald at Lincoln's Inn Fields on 9th March 1906. The object was to organise women for Labour representation; membership was open to women members, and wives and daughters of members of societies affiliated to the Labour Party.'[1] Thus there was a reaching-out to those women — mainly housebound wives and mothers — who had no access to information on public affairs as would be available to those who belonged to unions or to the Railway Women's Guild or to the Co-operative Women's Guild. Because the campaign of votes for women was being so steadfastly waged, year in, year out, it was inevitable that these women too, sooner or later would be enfranchised.

At that first meeting of the League, Margaret MacDonald took the chair and Mary Macpherson acted as secretary. Margaret had been a political activist and social reformer even before her marriage. One of her major concerns was women in sweated industries and she herself served as a hard working member of the Women's Industrial Council.

A month later, on 9th April 1906, a public meeting was held to set up the Central London Branch of the League. Ramsay MacDonald was present and of course, Keir Hardie who always supported 'The Women'. Hardie, Lansbury and Henderson always remained constant and staunch.

The League developed rapidly. The first League Conference was held in Leicester when over a hundred women attended and a wide-ranging set of resolutions were passed. Soon, branches were set up all over the country, the number reaching seventy by 1910. In Bermondsey, a seat was won in 1909 by Mrs. Ada Salter, the first Independent Labour Party woman to succeed in borough elections. As Patricia Hollis points out, the League 'by 1913 ... could claim six councillors, thirty one guardians, many women on education and care committees, and the full support of the Parliamentary Labour Party.'[2] Prominent members of the League included young university graduates; doctors like Ethel Bentham and Ethel Williams; nurses like Sister Kerrison; trade unionists like Mary Macarthur, Margaret Bondfield and Mabel Hope; women in public life like Ada Salter, Margaret Slesser, Edith Sellars and Katharine Bruce Glasier who chaired the Hull Conference in 1908. Most important of all, were the host of unknown devoted women — untold and unsung, the real backbone of the League, working selflessly for the good cause in branches up and down the country.

In 1907, Mary Macpherson fell ill and as a consequence Mary Middleton replaced her as Secretary and Margaret MacDonald became President of the League. In the same year it sought affiliation to the Labour Party, but to no avail, in spite of the fine work done by the women in local elections. The following year, however, the Labour Party Executive changed its mind and affiliation was granted in 1909. The League was thus entitled to send representatives to the Labour Party Conference though there still would be no representative on the Executive Committee. Meanwhile at the Hull Conference, the League's basis was defined as 'an organisation of women to work for independent Labour representation in connection with the Labour Party and to obtain direct Labour representation of women in Parliament and on all local bodies'. In addition, in the March 1933 issue of *The Labour Woman* Margaret Bondfield pointed out that at the Hull conference, 'a resolution was carried, amending the constitution to enable the Railway Women's Guild and the Co-operative Women's Guild to affiliate to the League, as they could not affiliate directly to the Labour Party, thus forming the nucleus of what subsequently developed into the Standing Joint Committee of Industrial Women's Organisations', on which Marion Phillips was later to serve with such distinction as Secretary.

From the beginning, a flow of leaflets and other literature, prepared by the faithful, emanated from the MacDonalds' home in Lincoln's Inn Fields. The pamphlets sought to identify social problems and to suggest how they could be overcome. The first League pamphlet began with a splendid declaration of faith. In capital letters too:

IT HAS ALWAYS BEEN THE PRIDE OF THE LABOUR PARTY THAT ITS MEMBERS STAND FOR THE EQUAL RIGHTS AND DUTIES OF MEN AND WOMEN AS CITIZENS.

The League certainly urged co-operation with men on committees and stressed that while women needed to meet on their own to discuss special needs and to develop their own policies and strategies, they also needed to acquire knowledge of political, social and industrial matters that affected the lives of everyone — men, women and children. Consistent with this, the first leaflet therefore, provided a list of topics that was engaging Parliament at that time: the Feeding of Schoolchildren; the Old Age Pension; the Inspection of Factories, Workshops and Laundries, and the Wages of Women in the Tailoring Industries. All these, as well as the work of town councils, education and unemployment were all regarded as matters of concern to *all* women. Consequently, the function of the League would be to inform, to educate and to promote intelligent discussion through the spoken and written word.

True to the declaration of its function, in the months and years ahead *The League Leaflet* —later on becoming *The Labour Woman*— would be dealing with a vast range of subjects from pit-head baths to open-air nurseries; from sweated labour to widowed mothers' pension; from insurance to nutrition; from housing to health; from infant welfare to international problems.

Women were also strongly urged to take part in local government, especially to become members of Boards of Guardians. It is, perhaps in Leaflet N° 6 — *Labour Women as Guardians of the Poor*, that one is most struck by the genuine concern and humanity of these women. Aware of the harsh treatment meted out to the poor in the past, they set out the need for reform in no uncertain terms, but if the mood was firm and uncompromising, the spirit was gentle and compassionate. Marion Phillips, visiting a workhouse, fulminated against the insensitive dubbing of old ladies as 'Grampsie 1, Grampsie 2, Grampsie 3,' *etc.* and sought with her colleagues the abandonment of such a dehumanising practice.[3] Twenty years later, Marion in a speech in the House of Commons was bitterly denouncing the practices of some of the Poor Law Authorities when pensioners were temporarily detained in hospital.[4]

The modern provision for the elderly in local authority residential homes, would without doubt, be the kind of establishment that the Labour Women's Movement envisaged so long ago. Then it was a distant goal, but in the meantime, being women of great practical good sense, they applied themselves to perform every immediate worthwhile task, starting, as it were, 'at their feet'. Marion Phillips, who was later to write *How to do the work of the League*, was an example of this. She never left a stone, nor indeed, a pebble unturned. These women appear to have beheld much virtue in the solutions of Mr. Dick in *David Copperfield* to pressing problems. It will be recalled that when Betsy Trotwood is suddenly confronted by the grimy, tearful face of the little runaway boy, who is seeking sanctuary at her home, she appeals to Mr. Dick for advice: '…what shall I do with him?' 'I should wash him,' he replies.

On the same practical lines, since the League women were deeply concerned with problems of health and nutrition, they produced a simple cookery book which they sold for sixpence. It was small — only six inches by four inches with a green cloth cover bearing the words, *My Favourite Recipes* — it sold well — going into three editions by 1912, and was excellent value for sixpence. The recipes themselves are very short, simple, economical and 'no nonsense', and therefore very useful for busy mothers. Many were submitted by eminent Labour women. Mrs. Keir Hardie, Mrs. J. R. MacDonald, Mrs. Mary Middleton, Mrs. Will Crooks, Mrs. Bruce Glasier were among the contributors. *Every* contributor, however, was a member of the Labour Party. There is even a vegetarian section in which 'Mrs. S. W. Thomas (Todmorden)' introduces her readers to 'Vigour Pie', which I am sure was appreciated by one and all.

The Women's Movement supported any project that brought hope and happiness into the lives of the deprived. Practical remedies had more meaning for them than defiant gestures. They did not burn their corsets. They set up a Baby Clinic instead.

In 1910, Marion Phillips, having completed her work on the Report for the Poor Law Commission, became more specifically involved with the question of women's franchise when she became the Secretary of the National Union of Suffrage Societies.

The National Union of Suffrage Societies, embodying five hundred affiliated suffrage societies of determined women, had been formed in 1897. Their President was Millicent Fawcett who had been battling on since 1867 when the first petition had been presented to Parliament by John Stuart Mill. Since those early days, convinced that votes for women could only be obtained through constitutional means, she had schooled herself in all the techniques of parliamentary procedure, and in spite of all reversals, had refused to be beaten. Throughout the years, she addressed huge gatherings, never failing to impress politicians of all parties by her sincerity and steadfast advocacy of the view that victory would come, one day, through democratic means. The headquarters of the National Union of Suffrage Societies was at Great Smith Street and with the help of Lydia Becker, the political secretary of the Suffrage Societies and a strong committee that included Eleanor Rathbone, Mrs. Corbett Ashby, Maud Royden, Margaret Ashton and Lady Frances Balfour, she carried on her campaign. Arthur Henderson, a staunch supporter of women's rights worked closely with Millicent Fawcett whose realism and respect for the democratic process, he admired.

In the meantime, Mrs. Pankhurst's movement — the Women's Suffrage and Political Union had been formed in Manchester in 1903 when she belonged to the Independent Labour Party. Already, however, opposition to her views and militant methods were being voiced by the Socialist women and Mrs. Pankhurst took her departure. Margaret Bondfield, Mary Macarthur, Jennie Baker, and Margaret Llewelyn Davies of the Co-operative Women's Guild supported the people's Suffrage Association in favour of complete adult suffrage, a goal to be pursued through constitutional and traditional methods. The official policy of the Labour Party from the outset had backed this view and the Belfast Conference of 1907 vigorously reaffirmed its total support for it. However, opinions were divided: Hardie and Lansbury in their enthusiasm to secure votes for women backed the Pankhurst line of a limited franchise, impatient to secure some sort of justice, as they saw it.

There were divisions too, within the League, but when Marion went to work for the National Union of Suffrage Societies, the increasing militancy of Mrs. Pankhurst's Women's Suffrage and Political Union was causing the rapid evaporation of sympathy for the women's cause.

Matters had, indeed, taken a turn for the worse since 1906, causing Churchill to say in 1909, 'I am bound to say, I think your cause has marched backwards.' In 1908, Mrs. Pankhurst was jailed three times as violence increased. Public property was vandalised and the fury of the Women's Suffrage and Political Union was directed not only at Liberal politicians, who were physically attacked, but at leading figures in the Labour Party as well. Henderson was one of those who did not escape their wrath.

During the time Phillips worked with Mrs. Fawcett's movement, the violence escalated, reaching its peak in 1912 and 1913. What became clear to more and more people now was that Mrs. Pankhurst and her supporters would have been satisfied if women had been accorded the franchise on the same terms as those men who already had the vote. In other words, the lower reaches of society — the working class of both sexes were no concern of hers. Indeed, it has been widely held that many of her supporters were actually opposed to giving the vote to women of the 'lower classes' as this might damage the servant situation. It was, therefore, natural that the Labour Party, supporting votes for everyone over twenty-one, should incur their fury. This growing realisation, as well as the increasingly dangerous tactics of the militants, now caused many of those most committed to the women's cause to abandon the Women's Suffrage and Political Union. The Pethick Lawrences, who had not only supported Mrs. Pankhurst solidly but had always paid the fines incurred by her followers until the money ran out, now left her movement. Charlotte Despard, a champion of children's welfare and a member of the Independent Labour Party left at the same time. Mrs. Despard, of Irish descent and the sister of Field Marshal French, was a distinguished and well-loved figure at women's meetings up and down the country. She would charm her audience by her appearance as much as by her oratory. She was tall, extremely thin and usually wore a cape and sandals. Occasionally, she wore a mantilla which added to her attraction as she spoke passionately about 'Socialism, Women's Rights and Vegetarianism'. Later she formed The Women's Freedom League — a short-lived enterprise. Her welfare work and her contributions to *The League Leaflet* and *The Labour Woman* and the activities of the Women's Labour League were of more lasting significance.

Denying the vote to women must have been incomprehensible to Marion Phillips, coming as she did from a country where women had long since been enfranchised. Vida Goldstein, her school friend was to become an Australian member of Parliament. She was, therefore, totally committed to securing votes for women in this country, in the quickest possible time. The best route to this end was a matter for conjecture for individual members of the Women's Labour League, as it was for members of the Independent Labour Party. The Women's Labour League Conference in January 1911 settled the matter irrevocably for Phillips, Dr. Ethel Bentham and Maud Ward and the rest of the League members. The Conference decided overwhelmingly in favour of full enfranchisement of men and women — full adult suffrage.

Phillips left the National Union of Suffrage Societies in the summer of 1911, but she was to keep the suffrage issue continuously to the fore in *The League Leaflet* and *The Labour Woman* which she edited from 1912 — 1932, and in meetings such as 'The Conference of Working Women's Organisations' convened by 'The People's Suffrage Federation' in 1911 and 'The Joint Campaign Committee for Securing Women's Suffrage' on a broad and democratic basis.

In an article entitled 'Labour Women and the next steps to Women's Suffrage' in The *League Leaflet*, of January 1913, she makes the following unequivocal declaration:

> We stand therefore, we of the League with a policy clear as daylight. A Government Bill granting manhood and womanhood suffrage, *there* is the strong demand of the workers. We will play with no other promises, work for no other compromises. The Labour Party has set its face against treachery and we have the Conference's [Labour] splendid declaration which lifts the Labour Party clear above all other political parties in its faith in the equality and comradeship of women.

The rest of the article is an impassioned plea for the political equality of men and women. She argues that in it

> ... lies the hope of release and freedom to the enslaved, whether enslaved by poverty or ignorance or weakness. There is only one side of the Women's Movement which is our concern — and that is the world's concern — and that is the side where women's cause marches with the workers' cause, the cause of homes made desolate by poverty, of children stunted and wearied before life has begun for them, of women growing old before maturity should have been reached, of wives and husbands straining old affections by the constant anxiety of

tomorrow's needs, of men and women looking with wan eyes as happiness is lost in the struggles of material want ... we want it not to have, but to *use* ...Our work is to drive home into the great slow-moving public, that we are honestly and surely convinced that we could do much to better the home conditions of the nation if we could get political power into the hands of the mothers as well as the fathers ...

Let us follow the paths of right and justice. Let us still show and explain and persuade. Let us win the way to the minds and hearts of those who make public opinion, who form the national will.

In 1913 too, the League Executive decided on 31st March to send the Prime Minister, the Chancellor of the Exchequer, the People's Suffrage Federation and the Labour Party, resolutions demanding immediate Government action to grant women the vote. Indeed, throughout those pre-war years, Marion Phillips was prominently involved in the cause of suffrage on the Westminster scene. She was particularly concerned about the coercion of women and the disgraceful 'Cat and Mouse' Act. She was, of course, as strongly opposed to the militant tactics of the Women's Suffrage and Political Union as she had ever been, but like most women shaken by the tragic death of Emily Wilding Davison, who threw herself under one of the horses in the Derby. Phillips wrote movingly about her martyrdom and heroism in the July 1913 edition of *The Labour Woman*.

Her time with the Suffrage Societies came to an end, when, in June 1911 she was invited to work with Mary Macarthur as organising Secretary of the National Federation of Women Workers. Mary Macarthur, Gertrude Tuckwell and Julia Varley — all representing the Women's Trades Union League, were also members of the Independent Labour Party, so close links were maintained between the two movements and of course with the Women's Labour League, with Mary Macarthur often writing a column in *The League Leaflet*.

It was intended that Phillips would deal with the complicated negotiations affecting the Unions, arising from the Chancellor's Insurance Bill. That Bill, presented to the House in May 1911, was described by Mr. Lloyd George as 'a measure that will relieve untold misery in myriads of homes ... and which will arm the nation to fight until it conquers 'the pestilence that walketh in darkness and the destruction that wasteth at noon day'.' It was modelled on Bismark's Health Scheme but less hemmed in by bureaucracy than its German prototype.

The Bill was indeed welcomed at first by all with great goodwill as a far-reaching measure of social reform. The sickness and invalidity section of the Bill, it was anticipated, would affect fifteen million people. The unemployment part of the Bill was confined to the building and engineering trades. It provided that the worker should contribute 2d a week, the employer, the same amount and the State should supply a quarter of the total cost. Favourable comment came from abroad. President Taft said that the Chancellor had 'translated the twenty-fifth chapter of St. Matthew into practical legislation.' Equally laudatory were the comments of the German Labour Party.

Soon, however, the euphoria gave place to a storm of criticism, partly due to antagonism, partly due to misrepresentation. There was also genuine concern. Many amendments were moved during the Committee Stage and a division was challenged on the Third Reading. Although the Opposition declined to say 'Yes' or 'No', they voted against the Third Reading of the Bill on the ground that it had not been adequately discussed.

The Chancellor however, was determined that this Act should go through, declaring, 'I will fight it through or I will fall'. Tirelessly he met deputation after deputation, representing a host of various interests. Among those who sought to change the Bill as it related to the contributions of the lower paid, was Mary Macarthur the doughty fighter for the rights of badly-paid women workers who called her 'Our Mary'. The daughter of a prosperous Conservative business man in Ayrshire, she had, after attending, at the age of twenty, a meeting of the Shop Assistants Union, going there, as she said 'to scoff' but becoming converted to their cause. Encouraged by Margaret Bondfield to continue her union activities, she progressed in a short time to becoming the Secretary of 'The Women's Trade Union League'. Later, she formed the 'National Federation of Women Workers', and could claim great success in raising the wages of women in a number of industries. Her most notable triumph was the victory of the women strikers at the Cradley Heath chain-making factory, which was of historical significance. Throughout her working life, her particular concern was the plight of women in the sweated industry. She was wont to say:

Don't think of the Empire on which the Sun never sets, Think of the wage that never rises.[5]

An energetic worker, passionately concerned, and impatient of delay, she tended to become emotional in times of stress; sometimes unfairly criticising those who best supported her. A self-confessed 'agitator', she may have been somewhat handicapped in complicated negotiations. Anyway, in the summer of 1911, she felt strongly that the provision in the Insurance Bill that every worker should contribute 2d a week should not apply to the lowest paid. She sought to amend the Bill and on 19th June 1911 she headed a deputation to the Chancellor to put objections before him. Lloyd George, apparently became very irritable, according to Mary Agnes Hamilton, and no progress was made. Mrs. Hamilton said that Mary Macarthur maintained that he had 'an animus' against her.[6]

Consequently, in July, when a deputation from 'The Special Committee for Safeguarding Women's Interests' under the Bill, went to see Lloyd George, the Women's Trades Union League was not represented by her but by Marion Phillips and Constance Smith. There would be subsequent occasions when Phillips served on committees with Lloyd George as Chairman after he became Prime Minister. Her negotiating skills on this occasion, led A. J. Braithwaite — the civil servant involved in these meetings to remark that she had 'the best brains of the whole lot' (of the women concerned).[7]

Indeed, after this July meeting, the Labour Party in the House did secure some substantial improvements in regard to the women, in the Committee Stage of the Bill. One example was that sickness benefit for girls under twenty-one was raised, to 5/- a week, and as for the exemption from contributions that Mary Macarthur had advocated for the lower paid, an adjustment was made, allowing exemption for those earning less than 1/6d a day.

Among the other consequences of the Act was the requirement to set up Approved Societies, so Mary Macarthur and Marion Phillips set out to establish an Approved Society as part of the National Federation of Women Workers, with a membership of twenty-two thousand. There was work to be done too, in connection with Trade Boards. Initially these had applied to four industries only. Now, the intention was to extend them to other industries.

It was at this time too, that Marion Phillips established 'the Industrial Women's Insurance Advisory Board' of which Mary Macarthur became Chairman. Both women in the coming years would work closely on further reforms of the Insurance Act, while Phillips ran a regular feature on its implications in the columns of *The League Leaflet* and *The Labour Woman*. Between 1911 and 1912, she was lecturing on State Insurance at the London School of Economics and giving the readers of her magazine the benefit of her expertise.

Meanwhile, in the stifling heat of a London August, while both women bent their minds to their pressing administrative tasks, a strike suddenly erupted in Bermondsey, where fifteen thousand women workers had 'come out' without warning. Mary and Marion put down their pens and rushed to the scene.

The sight that greeted them was not pretty and the stench of jam and glue was suffocating. Some of the women worked in pickle and jam factories. Others were tea-packers, biscuit makers, confectioners, manufacturers of tin boxes and canned products, but one matter was common to them all: they were not 'organised'. They did not belong to unions and therefore, union funds were unavailable to them. They had no savings and no means whatsoever to buy food. Children too, who worked in these factories came out on strike as well, as did the women's husbands who were mostly dockers. The average weekly wage for the women was between 7/- and 9/- and the children earned 3/- a week. The situation was desperate.

The two women made the Labour Institute in Ford Road their headquarters and soon found that they had to deal with twenty-one separate strikes. They immediately appealed through the Press for bread for the women and children. Mrs. Mary Agnes Hamilton described the scene, saying that within a week £500 had been subscribed with milk and other provisions, but there followed the tremendous problems of distribution in the heat and dirt and vermin. She continued, 'Dr. Marion Phillips organised daily processions to march through the City with collecting boxes. Meetings were kept going, assisted by all sorts of speakers like Dr. Salter and Herbert Burrows. At these meetings, recruitment drives for membership of the Women's Trade Union League took place. In one week four thousand membership cards were issued. Thousands of loaves were distributed daily while negotiations proceeded.' By the end of three weeks, increases in wages in most of the factories where the strikes had taken place, were obtained. According to Mrs. Hamilton, 'Dr. Phillips, presiding over a mass meeting at which results were declared, reported that no less than £7,000 a year had been won by way of wage increases, ranging from 1/- to 4/- per week.'[8]

The *Women's Trade Union Review* of October 1911 said that the greatest gain was 'the new sense of self- reliance, solidarity and comradeship which had been so gained, making it certain that whatever the difficulties and dangers of the future, they will never again be ... without hope.' As for Phillips, this experience in Bermondsey was to prove valuable. Outstanding organiser though she was, even her powers would be put to the test in the mammoth challenge that awaited her in 1926.

But 1926 was fifteen years away. This was 1911 — a year of joy and tragedy in the Labour Movement. On September 21st, Mary Macarthur married Wil Anderson, Secretary of the Labour Parliamentary Group. She had met him at that first union meeting which had changed her life. He was a fine man and a stabilising influence in Mary's life. They would one day have a little daughter — Nancy Anderson.

For the Women's Labour League, however, 1911 was a year of great sadness. In April, the League's Secretary, Mary Middleton, had died after a lingering illness. Then in November, unexpectedly, the greatly-loved and greatly- admired Margaret MacDonald died, leaving her husband, Ramsay and five children, the youngest, a child in arms. The double blow was devastating for their women colleagues. They were appalled by the tragedy that had befallen the grief-stricken families. They were equally resolved that the work started by the founding members should go on.

Chapter 4: The Crusade Begins

When Mary Middleton died, Margaret Bondfield was appointed by the League Executive Committee to the newly-created post of Organising Secretary, in order to help Margaret MacDonald with her duties. Margaret Bondfield, already established as one of the prominent leaders of Labour Women, was of course, welcomed by members of the League in this capacity. Then, after the sudden death of Margaret MacDonald and the ensuing illness of Margaret Bondfield, Marion Phillips was approached to see if she would agree to act as General Secretary of the League on a temporary basis. Phillips, in January 1912, was still lecturing at The London School of Economics, but she did agree to act in a part-time capacity. Later in the year, in September 1912, when Margaret Bondfield finally resigned from her post, Marion Phillips accepted the position of General Secretary of the Women's Labour League on a permanent basis and that of Editor of *The League Leaflet*.

The question must arise at this point: why did a woman of such outstanding intellectual capacity and drive consent to take up such a post? Surely there must have been more glittering prospects for 'the best brains of the lot of them.' Barbara Ayrton Gould, at Marion's funeral service, partly explained the motive of her mission. She said, 'Behind all her talents was a passionate love for humanity, a desire to do something for all the people of the world. She hated misery, injustice and poverty ... She built up the Women's Movement with her heart and soul and blood.'[1]

This of course was true. But there was something more specific. When Albert Schweitzer was once asked why he had chosen to abandon an idyllic existence to go to heal the sick in the dark forests of Lambarene, he answered that it was partly in repayment for all the wonderful gifts bestowed upon him: a happy childhood, the ability to learn easily and the loveliness of civilised surroundings. Yet he was always haunted by the spectre of suffering.

Phillips too — conscious of having been given so much in her own up-bringing, saw the struggle to secure for down-trodden working women and their children decent homes, proper health and educational facilities, justice, equality and a sense of personal dignity, as a challenge that had to be met. When seconding the second reading of Sorensen's 'Children and Young Persons Bill' in the House in 1929, she talked of her own 'protected and prolonged childhood' urging that those who had had a similar upbringing to hers 'were the very ones who should be most ready to assist in getting this Bill on to .the Statute Book. They know that an enormous difference lies between the children of the protected classes and the children of the working classes.'

Deep inside her there was always that sense of obligation to those who had been cruelly deprived of her own advantages.[2]

So it was that the happy warrior set forth upon her life's work, first for £1 a week that was later increased to the handsome total of £100 a year. Her professionalism soon set its stamp upon The League. She restructured its machinery, turning it into an efficient, well-organised, well-informed movement, capable of commanding respect and admiration. At local level, district committees and conferences were set up while there was an increase in the powers of the executive and central administration. It became a movement that could hold its own with the Labour Party as equal partners. Already, because of the women's help in electioneering and local propaganda work, the Labour Party began in 1911 to make a grant to the Women's Labour League. But if that grant had been given in the kindly, patronising spirit of 'The Ladies, God Bless 'em,' then it was inevitable that Marion Phillips would be out to change that attitude. By 1913 the grant was doubled — partly because Members of Parliament were paid a salary for the first time in that year, thus freeing some of the resources of The Labour Party. In the same year too, a Joint Committee of Labour Party and Women's Labour League representatives was set up to oversee their finances. This meant a growing feeling of joint responsibility and equality. Phillips, in 1914, because of all the extra costs incurred by the League in the form of office expenses, literature and general expansion of activities, decided to forego her salary for that year. Her work gathered momentum: campaigns for school meals, school clinics, for proper maternity and infant care — pursued so steadfastly over the years, continued enthusiastically under the new leadership. Badges were designed for the Women's Labour League and soon every Women's Section had its own distinctive banner.

The League grew in confidence and prestige. Indeed, the professionalism of the Women's Conference in 1914 made such an impression on the Press that Phillips reproduced their comments in the March 1914 issue of *The Labour Woman*.

> The possibilities are that the six hundred delegates (to the subsequent Labour Conference) will say in a long-winded and halting fashion what the women said in tabloid speeches and resolutions.

Not a bad start!

When Phillips first took up her post as Secretary, it was not all sweetness and light at the League Headquarters. Even before her arrival, there were currents of petty rivalries flowing into the mainstream of activity. Into this situation there came this high brow intellectual. Cleverness often carries its own penalty. Moreover, she was a newcomer — an Australian, albeit that her roots were in London. Most important of all though, she was seen to be totally different in personality and training from her predecessor — the well loved Margaret MacDonald, whose home was the headquarters of the League. In her life time, the work took place amid a welter of Government Bills and MacDonald babies, dolls and delegations, with Margaret herself calm amid the chaos. The picture is an appealing one that must elicit a great warmth and sympathy in any mother who has attempted to perform 'good works' in such circumstances.

Yet in 1912 it was a hard world, and however well-intentioned and hard working were Margaret and her colleagues, the battle against poverty and injustice called for single-minded and professional expertise and inexhaustible energy. Phillips was the right woman in the right place at the right time as events were to prove.

In the meantime, the memories of Margaret were fresh in the mind, and the transition was not easy for her friends and colleagues. Christine Collette in her book *For Labour and For Women —The Women's Labour League 1906–1918*, throws light on this, and on the antagonisms between various factions of the Women's Labour League on various issues. She refers too, to two letters written by Katharine Bruce Glasier to Ramsay MacDonald. The first letter indicates Katharine's reaction to his wife's successor in near-hysterical terms:

> ... the personality of Dr. Phillips is a real difficulty. If only your dear wife had lived to train her ... hold her, *compel* her to less egotism, she might have grown great as well as clever to a degree, and capable ... She is as hard and cold as glass. Brilliant as diamonds are, *none* of us can love her except Dr. Ethel Bentham.[3]

Dr. Bentham in whose house Phillips and Mary Longman had their quarters for some years, was a great benefactor of Labour causes, in particular the baby clinics. She also guaranteed the rent of rooms used by the Women's Labour League in Ramsay MacDonald's house. Dr. Bentham too had been elected to the Women's Labour League Executive Committee in 1910.

However, the volatile Katharine soon afterwards seems to have modified her opinion of Phillips, for in a further letter to MacDonald she announces that Marion had 'Identified the Women's Labour League with herself and toils for it untiringly ... we have accepted Dr. Phillips' amazing energy and powerful lead as the only thing to do in very difficult circumstances.'[4] Faint praise, perhaps but not altogether damning. Perhaps Marion's rimless glasses which she wore in those early days, like Susan Lawrence's monocle, gave an appearance of austerity and coldness. Violet Markham too, during the War when she first met Phillips said she was 'rather alarmed' by her but soon discovered her 'real depth of feeling' and 'human sympathy' as did the hosts of women with whom she worked. The 'motherly Dr. Phillips' described by constituents in Sunderland ill fits Katharine's description of her. The likelihood however is that Katharine had a good relationship with Marion who gladly published her articles in *The Labour Woman* praising her too, for her tireless battle to secure pit-head baths and other reforms.

Christine Collette in further reference to the change of leadership says that Margaret Bondfield in 1912 felt that she, as Organising Secretary, 'had insufficient say in policy-making.'[5] That, of course, meant that Phillips was indeed taking the reins into her own hands, but there is no evidence of any personal antagonism between the two women. Bondfield left office in 1913 but during the following years both were to work closely together serving on a great number of public bodies and in the March 1933 issue of *The Labour Woman* she was to refer to Marion's 'Magnificent Leadership' of the Women's Movement.

Phillips could no doubt be very brisk and business-like at her desk, and she could at times be autocratic. Her warmth, compassion and cheerfulness were mostly in evidence in her dealings with the downtrodden, and always present in the company of children.

Chapter 5: Babies and Children

i. The Baby Clinic

There is early evidence of Phillips's love of children. Len Fox, in a letter to me, relates how his sister Louise — now eighty-eight years old, has a special memory from her childhood of Marion. I quote from the letter: 'Louise remembered her as 'being very fond of children; big-bosomed; a lovely happy face; I loved cuddling her. I think of her as a person who was very compassionate to people in trouble'.'

This is how one very small girl responded to her. No doubt there were many others. We know that she, in freezing weather, during the winter of 1923–24, visited an orphanage at Helenov, some miles from Warsaw. She had been taken there by a friend — a Polish Deputy, who had made the running of this 'Farm School' for eighty destitute children, a major responsibility in his life. The little lost children — victims of the First World War, among them, Poles, Prussians, Jews, Germans, Lithuanians and Ukrainians, were cared for at this children's home by Polish socialists, relying on voluntary gifts and services to maintain it. The numbers kept growing as more destitute, orphaned children were taken in. Phillips, in a vivid article 'A Home for Waifs', published in *The Labour Woman* in January 1924, clearly touched by her experience, appeals for gifts of money and warm garments and picture books for the little ones...[1]

One of the projects closest to her heart was the setting up of the first baby clinic of its kind in this country, where treatment was entirely free and supported by voluntary contributions. There was in her, a deep compassion for deprived, pathetic children, as well as anger towards those responsible for their plight. The sight of happy, healthy children filled her with delight; she enjoyed their antics and often pressed them into service during an election. The woman who could make strong men quail became a warm motherly figure in the presence of little children.

In the early summer of 1911, Phillips was one of a special committee that met at Margaret MacDonald's house in Lincoln's Inn Fields, to discuss a suitable memorial to Mary Middleton who had died in April. It was decided to set up a baby clinic and Marion describes that meeting in the first Annual Report of the clinic, published in *The League Leaflet* of January 1913.

> Sheila MacDonald, dark-eyed, chubby and pink-cheeked, at that time only some six months old, played a larger part than she will ever know in the foundation of the clinic. It was the sight of the jolly little bundle that she made

that afternoon when we talked of a League Memorial to Mary Middleton, which turned our thoughts to other babies not so round and happy — not so free from doubt and pain.[2]

Alas, before the end of that year Margaret MacDonald had died too, and the clinic became her memorial as well as that of her friend. Little Sheila MacDonald was present in her father's arms at the opening of the clinic at 12 Telford Road, North Kensington, on November 13th, 1911. *The League Leaflet* for the following month described the opening as a 'quiet and beautiful ceremony'.[3] There was a description of the green and cream waiting room complete with toys and 'a fine doll's house'. The consulting room was said to be 'not at all terrifying and looks quite gay with its copper hot water geyser and bright table cover'. In the upper part of the house lived the resident nurse, with the caretaker installed on the top floor. 'The mothers begin already to feel how good a place the clinic is and very comfortable and jolly they look in the warm, cosy waiting room, chatting together, while the children play until their turn comes.'

The Hon. Lily Montague was the first Chairman of the Clinic Committee and the Treasurer was Mrs. Nodin of Kenley, Surrey. Dr. Ethel Bentham, one of the prime movers of the clinic and another doctor were in attendance on certain days of the week with a resident nurse present on a regular basis.

The clinic existed entirely on voluntary contributions though the Women's League hoped that it would be the fore-runner of many that would eventually be state or municipally controlled. Donations arrived from all quarters as well as gifts of medical supplies and other equipment from blankets to baby chairs.

Still, much more was needed. Locating the clinic in North Kensington went some way to meeting a desperate need, since the report of the Kensington Medical Officer of Health at the time, showing the infant mortality figures indicated a sharp difference between poor North Kensington and the affluent South Kensington areas. Care for infants from poor homes until now had been non-existent. It is true that in 1889 infant welfare centres had been opened in St. Helens, but simply to distribute free milk to needy mothers. In the early years of the century too, the idea of instructing mothers had resulted in a 'School for Mothers' at St. Pancras, but the situation generally was intolerable. Dr. Bentham in *The League Leaflet* of November 1911 said:

> We are going forward in faith …[4] We believe that this effort at preventative medicine in a small area will show that it is better to spend money doing things, than tabulating the reforms to be accomplished and that we should be wise to attack child sickness at the earliest possible moment, since by five years of age much mischief is done and much is irrevocable.

She stressed too a most important point: that the clinic was near the homes of the children in that district, so avoiding long journeys in all weather, and long waiting time in hospital. Doctors on the spot were there to advise too on matters of 'proper clothes, good habits, sufficient sleep and pure air'.

Month by month *The League Leaflet* would give a progress report on the work of the clinic, together with lists of subscribers. Describing the young patients in the first Annual Report on the clinic,[5] published in *The Leaflet* of January 1913, Phillips referred to one of them thus,

> Especially pitiful is the tiny figure on page fifteen — not a baby but a little old man of misery, puzzled at the strange world of pain and trouble he had tumbled into. Again on page seven is a baby so tiny that she is almost hidden by the doctor's hands. The children look quaint and pathetic, rolled in their blankets, ready for the doctor to see them...

By contrast, she referred to the 'lovely little design' on the cover of the Report, saying,

> The happy little angel with her very best Sunday wings is welcoming into her arms the chubbiest of little boys and girls — just such babies as we hope to see about us when the work of our clinic has been achieved. From the point of view of the Women's Labour League, that work will not be achieved until we have seen established in every district a baby clinic sufficient for the mothers' needs and established not only on the capricious basis of a voluntary fund, but on the basis of the efforts of the community as part of a state or municipal medical service.

She reported, however, that much was already being done in North Kensington. Publicity was being widely given to the clinic through the North Kensington Branch of the Women's Labour League (which she had established) and through the various Women's Clubs connected with it.

The clinic's first birthday attracted support from many areas. A 'nice little sum' was promised, for instance, as proceeds from a garden party held in Leicester. Other gifts arrived from various branches, while a special birthday meeting was chaired by Sir George Newman who laid stress on institutions such as the clinic and said that the high mortality rate was very often attributed to 'bad motherhood', applauding the organisation that cared for the health of little children by teaching mothers to feed them properly.

Meanwhile, supporters of the clinic on every hand showed great industry and much generosity. Talks (accompanied by collection boxes!) were given to the Froebel and other societies. Dr. Bentham, for instance, addressed the Ethical Society in Hampstead, similarly asking for contributions. There were 'drawing-room meetings' for the same purpose and Mrs. Gerald Montague paid for the services of a lady dentist for a monthly operations day. Important pieces of medical equipment were donated from time to time.

From the Report, we gather that in one month, eighty-five new cases were treated, in addition to the two hundred and fourteen already on the books. Quantities of cod-liver oil were required to remedy malnutrition, the Report added. The Clinic was indeed making headway.

In March 1912, a Conference on 'The Care of Babies and Young Children', organised by the Central London Branch of the Women's Labour League and presided over by Dr. Phillips, was addressed by Dr. Bentham. The Report of the conference was later published as a booklet called, *The Needs of Little Children*.[6] In her opening remarks, Dr. Bentham said scathingly that 'for fifteen years the Nation has been concerned with its infantile mortality, lowered birth-rate, slums, and about getting soldiers whose teeth are not entirely rotten.' After various inquiries and commissions to seek information, the results of recently instituted school inspections — revealing the state of health of children under the Poor Law, had she said, 'come like a thunderclap'. Dr. Bentham went on: 'We stand convicted of them ... of the worst possible business methods and reckless waste of natural resources'. She talked of wretched poverty with children on the verge of starvation. It was vital to see that they were fit enough to go to school. Thirty treatment centres had now been set up for school children but they were not enough.There should be more.

As for the under fives, the need for medical advice in this section was crucial. Indeed, the need was greater in the first five years of life than subsequently. She quoted that the death rate from tuberculosis in the first year was twice as great as in later years and that the death rate from other causes, between one and three years old, was four times greater than in any other five year periods up to thirty five years of age. As for the survivors, their general health was poor, particularly with eye and ear defects. The simple truth was, she said, that the majority of poor mothers could not get advice, and dared not spend any money on doctors, and that a third of homes have an income of twenty five shillings and often have to keep many children on that sum.

The setting up of the baby clinic, Dr. Bentham explained, was experimental. The advantages she explained, were 'that there is a clinic near to the homes of little ones who can be examined, weighed and given advice with weaning, teething and how to set their feet firmly on the right road'. She stressed in particular, the preventive aspect of the treatment: the keeping of reports and case papers and monthly monitoring of progress. Treatment by a nurse was advisable daily, and two doctors were available to deal with about a thousand cases a year and again she stressed that lack of food and adequate housing were the root causes of tuberculosis, malnutrition, rickets and other ailments.

The following year, 'The Report of the Registrar General dealing with Births in England and Wales' was printed in the October 1913 issue of *The Labour Woman* and given the greatest prominence by Marion Phillips.[7] She pointed out that the Report showed that 'the infant mortality rates among the middle classes are only sixty one percent of the infant mortality rates among the working classes.' The infant mortality rate among the working classes for 1911 was one hundred and thirty per thousand. The words of the Registrar General were then further quoted:

This suggests that at least forty percent of the infant mortality ... could be avoided if the health conditions in infant life in general could be approximated to these met with in Class I — the upper and middle classes.

Phillips herself continued, 'there is the official text to save the babies, make the life of a worker's baby as nearly as possible like that of the baby of the well-to-do.' There followed a short account of health hazards under headings in heavy type: 'Poverty kills children; bad sanitation kills children; overcrowded areas mean death for children'. Statistics were provided too for various areas throughout the country, showing the stark differences between prosperous and poor areas.

A ringing plea was then made for the establishment of baby clinics in all areas assisted by Treasury grants and set up by local authorities or even voluntary agencies.[8] Again she quoted the Chief Medical Officer for the Local Government Boards who had maintained that the object of child welfare work was to see that parents were given proper advice as to hygiene and domestic conditions, and emphasising the need of early treatment to prevent later serious disease.

But, commented Marion Phillips, 'we cannot get this high standard realised except through the open door of the baby clinic'. It was most urgent, she said, that support should be given to the campaign being waged by the Women's Labour League for the inclusion of baby clinics in the Education Bill to be introduced in the next session of Parliament. Nor, she stressed should these clinics be confined to consultations only. 'The mothers must be able not only to 'consult' the doctors, but it is imperative that the little ones be treated as well.'

She noted too, that while the principle of 'School Clinics' had been accepted, reports of children medically examined on entering schools showed that a high percentage of them suffered from 'malnutrition, adenoids, enlarged tonsils, deafness, bad teeth, rickets and other defects,' quoting the relevant statistics. She concluded by urging her readers to obtain the Report of the Medical Officer for Education for their own districts and pleading with them once again, not to wait but to press hard for the remedy of a baby clinic in their own areas.

The 'Needs of Little Children' were to occupy a great deal of Marion's time as well as that of her colleagues in those pre-war years. During the conference held in March 1912, in which Dr. Bentham had spoken so forcefully, many others, deeply concerned with the welfare of little children, had made impressive contributions. Margaret McMillan, who, with her sister Rachel, had set up nursery schools, stressed the importance of nutrition, which she said was the basis of growth and excellence. She urged too, that every school clinic should have an attached nursery with the conditions of home. Keir Hardie stressed the necessity for the removal of poverty as the root cause of the evils of ill-health. Mrs. Pember Reeves deplored that the lying-in hospitals only dealt with abnormal or 'interesting' cases while out-patient departments were totally inadequate. She emphasised that generally, among the poor, giving birth was sheer misery, confinement often taking place in the room where the family lived and motherhood was often regarded 'as a penalty.' There was a need, she said, for experienced midwives. Mrs. Pember Reeves referred to her experience in investigating the poor in Lambeth, the findings of which were published in the Fabian Tract N° 10 entitled 'Life on a Pound a week'.[9]

Following Mrs. Reeves, Mrs. Model — from the Association for the Promotion and Training of Midwives — said that the contribution of a penny or two a week would provide more midwives to help poor mothers and to provide lectures for young girls in hygiene and preparation for motherhood.

The latter point was taken up by Mrs. Charlotte Despard — a member of the Baby Clinic Committee who made a special point that older boys and girls in school should be trained for parenthood and citizenship. Almost a century later the need emphasised by Mrs. Despard is still valid.

Sister Kerrison, a member of the West Ham Board of Guardians, complained of her difficulty in persuading the Guardians 'as well as a good many mothers' that milk should be given to children as a 'proper food.'

A full report of the conference was published later in 1912 under the title 'The Needs of Little Children.'

ii. Open-Air Schools
In the same year — 1912, in the October issue of *The League Leaflet,* an article by Marion Phillips called 'Into the Sunshine', shows her enthusiasm for open-air education.[10] This account was later followed by her booklet, 'The School Doctor and the Home'.

'Into the Sunshine' is written in her usual lively fashion. She starts by deploring the dark, unsatisfactory schools of the time, badly situated and badly designed, in towns and cities, away from 'trees and grass and flowers.' Nature, she says, should play a part in the early education of children and she quotes from the 1910 report of Sir George Newman, the Medical Officer of the Board of Education, who had clearly declared in favour of open-air education.

Even when complete open-air schools are unavailable, she suggests two ways in which children can benefit from open-air education. In Switzerland and Germany, children are taken on long walks and even away from home for week-ends in the summer. Not only do they return with arms full of leaves and flowers, but also, she contends, 'with minds glowing with beautiful pictures, while their quick and observant eyes have taken in a hundred facts which their teachers, next day, turn into knowledge of geography, or the science of stones, or tales of the history of the places they have seen.'

Halifax and Birmingham are mentioned as examples of places where this worthy practice is followed. London too, although she regrets that there, the visits are usually to picture galleries and museums and historical buildings — visits that would best be postponed until winter, leaving the summer free for open-air activities.

The second open-air option is the 'playground' class in which lessons take place in a verandah-type structure enclosed on three sides only. With delicate children well wrapped-up, this room could be used in the good weather of every season.

The third type is the Open-Air School itself. She is glad that good authorities have already set these up, although they are only available to delicate children. The emphasis is laid on good meals and plenty of rest with the maximum time spent in the garden, in the Open-Air School. The more formal lessons are taken in the verandah room. Phillips sets out in detail the timetable of a day at such a school, applauding the priority given to good nourishing good, rest and hygiene.

There is too, she tells us, the Residential Open-Air School, where delicate children remain even for weekends for greater benefit, especially those who came from 'crowded and shut in' houses. She again praises Halifax for providing one of these schools, where the children are kept until they 'are thoroughly strong'. They have formal lessons with the day pupils, and then become day pupils themselves when they are fit enough.

Phillips is also in favour of those residential schools that operate as summer camps out in the country. She maintains that improvement in physique takes place after a period spent at these schools and in a high proportion of the children tuberculosis disappears.

The cod-liver oil and orange juice presented by the Welfare State after the Second World War to pregnant women and to babies (in addition to other advantages), produced generations of sturdy youngsters. Older folk, though, will remember the thin pallid children of long ago who suffered from 'weak chests' or anaemia or malnutrition, and for whom these schools — as a kind of junior sanatoria — provided timely help.

Marion Phillips, at the end of her article urges mothers to campaign hard for one or more of these schools in their districts, and to do so, particularly during the municipal elections! Cheerfully she addresses the young ones:

Forward children into the Sunlight.

It is not a 'governessy' command. Rather a kindly gesture of shepherding little children into a healthier and happier life.

iii. The School Doctor and the Home
In 1913, following the pamphlet on 'The Needs of Little Children' and the article on open-air education, Marion Phillips published a booklet called *The School Doctor and the Home*.[11] It was based on the results of an inquiry into the inspection and treatment of school children. Since the 1907 Act making school medical inspections compulsory, the Board of Education had strongly encouraged local education authorities to submit schemes of medical treatment to them for approval, leaving the funding of such schemes however to come from the rates. Now, unless treatment would follow rapidly after the identification of a defect,

the whole process would be self defeating and Phillips in her booklet, endorsing the need for immediate treatment, quoted from the report of the Chief Medical Officer for the Board of Education, published in 1909 — 'We want a single effective organisation which shall conduct an ailing or defective child, through the process of medical inspection ... without waste of effort ... into the hands of those qualified to treat him.'[12]

The aim was laudable, but the whole organisation of inspection and treatment was far from satisfactory. To begin with, Marion Phillips urged that no child should be regarded as one unit in a mass of dirty children suffering from ailments and defects within the confines of a school building. The child, she insisted, was an individual human being from an individual home. There was therefore, need, she said, to treat the child as a complete human being, instead of merely treating his infected eye or ear. It seemed to her that since there was so much ignorance about the inspection and treatment of children and so much need to elicit necessary information, a detailed questionnaire was sent out to homes and to the local education authorities. It was vital to know, she said, answers to questions such as 'How have inspection and treatment affected the home life of the child?' or 'To what extent have they allayed parental anxiety?'

Thus a wide-ranging questionnaire was distributed among all kinds of people concerned with the administration of the Act, in all parts of England and Wales. It was found that children were inspected when they entered schools and when they left, that is, about a quarter of the pupils of a school would be inspected at one time. It was 'patchy' to say the least. It was found too, that many mothers were unaware of the inspection, which was in any case, cursory. Marion Phillips insisted that it was necessary for the mother to be present. She insisted that 'medical evidence is still a formal, technical affair. It has not been humanised'. She stressed too, the importance of women doctors for the older girls.

Further, she condemned outright the system where there was no connection between the inspecting authority and the treating authority, and that the inspecting doctor rarely gave details of a defect, only identifying its location. She quoted as an example, that a cleft palate would simply be referred to as 'mouth' or even not that! Sometimes the defect would be described as a vague 'needing treatment'. Equally vague would be the message sent home by a child, conveying the result of an inspection, or the useless statement made by a teacher. Phillips quoted as an example of the latter: 'Weakly, but no definite illness.' She concluded that the system was woefully inadequate. An absentee child would not be inspected at all. Quite often, it was only after children left school that a serious defect was found.

Phillips said quite plainly that it was time for parents to 'stir' in the matter and insist on improvements. Insist, for example, she said, on the presence of a parent during inspection and on being fully informed. As for medical treatment, she referred to Sir George Newman's Report of 1910, in which he mentioned those school clinics already established — with five dental clinics among them. Others dealt exclusively with skin, eyes, ears and ringworm. Sir George said that the simplest form of treatment would be 'a general clinic for the treatment of minor ailments'.[13] The removal of adenoids, enlarged tonsils and eye-testing and X-ray treatment for ringworm could be dealt with separately. He added that efficient treatment for school children could only be obtained in very few places ...

Declaring that 'We feel strongly that the work of school clinics is far too narrow,' she referred to the splendid pioneer work performed in the clinic established by Margaret McMillan at Deptford where, in addition to general treatment of the usual child ailments, there is treatment too, for anaemia, debility, heart disease, spinal disease and tuberculosis, with doctors, dentist and nurse in attendance. In Deptford too, there was a special remedial room for remedial and breathing exercises under the supervision of a qualified teacher. The aim should be, said Marion Phillips, to establish such clinics in every school or at least in certain groups of schools. There was no charge made at Deptford she added, nor at Bradford. A small charge was made at Kettering and at Abertillery in Wales.

Phillips too, criticised the location of clinics in municipal buildings and dark town halls. She thought a better idea would be a travelling doctor, with a resident nurse on location. As it was, some hospitals received subsidies to treat ringworm, while verminous children were taken to cleansing stations. Hospital treatments in any case were haphazard. Sometimes letters were required. There were always delays, and refusals to treat skin diseases. Hospitals too, were a good distance away from homes, and there would often be long waiting hours. Where hospitals received no subsidy to treat certain diseases, the situation was worse. All in all, the hospitals were unable to cope and outpatients' accommodation always overcrowded, especially the Ear, Nose and Throat Department.

Neither was there any co-ordination between school and hospital. Dr. Phillips gave many examples of this — all resulting in hardship and neglect. She saw, in short, three main drawbacks to hospital treatment: a waste of time and energy for all concerned; the unnecessary costs of treatment and travel and finally, the very small average number of children treated.

The Education Authority she went on, should make provision of proper meals and open-air establishments for the treatment of tuberculosis and malnutrition. She again expressed her enthusiasm for open-air schools which, she said, could be opened anywhere quite easily. Phillips then gave a list of the provisions necessary to cater for the needs of little children.

First
More doctors to each Education Authority.
Following inspections, with mother present, there should be treatment at clinics with qualified dentists on the spot.

Second
    Arrangement for cure or prevention were listed as follows:-
    the need of general supervision of schools for health reasons.
    She criticised badly-designed classrooms with windows in the wrong place.
    The need for separate pegs for hats and coats.
    The need for a proper dining-room, and consultations with a doctor about
    nutritious food.
    The need for baths and other washing facilities at school.
    The need to have a school clinic with a room for remedial exercises.
    The need for mothers to have the opportunity to hear lectures on food, hygiene,
    clothing and dental care.
    She pointed out that these things were already in the reach of the well-to-do.
    There were, however, two other requirements, she said.
    One was the supply of drugs, spectacles, X-Rays and other equipment for
    dental treatment and for the removal of tonsils and adenoids.
    The other was the setting-up of Open-Air Schools and sanitoria.

These, she said, constituted the Health Department of a school. The thoroughness of her thinking and her attention to detail covered the whole scene — down to the provision of separate clothes' pegs to prevent the spread of vermin.

She acknowledged that bad housing and low wages must be tackled as root causes of so many diseases, but it was vital, she argued, to start immediately on a scheme of preventative and curative doctoring of the children of the workers. It had to be done immediately. Like Dr. Bentham who spoke of the need of urgent action instead of merely tabulating reforms, so Phillips would brook no delay.

The gap between birth and school, though, was still a problem. She saw the snag in that local education authorities had no contact with a child until he was five years old. The answer then was the establishment of baby clinics like the pioneer clinic at Telford Road, throughout the land, thus ensuring a complete health structure for babies and children of all ages. Phillips ended on a typically optimistic note:

> There is no task which ought to come as a more welcome one to mothers and fathers than this of founding a National Service which will bring such estimable good to their children ... We all know too well, the little battalions of the ragged children of the slums, undersized and underfed, marred by preventable disease, shut off from joy by needless suffering. But next to them come the host of children of the wage-earners — more fortunate than they, but bringing their pitiful tale of lost opportunity.

> The aim of these pages has been to help on, the parents' campaign in gaining for their children every chance of escape from present pain and future lack of strength. The Women's Labour League is looking to the future - looking to see draw near the rosy, sturdy band of boys and girls, clear-skinned and fine-limbed,

bright-eyed and glowing with vigour and joy. As such children take their place in the world's struggle, the victory of happiness will be secure.

Alas, apart from witnessing a few piecemeal improvements to the medical service, Marion and her colleagues did not live to see the implementation of a complete health structure for children of all ages — for which they had fought so gallantly. It was not until after the Second World War that a National Health Service became a reality and with it the arrival of the first generation of the 'cod-liver oil and orange juice babies'.

Chapter 6: 1912

It must have been the memories of her own happy childhood that enabled Marion Phillips to enter into the world of children so easily. Twenty years later, in Parliament she was again to refer to her early happy days.[1] At the beginning of her political career she loved organising children into processions, the noisier and more colourful the better, whether they carried collection boxes to feed the hungry — as they did during the Bermondsey strike — or whether, equipped with kitchen utensils to attract the attention of voters, they paraded the Kensington Streets during the Borough Elections of 1912, in support of the two lady doctors who were standing as Labour candidates. They were of course, Dr. Ethel Bentham and herself, and entering into the spirit of the fray, she described the enthusiasm of the youngsters: 'In close battle array, they marched the streets bearing on high the Labour Party colours and portraits of the candidates. It was not a little straggling knot of children but a procession of some hundreds which marched to the orderly beatings of tin kettles and trays.'[2] The children apparently, held their own street corner meetings, laden with propaganda against their opponents — the Progressive Party. They sang lustily ditties that certainly would not have been compiled by the Bard of Avon, but were no doubt, effective enough in stirring up emotions.

In the event, both doctors succeeded in becoming borough councillors, using their extra influence to further welfare schemes and to enlist more support for the Telford Road Baby Clinic, the Co-operative Stores and Meeting-rooms which they had set up in Bonchurch Street. The local branch of the Women's Labour League were further strengthened by their presence on the Council.

It was probably during this election that Phillips saw the value of explaining to growing children that welfare matters, closely affecting their lives, were dependent on political decisions. Always the teacher and advocate, she saw that well-informed young people given responsible leadership, could be taught that through democratic means, they could, in time, improve their own immediate environment.

The result was the appearance a little later of *The Green Sprig Party* — described by its author, Marion Phillips, as 'a story for young people,' in booklet form and published by the Women's Labour League. She had anticipated running *The Green Sprig Party* in serial form. Unfortunately, the sequel, due to appear in May 1914, did not materialise.

The first *Green Sprig* story — 'The Election', was a bright, fast-moving tale of young, intelligent school children who wish to put right certain wrongs in the community. They are carefully advised by a wise teacher who explains to them the democratic processes that they must follow. After unsuccessfully seeking the help of Conservative and Liberal candidates in the forthcoming local election, they find that it is the Labour Party that listens and helps!

Phillips, very happily enters their world. The action proceeds at a good canter; crises occur and are resolved; there is more progress and the battle is won. The story is simply told. Marion's observant eye, her keen ear, her understanding of the human heart and perhaps above all, her zest for life, produces a lively tale. She must have met at some time a character like 'Thomas O'Brien ... a freckled, wiry boy not much past his thirteenth birthday but already a notable fighter'. Her other characters too, are sketched deftly with a few broad brush strokes.

The story itself, about a secret society of young adolescents, with codes and emblems, esoteric oaths and tunes and plots, is an echo of the activities of an earlier generation. Len Fox gives an interesting account of a solemn meeting of children recorded by Mondle Phillips, P. D. Phillips's brother, at the age of fifteen. Mondle's younger brothers — Edward and Lewis mentioned in his account, were then thirteen and eleven respectively, but awarded all the formality and dignity of adulthood by their brother. The chronicle of the fifteen-year old Mondle reads thus:

> At a meeting held on the twenty-eighth of October 1856, by Mr. Mondle, Mr. Edward and Mr. Lewis, it was agreed that they should meet every Monday, Wednesday and Saturday evenings, for the purpose of improving themselves in the most useful of studies and the following programme was adopted for the furtherance of the above-mentioned project.

Another entry indicates that at another meeting there was a discussion of 'The Laws' and that a later meeting the following item was recorded:

> It was also proposed by Mr. Mondle (Chairman) and seconded by Mr. Lewis, that Miss Hannah be admitted as member of this society.

Their sister Hannah, was ten at the time![3] Mondle Phillips, who died at the early age of twenty-four was apparently — from the later extracts of his diary — a shrewd and most amusing character. Some of these early entries may well have been the seed that grew into *The Green Sprig Party*.

Shortly before the Urban District Council Elections, Phillips was so gratified that women were coming forward to serve on public bodies, that she published lists of their names in the November 1912 issue of *The League Leaflet*. In the same issue, she made a special election appeal to women. It concentrated on the following matters: on the need for well-built homes with all the necessary facilities; on the needs of children — playgrounds, libraries, medical inspections and treatment, scholarships for further education, and above all, food for those who were hungry, whether in school or in holiday time; on the necessity of the daily collection of refuse and its disposal, together with the provision of overalls for dustmen and the provision for them to be washed outside the home; on the careful inspection of all food products including milk; on a living wage for all those employed by the Council from the office charwomen upwards, and finally, on allotments sited fairly near home, at reasonable rates for those who wanted them.

Phillips was always advocating the availability of allotments as a source of fresh produce that would benefit the health of the poorer members of society. Later she would raise the matter many times in Parliament.

Both Ethel Bentham and Marion Phillips served as councillors in the Golbourne Ward in the Royal Borough of Kensington until they resigned their seats after the war because of the pressure of additional duties. They were seven years of arduous often frustrating toil. Even as early as 1913, Ethel Bentham indicating the uphill nature of the task, told the Women's Labour League Conference:

> Whatever happens, we shall not want for work ... The meetings and the committees and the discussion, the socials, the struggles on Boards against an overwhelming majority ... and the everlasting difficulty of finding funds. But, after all we sometimes win[4] ... and now and again we score over points.

Their struggles 'against an overwhelming majority' — in Kensington of all places — was surely heroic though Patricia Hollis referring to reports in the *Kensington Express* noted that Phillips's 'indecorous' tactics in pressing for action to reduce unemployment and to provide municipal milk and more baby clinics in the area probably hindered rather than helped her cause.[5]

Proper housing was always one of the high priorities of the Women's Labour League. *The Working Woman's House*, produced by Marion Phillips and Averil Sanderson-Furniss after the First World War, set out in great detail what they considered to be essential features of any designs of municipally built homes of the future. These houses, they maintained, should also be situated in pleasant, green surroundings provided by the spaces left after slum clearance. Already, at the beginning of their tenure as councillors, Bentham and Phillips were seeking to influence the design of working-class houses. They claimed,

> that sitting on Kensington Borough Council, they had become an architectural panel of two: they had, for example, redesigned the cottages built by the Great Western Railway to include hot and cold water, a bath, and well-arranged windows and doors.[6]

This of course, underlined the need for more women councillors who could apply their practical experience to these tasks.

Later too, in *The Working Woman's House*, Phillips was to complain that workers' homes were always situated in depressing areas and lacked the amenities of well-to-do districts. It was hardly surprising then, that according to Patricia Hollis she 'was to complain bitterly in Kensington that Holland Park got the street trees at the expense of the poorer North Kensington.'[7] It was wholly predictable too, that she would press for the appointment of more women sanitary inspectors. Patricia Hollis again: 'Together, women sanitary staff and women councillors such as Margaret Ashton, Eleanor Rathbone and Marion Phillips took the lead on their councils in exposing and denouncing sweated labour.'[8]

All these matters, of course, were consistently discussed over the years at meetings of the Women's Labour League and articles about them featured regularly in *The League Leaflet* and later in *The Labour Woman*. Hours of work and factory conditions were prominent among matters to be pursued by Phillips throughout the war years and afterwards on the National and International scene.

In February 1912, she was caught up in the aftermath of the London Dock Strike. During the strike the I.L.P., the B.S.P. and the Children's White Cross League, in concert, organised help for children of the strikers by removing them — about a thousand of them — from their homes and setting them in more comfortable surroundings. This action had a doubly-good effect: on children, obviously, and on public opinion. After the strike had been settled, it was felt by many of the Women's Labour League who had been deeply involved, this planned help should continue and so be available to the small hapless victims in any future dispute. Consequently, at the W.L.C. offices later in the year, a Provisional Committee was set up with Dr. Parker of the Marylebone I.L.P. as Secretary, Dr. Tchaicovsky for the children's White Cross League, and Dr. Marion Phillips as Chairman, and a constitution for The League for the Strikers' Children was formulated.

This resulted in a large meeting where delegates from all branches of Socialist and Labour organisations in the London area gathered and 'The League' was set up and its constitution adopted. It was hoped that it would spread to other areas.

This development was intensely significant as far as Marion Phillips was concerned, for fourteen years later, during the miners' lock-out, it fell to her and her little band of helpers to mount a massive rescue operation in the mining areas devastated by the dispute. This 1912 project and her earlier experience during the Bermondsey Strike must have been of help when the time came for her to organise a country-wide evacuation of deprived children from the distressed areas into kindly, comfortable homes in the Home Counties.

She was busy too, in 1912, speaking and canvassing in three of the four Parliamentary by-elections of that year — at Hanley, Crewe and Midlothian. It was, apparently, very difficult for her to go to Midlothian where the election lasted three weeks and took place during holiday time. But go she did, and was pleased that as a result of the political activity in Hanley and Midlothian, branches of the Women's Labour League were formed there shortly afterwards.

In connection with the Parliamentary by-elections too, she issued another ringing appeal to women to support the Labour candidates, in the form of a leaflet — *A Call to Working Women*. It was written in a friendly, chatty style about the privations of unemployment, poverty and disease and the pitiful plight of widows and children of workers, presented with the stark choice of either the Poor Law pittance or the workhouse.

She stressed that these evils could only be destroyed by better representation in Parliament. Always the realist, she declared, 'We have learnt that STRIKES, in spite of magnificent bravery with which men and women have stood together and faced starvation, cannot get us what we want — that all the sacrifice they call for, brings but a small reward.' Phillips had this knack of identifying with women and their families in a warm, sympathetic way. She went on to plead for support for the Labour Party which was fighting to gain:

The Parliamentary vote for every man and woman

A living wage for every man and woman

A universal eight-hours day

The break-up of the Poor Law and the abolition of the workhouse

The maintenance of the widow and her children

Safety for the workers in the mines and on the seas, on the railways, in the potteries and in the workshops

The feeding of hungry children whether in school days or during the holidays

It is interesting that in *A Call to Working Women* Phillips declared her conviction that strikes as a means of securing justice for working men and women were hopelessly ineffective. As far back as 1912, she realised clearly that they could never win in such an unequal contest and that new machinery needed to be devised to settle disputes in a modern industrial state. The Sacrifice of the Innocents — a sacrifice made in vain, appalled her. However, in *A Call* she couched her convictions with a certain gentleness, well aware of the vulnerability of the wives and mothers of those days.

More forthright and cutting were her comments on a totally different matter in the December leaflet. The Criminal Law Amendment Bill was on its way through Parliament and the Commons had already decided that there would be punishment by flogging for all male procurers. She quoted approvingly from *The Nation* that had stated that since the House could not consent to the same brutal punishment for procuresses, the trade would go more and more into their hands.

In condemning the proposed punishment, she wrote:

It would be better to lose the Bill altogether than to bear the shame of passing an Act today which will require the payment from National funds of men whose duty it will be, in cold blood, to flog fellow men — prisoners — helpless creatures, however vile their crimes. A blow in hot passion — there is excuse in that. But the parade of brutal punishment, reform through fear of the flogger — these surely belong to a hideous past in our civilisation. It is simply revenge taken by society in payment for its own shame. Poverty, ignorance, greed and luxury lie at the base of the White Slave Traffic. None of these will be cured by the use of the lash.

Her acute mind was already turning to the problems of crime and punishment and to alternative forms of the treatment of offenders, though it was not until after the First World War that she, with Gertrude Tuckwell and Mary Macarthur, became a magistrate and was to find merit in some of the proposals offered by the then budding Probation Service.

Earlier in the year, Phillips had found time to write a brief review of J. Ramsay MacDonald's book on syndicalism. Since its political philosophy seized the imagination of many in the Labour movement at that time it may be interesting to record her comments. She first described how syndicalism in England differed from syndicalism in France. Then, concentrating on the former, she proceeded,

> ... broadly speaking this Syndicalism is less a thought-out scheme of revolution than a wild and idealistic impatience with the slow movements of men's minds, It does a certain good in waking up Trade Unionists and giving to them a sense of war-like fervour. But while at one moment it preaches the General Strike and the unity of all workers — at the next it proclaims that not nationalisation of industries is to be aimed at, but that each section of industry should own and control its own section. This would mean that the whole welfare of the community, would depend on that particular industry which was most necessary to it and thus Syndicalism would lay the foundations in a new tyranny over society.
>
> The denial of the worth of Parliamentary activity is perhaps the feature which shows Syndicalism in its real impossibility. It is natural that eager men should become impatient with the slow conversion of the electors. But it is clear that not even avowed Syndicalists are able to keep to their principles and abstain from Parliamentary action — while even their own schemes would require a large amount of law-making to become in any way operative.

One might conclude that in a nutshell, Marion Phillips thought the whole idea was half-baked. She ended, however on a kindly note. 'The Book', she wrote, 'is well worth reading, if for nothing else, for the analysis of the class war in chapter VII and the hopeful words of the conclusion!'[9]

All in all, 1912 was an extremely busy year for Phillips, with its welter of various duties, but possibly it was the working of the Insurance Act, in particular those aspects of it affecting women, that claimed her best attention in that year.

Chapter 7: Take Your Tickets, Ladies

Even before the Insurance Bill of 1911 had become law, Marion Phillips had set up the Industrial Women's Insurance Advisory Board to safeguard working women's interests. The Chairman was Mary Macarthur, Phillips was the Secretary and many prominent women served on it: Mrs. Webb, Dr. Bentham, Miss Weaver, Miss Llewelyn Davies, Mrs. Salter and Mrs. Spink as well as that great supporter of women in the trade unions — J. J. Mallon.

As Secretary of the Women's Labour League and editor of *The League Leaflet* — which from May 1913 became *The Labour Woman* — she was to deal with every aspect of the Insurance Act, seeking to inform, to explain, to warn and to direct her readers in great detail as to the way forward. The range of her concern extended from the precise interpretation of the Act to the matter of expenses incurred by the hard-pressed members of local committees in pursuance of their duties.

In the February 1912 issue of *The League Leaflet*, Phillips explained that the Board, which had now become 'The Industrial Women's Insurance Advisory Board', consisted of a number of Bodies, namely:

> The Women's Trade Union League
> The Women's Co-operative Guild
> The Women's Labour League
> The Railway Women's Guild
> The National Federation of Women Workers
> The National Union of Shop Assistants

'Other organisations, too,' she stated, 'could apply to join and the Board would vote on the question of membership.' She explained that it had been formed so that all working women might get the maximum benefit from the Insurance Act. The Board aimed to do two things: to get representatives of working women on all advisory committees, insurance committees and committees of approved societies on a central and local level; secondly, to get all working women to join a trade union and to insure through it. Where no special union existed for a particular trade, the National Federation of Women Workers would recruit them and seek in addition, the enrolment of domestic servants. A great effort would be made to keep all working women out of the Employer's Shop Club, the Post Office Deposit Fund and out of the collecting societies like the Prudential.[1]

Phillips lost no time in seeking to accomplish both aims. Already in June 1912 in fine style in *The League Leaflet*, under the heading 'TAKE YOUR TICKETS, LADIES' she was urging her readers to join unions so that they could enrol with approved societies.[2] Her regular column on the work of the Industrial Women's Insurance Advisory Board, set out the issues. In Leaflet N° 16 she emphasised the importance of 'taking the ticket'. She began:

> The National Insurance Act has been well described as a leap in the dark. Whether, as far as women are concerned, it is a leap towards the light will depend largely upon the efforts put forward by adherents of the Labour movement during the next three months.
>
> Let it not be doubted there is light. Four million women are to join, almost at once, some organisation, and a pull-devil, pull-worker struggle is beginning to take possession of them.
>
> 'Wheresoever the carcase is, there shall the vultures be gathered together'. That four shillings per head of administrative money is calling vultures of insurance from all quarters of heaven (and elsewhere?)... The motive of these is to despoil the Trade Unions already leavening the great lump of the indifference and despair of women workers.[3]

She warned strongly too, not only against the employers and collection societies but against the less insidious bodies: the friendly, philanthropic and religious societies who were all deflecting money away from the approved societies of the trade unions and therefore, to her mind, acting against the interests of women workers.

In the same column, Phillips discussed the other aim of the Board. The Act, she wrote, offered women opportunities for 'useful and varied service' and 'it should be made a school of experience for those who have the aptitude for the work of Government'. She turned to the League to set up a 'representative committee of working women who will see that the number and quality of the women on the local committees are what they should be ... Enthusiasm, organisation and hard work' were necessary.[4]

She urged too, that in order for the work of the Board to be effective, all branches of its federated organisations should form their local joint committees, similar to the Board, in every county and borough and that nominations to committees should be made at once. She also invited questions and appeals for advice from various parts of the country. In this way, Phillips was assembling a network of suitable nominees for service on the nationwide system of insurance committees.

There was too, the need to ensure that such committee members should be properly qualified, and in May, she announced that the Commission, at the request of the Board, had agreed to start special classes to explain the Insurance Act. Thus all women engaged in administering the Act would be given the opportunity to understand its provisions fully. Phillips welcomed this move, calling it a good democratic scheme and appealing for a good number of women to serve, and attend these classes. Her exhortations did not go unheeded. There was, for instance, enough enthusiasm to provide good attendances at 'Insurance Lectures' at Leeds, Manchester, Hull and elsewhere, while the Islington branch of the Women's Labour League was open on one evening a week for enquiries. It is clear from LIFE AS WE HAVE KNOWN IT[5] that many house-wife members of the Women's Co-operative Guild across the country soon became members of local insurance committees.

In the July issue of *The League Leaflet*, Phillips spoke of the great progress that had been made. Many local joint committees had been formed and large numbers of lectures had been held. A good number of women had been accepted to sit on Provisional Insurance Committees and a list of their names was provided. 'There was also a need,' she said, 'for further nominations for the District Committees in Counties and large Country Boroughs'. She stressed that those who were nominated to serve on District Committees would themselves be insured persons. 'There would be,' she explained, 'in addition to District Committees, representatives of the Deposit Contributors,' and she quoted from a circular issued by the Commissioners, giving instructions to the Provisional Insurance Committees and adding, 'Women of the League and the Co-operative Guilds are especially concerned, and it is from these organisations that we should get nominations of women able to look after the interests of Deposit Contributors'.[6]

She appealed again for influence to be exercised on factory workers to persuade them to enrol themselves in their Trade Union Approved Society. In the same issue of *The League Leaflet*, however, her concern for charwomen in relation to the Insurance Act, gave them pride of place on the front page of the paper. The situation, she explained, was very complex. The Commissioners, she wrote, with reference to the regulations, '... have evolved a very ingenious method of removing some of the inequalities — but far too many remain'. She suggested that each branch secretary should obtain a supply of the relevant official leaflet and should try to understand '... the distinctions drawn between the casual woman who *cannot* be insured, and the casual women who *must* be insured.' She herself, then dealt in great detail with the content of the Official Explanatory Leaflet N° 19, and also advised all League members who employed charwomen, '... to urge them to choose the National Federation of Women Workers as their Approved Society, and to encourage the signing of agreements among those who employ the same charwoman, so that employers will pay in turn, and the women will get steady and regular work.'[7] Not a stone was left unturned.

During the summer of 1912, Phillips continued to advise working women. Clearly in response to the anxiety felt by them, she stated firmly: 'Those workers who felt afraid that under the Insurance Act they would have to tell their employers their ages may set their minds at rest.' She explained the procedure, adding for good measure: 'Don't answer too many questions. No employer,' she stressed, 'could, under the terms of the Insurance Act, make it a condition of employment that a worker should belong to any specific Society for Insurance purposes, nor could a worker be dismissed on the ground that she was insured in a Trade Union. She should not disclose the name of her Approved Society unless she chose to do so. The Law,' wrote Phillips firmly, 'specially says that your employer has no right to know.'[8]

The question of expenses incurred by working women sitting on Insurance Committees was to present real difficulties in these early days of administering the Act; it was to concern the Board, as it feared the issue might prevent the women from performing such an essential task. The Commission was therefore being approached about the matter. Nothing, however, was done and, in the February 1913 meeting of the board, Phillips voiced her fears that '... the financial demands on the pockets of these women will lead to their resignation. Yet,' she said, '... the needs of a working woman to voice the desires of working women on these Insurance Committees is a pressing requirement. Administration will become a tyranny if we are forced to withdraw from these committees.'[9] Therefore, the Chancellor was being asked to receive a deputation to consider the problem, and in order that the women's case could be properly prepared, they were being issued with a questionnaire consisting of eight items, with a request that they should be returned promptly to her.

Meanwhile, in the August *League Leaflet*, Phillips strongly criticised the permit given to Industrial Insurance Companies to become Approved Societies. 'It had,' she wrote, 'proved the greatest blot upon the Act ...' She condemned the pressure brought to bear on defenceless people such as illiterate domestic servants; for example, agents would persist on calling upon them and produce ready filled-in cards for final signature. In factories, too, employers encouraged such agents and provided them with the necessary facilities to address the workers. Girls were urged by manageresses to join. 'Never,' wrote Phillips, 'was the need for trade unions made greater because only a strong organisation of the workers can fight against the contravention of the Spirit of the Act.'[10]

In September 1912, she published a list of those bodies that comprised the administrative structure of the Act and gave advice on two specific benefits that would concern members of Committees. The first was Maternity Benefit. She informed her readers that as the Insurance Committees would administer Maternity Benefits altogether for Deposit Contributors, she suggested that Labour women should make every attempt to become members of any sub-committees dealing with benefits for Deposit Contributors. She advised members of such committees that they should resist any arrangement made with doctors that would result in an increase in maternity fees; that, mothers — in accordance with the Act, should be given every opportunity to be attended by midwives if they so desired, and that Maternity Benefit schemes be given to the mothers in cash, unless she herself preferred a different arrangement.[11]

The second provision concerned Medical Benefits. 'There was,' she said, 'bound to be a delay in this area, as the difficulties with the doctors are not yet settled.' She warned, however, against any attempt by committees to

> Make use of the power given to them by the Act to place people with incomes over a certain amount (the suggested limit being £2 per week), outside the general scheme for Medical Benefit leaving them to make their arrangements with the doctors as best they may. We are sure that all working-class people will agree that all those who are manual workers or whose income is below £160 should be treated alike.[12]

She was to warn again of the great difficulties arising from the attempt to differentiate for the purposes of medical benefits — between persons of different incomes, and she enumerated all the pitfalls in another article.

She complained bitterly of the attitude of doctors, accusing them of holding up the administration of the Act in every direction. Thirty-four years later, the British Medical Association was to resist, quite as fiercely, Aneurin Bevan's proposals for a National Health Service. In 1912, Marion Phillips harboured a hope that the 'doctor's crisis' and their continuing obduracy of the profession might 'end in the establishment of a Public Medical Service.' The British Medical Association, she maintained, still regarded such a scheme as 'unmitigatedly shocking and socialistic and no doubt, if it were forced upon them, they would then regret having fought against the sum of 8/6 offered by the Chancellor. What we need now' she went on, 'is a little pluck on his part and the great boon of a Public Medical Service will become a reality.'[13]

She was particularly exasperated with the reluctance of doctors to refer patients suffering from tuberculosis to sanatoria, observing crisply that it was in the interest of everyone '... that such people should be removed from their homes where they act as an infection centre for the rest of their families'.[14]

That comment was made in the December 1912 issue of *The League Leaflet*. The following April, she was again referring to patients suffering from this scourge. In the form of a letter, published in that edition and addressed to all working women on insurance committees, she first dealt with those patients who were being treated at home, under the heading: SANATORIUM BENEFIT. An insurance committee, she maintained, was entitled to allow as 'Sanatorium Benefit' anything that the doctor attending the patient deemed to be necessary. She went on: 'This not only includes medicines, cod-liver oil, sputum flasks *etc.*, but nourishing food, milk, meat, eggs *etc.*, and even blankets, warm clothing or air cushions.'

In reply to the question of a committee member as to whether it was necessary, first, to inquire into the income of the household, she stated firmly, '... the Board is of the opinion that *no Insurance Committee has any right whatsoever to make any inquiries into the income of the family of an insured person. It was,'* she went on, 'extremely unusual for luxuries such as fresh eggs, quantities of milk, meat or warm blankets to be within the buying power of the patient ...' She added, 'fight strongly against any system of income inquiry in such cases.'[15]

One other matter claimed her attention in her April letter. It concerned Maternity Benefit for Deposit Contributors. In reply to a query about the propriety of a proposal that committee members appointed to act as visitors, should demand the production of marriage certificates from claimants, Phillips declared that such a procedure was unnecessary and that it would be quite enough for the husband to sign a statement when applying for the benefit. She added that at such a time no wife should be worried by matters of this sort but left in peace.[16]

Phillips also made the sensible suggestion that committee members should establish 'friendly relations' with women sanitary inspectors and health visitors in their areas, because of their special local knowledge of mothers of new babies. She was also anxious to know to what extent the Notification of Births Act was in force in each district.

Throughout 1913 and into the war years, she continued to inform and advise committee members with warmth and practical good sense, and to impart that quality so much admired by Florence Nightingale: the 'battering ram' of a woman's attention.

In the summer of 1912, Marion herself 'took her ticket', albeit one of a different kind, and set off for a short holiday in Switzerland. She loved walking and could never contemplate a holiday at a seaside hotel. Holidays on the Continent invariably consisted of a few days snatched away from her duties, often following meetings of International Women's Conferences. This time, she went on a planned holiday with two companions in the Swiss mountains and wrote about her experiences in the August (1913) issue of *The Labour Woman*.

She found the long walks in all weathers invigorating, enjoying too the fare at a small inn, and the fun of the company of young, colourfully-dressed Italians. She was then, thirty years of age, and clearly relaxed and happy in those surroundings. She was not enamoured though, of the Rhône glacier when she and her friends arrived at it, describing it as 'one of the most curiously ugly things that people could go and see. It lies along the hillside, all bright blue ice and peaks and crags (which brings back visions of Earls Court and artificial grottoes) fading away at the base into a long moraine of dismal grey.' She was glad to leave 'this piece of stage scenery' and to bid farewell to the Rhône Glacier Hotel which she likened to a '... busy railway station, crowded with people.' Phillips soon escaped from them and she and her friends eventually found themselves in '... a charming narrow valley where the most perfect peace spread its gentle hands over all.' More happy days were spent among the flowers and fields and streams.

Her realism, however, soon re-asserted itself. It might seem an idyllic existence up in the valley in summer, but for local families, life all the year round, meant hard toil for little reward. The next valley also, though once a place of great beauty, had been reduced to a near-slum by human needs. Indeed, Phillips felt that the 'battered old tenement houses without drainage, overcrowded with families and animals, would compare unfavourably even with the slums of Liverpool.' Ceaseless daily toil, few pleasures and no formal education seemed to her to be the lot of these valley people. She commiserated especially with the women, who, old before their time, toiled in the fields and indoors, and were further reduced by natural hardships.

This unhappy scene prompted her to ask, 'How are the lives of these people to be fitted into the commonwealth of the future?' For her, there were no frontiers to suffering and injustice. The challenge that lay ahead was to lighten the load of everyone, in every land. In her own words:

> We have little message to take to these hard-driven women of the mountains, and no greater task lies before the Labour movement than that of building up a programme which will mean to those also, a lightening of the burden of poverty and toil that presses on them today.[17]

Chapter 8: Grass Roots and Brass Tacks

The years between 1910 and 1914 were marked by increasing industrial unrest in spite of many advances in social reform. Apart from the National Health and Unemployment Insurance Act, there was the Shops Act, followed by the Trade Union Act of 1913. Indeed, since 1906, progress in social legislation had been substantial. It included the Trades Boards Act, the Miners' Minimum Wage Act, the Acts establishing Labour Exchanges, the Old Age Pensions Act and the Act in which local authorities were given the power to provide school meals. Finally, there was the Lloyd George Budget that introduced a tax upon land values for the first time in the history of this country.

Yet, militancy was in the air. It expressed itself not only in the more violent actions of the Suffragettes but in the obstinacy of both sides to settle industrial disputes. The number of stoppages increased between 1908 and 1912 mainly because of the disparity between growing profits and rising prices on the one hand and stationary wages on the other.

There was too, in the Labour movement itself, in the words of Francis Williams, a feeling of 'general malaise.' He attributed it partly to indecisive leadership and to divided opinions on many of the major issues of the day. Belief in socialism was as firm as ever, but as Williams pointed out, there was 'a divorce between the organisation of the Labour Party and its campaigning and propaganda branch.' He went on, 'The Labour Party was in a state of transition ... the nation was in a state of transition also ... A great many new social forces were assailing all the organisations of society and the Labour Party among them.'[2]

Arthur Henderson was foremost among those who saw how vital it was to strengthen the links between the various components of the Labour Party, in order to consolidate and increase support for the party as a whole. Marion Phillips was equally alive to this pressing need in those difficult days. Most urgent was the necessity to prepare women for the time when they would be given the vote. This meant improving the machinery of the organisation of the Women's Labour League, and to this end she wrote an excellent manual called *How To Do the Work of the League* It was published in 1914 but re-issued after the 1914-18 War for the benefit of the New Women's Sections of the Labour Party and re-named *Women's Work in the Labour Party*.

It was Margaret MacDonald who had first conceived the idea of setting out the aims of the League and explaining how it should operate to maximum advantage. Phillips met the requirement admirably in this manual. Her organising talent is at once perceived in her opening remarks as she briskly explained in simple language, the purpose of the League, its structure, the method of election of its executive and officers and details of its affiliation to the Labour Party.

She noted that 'The great difference between the Women's Labour League and all other organisations in the Labour Party is that it is the only political national organisation for working women, and that it is the only organisation in the Labour Party into which women, who may not happen to be wage-earners and therefore cannot become Trade Unionists, and who are in general sympathy with the Labour Party, though they may or may not be Socialists, are admitted.'

Here was Phillips holding the door wide open to a broad span of women voters of the future. She explained further, that the League performed the functions of 'Keeping the Labour Party well informed of the needs of women, and provides women with a means of becoming educated in political matters and thus better able to take a full share of such work as the Party, men and women together, feel is needed. Its special work is to give expression to the wants, and the means of satisfying the wants of working women'.

The handbook is divided into sections containing detailed instructions and suggestions under headings like 'How to form a Branch', 'Officers of the Branch', 'Branch Meetings', 'How to make New Members,' 'How to raise money', 'Organisations connected with the Women's Labour League', and other matters.

Her comments throughout showed commonsense and understanding. Considering her own background and training, her insight into the everyday lives of working-class housewives was extraordinary. Her approach was always intuitive and sensitive. Not a single wrong note was struck.

As she carefully spelled out instructions on forming a branch, she anticipated minor difficulties. 'Some branches', she wrote, 'charge an entrance fee of 6d or 1/- but in adopting this system, a branch should always be sure that it is not keeping women from joining because they cannot afford the fee'.

Referring to the role of branch officers, she stressed the need for punctuality and added that the chairman should always 'have a cheery word or two in starting the regular meeting'. The chairman, too, she urged, should always explain the purpose of the League and make a plea for new members in addition to drawing attention to the literature that was to hand. Phillips attached great importance to creating a happy atmosphere at meetings with welcoming greetings to members and she suggested starting and ending each occasion with a song — 'very exhilarating if you have a piano and good singing!'

Sensibly too, she indicated that a committee was not really necessary in small branches as it might prove counter productive. Even in larger branches she suggested that all decisions should be made at the General Meeting, lest members might lose interest, because of lack of involvement.

She advocated that branch meetings be held on a fortnightly basis, alternating between afternoons and evenings. Their work should concentrate on business, education and propaganda, with social functions providing opportunities for short speeches explaining the work of the League.

Phillips was anxious that members of the League should continue to be outward-looking and in her handbook, she provided information about those organisations to which the League was affiliated. In addition to the Labour Party there were others like the W.E.A; the Women's Suffrage Advisory Joint Committee, and the Women's International Council of Socialist and Labour Organisations, British Section. She further explained that the chief work of that Council was to keep the different organisations in touch with the Women's International Socialist Movement and to organise the British Section at the International Women's Socialist Congress. Its official organ, she added was *The Labour Woman*.

She emphasised too that the League sent representatives to conferences and committees of other organisations and urged branches to discover information for themselves about various local organisations so that delegates might be sent to their councils. In this way, Phillips was preparing members to cast their net as wide as possible, to interest new recruits in the work of the League, and to extend its activities into every area, town and city. Conscious of the splendid electioneering work already performed by many branches of the Women's Labour League, she stressed that in every constituency the League should affiliate to the local Labour Party, L.R.C. or Trades and Labour Council, so bringing women into the work of the Party to watch over women's interests as well as to fit themselves to take their place in politics. This dual role of members of the Women's Labour League was always of paramount importance in her eyes. Local government was clearly an area in which they could operate. To begin with, she suggested that appointed members should attend meetings of local governing bodies — the municipal, urban or rural district councils and report the proceedings to the branch. When there were unusually important discussions she felt that all members of the branch should attend to hear what councillors had to say and how they voted.

In connection with local issues, she pointed out the importance of letters to the press and letters and deputations to councillors when occasion demanded. Members too, she pressed, should monitor carefully the work of the Poor Law Guardians and present themselves as candidates for election to these boards and to local councils. This activity would be allied to their efforts to get Labour candidates elected to Parliament. As for those members of branches already serving on local bodies, she suggested that they should always bring back reports to their branches.

Close contact, she further urged, should be kept with 'the Women's Co-operative Guild, the Socialist Sunday Schools and the Suffragists, in their area'. She also encouraged branch members to become involved with the work of the Women's Trade Union League, adding: 'We suggest that the case of women employees of public authorities may be made one of a branch's first causes.'

Phillips's advice on how to recruit new members was homely and imaginative. In the first instance, she suggested that a good way of keeping members of a Branch interested was to give them plenty to do. One way was to allocate the names of potential new members — one or two per person — to them so that visits could be paid, followed by more visits with literature. She was prepared too for all contingencies in the work of enrolling new members. Anticipating the upheaval in a family following the arrival of a new baby, with all the extra work and new time schedules that would prevent a mother from attending a meeting, Phillips pointed out, 'It is of the utmost importance for members to show their comradeship with her and not let her drop her connection with the Movement altogether. It is a crisis in most young mother's lives and as we want those who have children to be foremost in the political world of the future we must not let the new ties narrow a mother's life to a monotonous round of child-minding and housework.'

It was for this, that Phillips was to fight throughout her life: the chance for the working-class housewife to enter the world of politics and social reform; to develop her talents outside the home; to be a citizen of the world as well as a wife and a mother.

After making some more useful suggestions on ways to enrol new members, Phillips proceeded to look at the possibilities of raising money. She mentioned about a dozen fairly orthodox methods, but was realistic enough to dismiss the idea that propaganda meetings would bring in much cash. On the other hand she commented laconically 'Teas are a sure thing'. As for collections at public meetings she seems to have hit on the right psychological moment: 'These should be taken after the best speaker has spoken, before the close of the meeting and should be clearly announced by the chairman'.

Then, in order to stimulate general interest, before proceeding to discuss in more detail the work of the branches, Phillips drew attention to a few 'miscellaneous matters'. Among these, pride of place was given to the Baby Clinic. She suggested ways in which the branches could support this excellent cause.

Three Labour publications were then mentioned. *The Labour Woman* received from its editor a small pat on the back: '... in less than two years' she wrote, 'it had grown from a tiny four-page leaflet to a well-produced paper of sixteen pages. It is full of good articles, stories and notes on current affairs and is by far the best paper published for working women. Every Branch will find it of the greatest value in bringing in new members and keeping old ones up to the mark'. *The Labour Leader* — the weekly organ of the Independent Labour Party, which regularly included a column of Women's Labour League Notes, and *The Daily Citizen* — the daily paper of the Labour Party, received more than an honourable mention! Both were prepared to publish views held by League members, she gladly informed her readers. Then returning to the work of the branches, Phillips set out her *Notes on the Conduct of Business.* This is an informative and valuable section, providing a clear, detailed account of procedures, and in case they might prove daunting to the uninitiated, she had a word of comfort: 'It saves time and trouble if these rules are followed and they are really less complicated than they look at first.'

She then offered her suggestions for the content of meetings. Emanating from her bright resourceful mind, they are truly first-rate. She dealt in turn with the available options, providing all the necessary information in each case. Books and pamphlets, she suggested were good subjects for discussion but if a pamphlet was chosen, it would be an advantage if all members had a copy to study, while one member opened the discussion on it. If a book was chosen, it could either be read aloud or a synopsis given at the meeting with a discussion to follow. Each Branch, she suggested might make use of the Fabian book boxes which were lent at a low cost.

The writing of short papers would be very valuable educative work, she thought. It was indeed a splendid idea for members to do their own personal research into special institutions and then produce papers on their findings.

In order to spur them into action, she supplied a short list of the institutions she had in mind: municipal lodging houses for women; training colleges for teachers; open-air schools for children.

Lectures too, by outsiders were suggested. There was a possibility that civil servants might care to come to talk about their work, in a private meeting. The W.E.A. of course, was mentioned as an organisation always prepared to set up a course or single lectures on any subject of interest to a Branch. Lectures could also be provided by the Fabian Society, the Fabian Women's Group, the Industrial Law Committee, the Independent Labour Party and the Anti-Smoking League. Nevertheless, she stressed that the participation of the members themselves was most important because she explained, 'We want especially to train speakers in our own ranks and every one should have a try. Subjects should be chosen on which every woman in the Branch will want to express her opinion'.

This was very far-seeing. So many politicians of the past deprived of formal education, learned to make fluent and often impromptu public speeches through their early training in church and chapel literary and debating societies, where the invaluable practice of 'giving papers' on selected topics before an audience promoted poise and confidence that would always remain with them. Very wisely Phillips suggested examples of subjects for discussion and short speeches which were most immediate to every woman — those precise matters that affected her and of which she had daily knowledge: bathrooms, school uniforms, mid-day school meals, sculleries or larders, the school-leaving age, taxes on food, baby and school clinics, marriage and divorce laws, child labour. Questions could be discussed such as 'Should girls be taught care of babies at school?' or 'What is the best employment for girls after leaving school?'

Most of these topics would be within the orbit of mothers attending any Branch meeting and Phillips understood that once launched into discussion, their shyness would fall away and in time they would be ready to venture into more complicated issues. It was her imaginative insight that endowed her with such qualities of leadership and direction. Anyone who knows of the difficulty of bringing shy, inhibited people into general discussions cannot but admire the sensitivity and perception of this woman in her approach. She sought to turn every Branch into a mini-adult education centre, aiming high, while keeping her feet firmly on the ground.

As for directions for holding public meetings, all her public relations skills are seen to swing into action. Not a detail in the arranging of such events was overlooked: handbills and posters to be distributed; tickets to be sent to every newspaper accompanied by notes about the speakers and their chosen subjects; table and chairs for reporters to be provided near the platform, and so on. If no reporter was sent she advised the Secretary to send a report of the meeting to the newspaper. All meetings, she also suggested, should be supplied with literature for sale.

Branches everywhere, one would assume, would have been kept on their toes, following all Phillips's explicit directions. Roger Levy, her nephew recollected a story about her going to speak at a small public meeting clearly *not* arranged by one of her branches. She found that the rear half of the hall was occupied, and everyone knows that addressing an audience across a sea of empty seats is a peculiarly uncomfortable experience. Her audience however resolutely refused to move forward, and Marion who had put on much weight in her middle years finally said, 'Very well then, the Mountain must come down to Mahomet' and trotted down to join them in the centre of the hall.

Two brief comments complete the Manual. First she dwelled briefly on the work of the League with regard to International Relations. She explained that it was represented at the Women's International Socialist Congress to which came representatives from nearly every nation in the world. Between these three-yearly meetings she went on, contact was maintained by international women writing in *The Labour Woman*, and League members writing from time to time for international papers. Messages were interchanged on all important occasions and she assured her readers that 'the feeling of international solidarity among working women is growing steadily greater'.

Then returning to the grass roots of the League — to Branch activities, she expressed the view that social functions: receptions, dances and concerts, were 'not to be despised' as they helped to form lasting friendships within the movement and the warmth of the atmosphere and sense of enjoyment were bound to have a good influence on the children and young people who attended them. However, she cautioned that the social aspect of the League should never 'degenerate merely into a means of making money, without consideration of the primary objects of the Party as a political body'.

In conclusion, she provided a long list of the addresses of organisations that could be useful to branches, and offered her own help to new secretaries with any inquiries.

So ended this first-class publication — a model of its kind. In 1918 when the Labour Party was reconstituted, Marion Phillips became its Chief Woman Officer and in that capacity brought a quarter of a million women into the Party, thus — as Beverley Kingston maintains — 'creating the largest mass movement of working women that had yet been seen.'[3]

Chapter 9: The War Years

During 1913 an article by Marion Phillips called 'Women and War' appeared in *The League Leaflet*. 'There are', she said, 'two sides to the war against war: the economic and the humanitarian, but both spring from the same impulse, that of fostering and beautifying human life. If we are fighting to destroy and to prevent the ravages of poverty, we must fight also to prevent the ravages of war ... Just as poverty cheapens human life, so war mutilates it. We stand, the Labour and Socialist forces of the world, the champions of human life, proclaiming a sacred right to freedom from the hideous nightmare of slumdom and the rule of force and the murderous threat of the world's great armies'.

She went on to condemn the international interests that profit from war and she made an eloquent plea to the women of the world. 'Here lies the task of women, so often told that it is they who guard the morals of the race. Their task it is to teach the true heroism of self control, of love of truth, of the striving of the soul to remain on the highest summits of wisdom it can reach ... Real love of country lies in the desire to develop the higher qualities of national life - sacrifice for love of country is not met by chancing death in war but by braving and bettering the chances of life in peace'.[1]

The Women's Labour League had, since its inception, believed that the chance of world peace and social reform would be greatly enhanced by close international bonds between like-minded women. The Independent Labour Party already believed passionately in international co- operation as the road to peace, and when Mrs. Ramsay MacDonald spoke at the inaugural conference of the Women's Labour League in 1906, she sounded the international note loud and clear. Margaret MacDonald, like Marion Phillips who followed her, understood full well that women the world over are seized with the same preoccupations: their hopes and fears are the same; their children make the same sound when they laugh; their babies make the same sound when they cry.

Therefore, when the first international women's meeting took place in 1907 at Stuttgart — the home of Frau Clara Zetkin — the German champion of Women's Rights, the Women's Labour League, though only a year old, accepted the invitation to send delegates to Stuttgart. Then, the idea of an International Women's Conference took root: Frau Zetkin was appointed International Secretary and at the conference held three years later, in 1910 at Copenhägen, delegates arrived from Britain, Germany, Austria, Finland, the Scandinavian countries and Portugal. In the same year, Frau Zetkin proposed that an annual

International Women's Day should be observed on 8th March — the date on which the garment workers in New York had made their historic march in 1907 to protest against their working conditions.

Soon afterwards, the British delegates decided to form an International Committee of British Women Socialists, to include women representatives of Socialist Societies, Trade Unions and other bodies eligible for affiliation to the Labour Party and International Socialist Congress. The body formed in accordance with the resolution taken at the meeting was called 'The Women's International Council of Socialist and Labour Organisations, British Section', and Marion Phillips became its Chairman in 1912. She was to figure prominently at these International Conferences, particularly after she became Chief Woman Officer of the Labour Party.

Discussions of various topics of interest to women, and the correspondence between the British Section and their counterparts in other countries, formed the basis of a regular international column in *The League Leaflet* and later in *The Labour Woman* written by Mary Macpherson for many years and afterwards by Mary Longman and then Jennie Baker.

These 'International Notes' recorded faithfully the progress of the socialist women's movement overseas. At the Sixth Annual Conference of German Women at Jena in 1911, described by them as 'this little Parliament of Women', one of the matters discussed was the need for the protection of mothers and infants in industry and for the maintenance of widows and orphans. This would be a recurring theme for many years to come, at home and abroad. It is noteworthy too, that even as far back as the 1840s there had been efforts to evolve standard codes of practice throughout Europe, relating to the protection of women and children at work, and the limitation of hours. In 1897, the International Labour Congress set up by the Swiss Labour League discussed equal pay for equal work, maternity leave, the introduction of an eight-hour day, the protection of women in domestic work and as a result, the same year saw the establishment of the International Association for Labour Legislation with its Headquarters at Basle.

From the *Notes*, too, it is clear that by the end of the first decade of the twentieth century, women were now on the march throughout Europe, to seek long overdue reforms for themselves. In 1911, we find that the Austrian Socialist Women's Conference at Innsbrück was discussing equal rights and the organising of domestic servants. The plight of this particular section of women workers was of special concern to Marion Phillips when she became the first Secretary of the International Federation of Working Women in the post-war years. In 1912 Frau Adelheid Popp represented the Austrian Socialist women in the first Convention of Domestic Servants held at Berlin.

By 1912 too, women's suffrage had become internationally a burning issue. We read that in that year a paper called *Women's Right to Vote* (*Frauenwahbrecht*) was published by Frau Zetkin in Germany, while a similar paper — *Frauentag*, was published in Austria to celebrate a special Women's Day. Belgium women too, were making some gains, since for the first time they were eligible to stand as candidates for the councils that settled disputes between workers and employers.

Such then, was the regular correspondence between the women Socialists internationally, that readers of *The League Leaflet* were kept fully informed of developments overseas. They learned for instance, that there was a considerable increase in the number of women doctors, dentists and public servants in Germany, Austria, Denmark and Holland during these pre-war years, and that in Italy not only was a woman advocate appointed for the first time, but that a new law prevented women from working in factories for a month before childbirth, entitling them also, for a 'motherhood' grant for each confinement. Similar news soon arrived from Switzerland. In Zurich, free medical attendance during childbirth was being made available to mothers receiving income below a certain figure, while similar schemes were established in Lausanne, Tessin and Offenbach.

The women's crusade was spreading through America too. Californian women called for suffrage reform, while in Ohio, Michigan and Illinois, there was a strong demand for financial provision for the widowed mother 'as a right' so that she could stay home and care for her children.

In all these countries, women were concerned about the same issues and campaigning for them along the same lines. At home, discussions continued in the British Section on a variety of subjects, including the welfare of infants, the care of the mentally handicapped and the abolition of child labour. Conscious of the common purpose to which they were all committed, the British women were enthusiastically preparing for the International Congress of Socialist Women to be held in Vienna in 1914.

Then the curtain came down, with the outbreak of war on 4th August 1914. The conference had to be abandoned, but the bond held firm, even in the darkest days.

The war was unexpected in Britain, since few were privy to the secret pact made with France by Prime Minister Asquith and Foreign Secretary Sir Edward Grey. Even as late as August 2nd it was hoped that Britain might remain neutral, working with might and main to seek a settlement between the belligerents. Women's organisations held a splendid anti-war rally at the Kingsway Hall, and on 2nd August, a massive meeting was held at Trafalgar Square, at which Marion Phillips was one of the speakers. On that same night, however, hope died when the news that Germany had attacked Belgium, made Britain's entry into the war inevitable. Even among the anti-war citizens in this country there were plenty who felt that this conflict nevertheless, was inescapable, in order in the words of H. G. Wells, 'to be done for ever with the drilling and trampling foolery in the heart of Europe.'

The first months of the war though, did not deter the women of Europe from making every effort to retain contact with one another across the national frontiers. The British Section published their manifesto in *The Labour Woman*[2] and this reached the correspondents in the allied and neutral countries while every effort was made to convey messages of goodwill and unity between the sisters living in all the countries involved in the war. Even after a few months of hostilities, the women still felt that an International Conference might be held, and it was the intrepid Frau Zetkin who convened it with the help of friends in neutral Holland and Switzerland. It took place in Berne in March 1915. Thirty delegates from eight countries attended, the German women doing so at great risk to themselves. Mary Longman, Margaret Bondfield, Ada Salter and Marion Phillips represented the British section. Mary Longman in her article 'Women and Internationalism' published later in *Women and the Labour Party* described the meeting.[3] 'It was the most impressive gathering in which those present had ever taken part. Our delegates returned full of hope and bearing with them the text of agreed resolutions expressing the united mind of the conference'. Its aim was to press for a swift end to the war, followed by negotiations for a just and honourable peace. Indeed its peace terms were afterwards repeated in the memorandum adopted by the Allied Socialist and Labour Conference held in London two years later. Mary Longman concluded her article by stressing the importance of contact between women of all nations. 'Labour Women', she said 'have taken a definite part in maintaining the union of the workers of the world and being women and non-combatants, they may have found it easier than men to remain comrades of their sisters in all countries. They have had a share in saving inter-nationalism from being wrecked in the storms of war'. Marion Phillips too, in her introduction to the publication, paid a similar tribute to the women saying: 'Politically, women have a clean slate. They cannot bear any direct responsibility for the catastrophe that has overwhelmed Europe and drawn the whole world to disaster'.[4]

But while deploring the coming of war and the untold suffering in its wake, Phillips spent the duration working like a Trojan to allay its effect on working women. Immediately after the outbreak of war, she had become a member of the War Emergency Workers' National Committee. The Labour Party, conscious of the distress, fear and uncertainty that was bound to lie ahead, had moved swiftly to safeguard working people. The day after war was declared, Arthur Henderson called a meeting at the House of Commons and so the War Emergency Committee came into being. Representatives of all trades and callings sat upon it: trade unionists, miners, railway workers, teachers, factory workers, members of co-operative fields and others. Marion Phillips as General Secretary of the Women's Labour League was there to look after the interests of women. She was to speak for them, loud and clear, in the years that followed, and to them in the columns of *The Labour Woman*. Through this medium she explained issues to them, advised them and supported and comforted them in the darkest days of the war.

MacDonald and the I.L.P. opposed the war, just as Liebknecht and his followers had done in Germany. MacDonald had therefore, resigned the leadership of the Labour Party and Arthur Henderson had taken his place remaining at the helm throughout the war. J. S. Middleton became Secretary of the War Emergency Committee, the work of which is described in *The Book of the Labour Party*[5] thus:

> The general industrial and social outlook was examined and a programme of recommendation issued with a view to the prevention of unemployment; purchase, storage and distribution of food by public authorities, fixing of maximum prices; provision of meals for school children and the supply of milk to nursing mothers, infants, young children and sick people.

The Women's Committee of the Workers National Committee representing all the women's movements, safeguarded the interests of women workers throughout. In 1915, the 'Appeal to the Women of England' meeting was held at Caxton Hall, urging women to be vigilant of their rights. *The Labour Woman* published the 'Appeal to Women Workers' under the heading 'Equal Conditions and Equal Wages' for those who did the same work as men, whether as salaried workers or wage earners. They were urged to join the appropriate trade union or association for professional workers immediately upon taking up war work and through them to demand the same rate of pay as men and warned 'that in no case should any woman be employed at less than an adequate living wage and that the stereotyping of sweated conditions must at all costs be avoided'. A warmer note is struck when women are advised to try to 'preserve their strength' in view of the heavy burdens they carry in wartime in addition to caring for their children.[6]

During the war too, Phillips published a series of articles in *The Labour Woman* on 'Women in Munition Works'. In the first of these, she explained that 'munitions' included not only 'actual shot and shell but everything which is needed in any way for the equipment of army and navy. Thus food preparation, clothing, the making up of any raw material needed in the manufacture of anything for the armed forces as well as for the transport of such things is equally 'munitions". She had gone into this detail to explain that all these services brought the women workers engaged in them under the provisions of the Munitions Act. Ever the advocate, she explained that under the Act, a woman worker would become 'liable to all the compulsory clauses of that Act with its complicated provisions against strikes and its difficult process of getting leaving certificates. It makes her liable to the jurisdiction of the Munition Courts'. Having elaborated on the position she urged women workers to join trade unions so that they could be properly represented. Without that representation, she explained, 'pressure cannot be brought upon the Munitions Department or the employers to improve and equalise over the country with due consideration of local differences, the conditions and wages of women'. Examples of such 'irregularities' were then provided.

Phillips continued, 'exhaustion is due to lack of rest, impossibility of getting comfortable housing or sufficient food, frequently unhealthy conditions in the factories themselves, and all the consequences of low wages will play havoc with our women workers if left unchecked'. In an attempt to safeguard them, she issued a list of their 'primary needs'. They ran as follows:

> There should be a joint effort by all Trade Unions taking women members, to organise munition works, and there should be an 'exercise of the powers of the Munitions Department to get returns as to women's wages and to enforce compulsory increases ... where women are shown to be receiving less than men for the same work.

She suggested too, the establishment of an advisory committee of representatives of women workers to ensure this.

Wherever night work was needed, Phillips suggested an arrangement of three hour shifts, and canteens and rest rooms should be provided at factories and workshops with women workers participating in their management. There should be stringent factory inspection with additional women inspectors in those establishments that involved 'processes dangerous to health'. Finally, she recommended the provision of hostels whenever large numbers of women were brought to a new place to work.

So, human and industrial problems, besetting the lives of working women in wartime Britain, claimed her almost daily attention.

The Labour Woman of February 1916 published an account of the Chairman's address, delivered at the 10th August conference of the Women's Labour League, held at Bristol in January under the title 'A Working Woman and the Problems of War'.

The magazine article first emphasised Labour's faith in international co-operation, re-iterated the stance taken towards the war by the Women's Labour League, and calling attention to the resolution passed by the Berne Conference in March 1915 as the foundation to a just and lasting peace.

The article went on to indicate the unease felt about the situation at home. 'The Workers' it said, 'are fighting a battle waged on two sides. They are fighting the enemy abroad and they are fighting the forces of reaction at home'. While the lack of Labour leadership caused dismay, the National War Emergency Committee was praised for its work in protecting the weak and vulnerable in society. There was praise too for Labour's firm stand against the Compulsory Military Service Bill.

Attention was then focused on the plight of the helpless in war-time Britain. The Old-Age Pension was described as a pathetic figure. 'Today the pension is worth little more than 3/- and the war has not a sadder victim than the starving old people', she said. As for the children, they too, bore the 'burden of war', with further restrictions placed upon their 'scanty educational advantages'. They would reap a bitter harvest in later years.

The position of working women after the war, the article continued, was fraught with difficulties. Before the two million serving men returned to civilian life, much thought should be given to produce a policy, by the political and industrial arms of the women's movement. 'Clearly' it went on, 'the position of women will be one of the greatest delicacy and urgency. From two sides we must view the problem. On the one side, women admitted to the better paid classes of employment and finding their capacity equal to and sometimes even surpassing that of the men they have replaced, learning what it is to have a man's wage in place of a woman's, will refuse to return to their old rank of industrial drudge. On the other hand, women who are not themselves wage earners, but are dependent upon their husbands, will have to consider how far the presence of female labour with all its traditions of low wages and weak organisation, will mean the lowering of the whole standard of life for the working people. And further, what will the re-instatement of the old Trade Union rules mean to women workers'? Here was a statement of the chronic problem that had bedevilled the equality of the sexes for far too long a time, but it would have to be tackled by members of the Labour Movement. Co-operation was therefore urged with other women's organisations: The Railway Women's Guild, The Women's Trade Union League and the Women's Co-operative Guild. Finally the links with friends in other countries should be firmly forged after the war through the Women of the International and Labour Movement. In that way, the wounds of the past would be healed and together they would help to rebuild a peaceful world.

The magazine too, throughout the war, continued to give prominence to lectures on the effect of the conflict on family life. There was, for instance, a lecture on 'The Effect of War on Children's Lives' delivered by Mrs. Bruce Glasier in the Midlands and in Newport. Other lectures concerned disabled soldiers and sailors, and pressing Labour problems were aired by Margaret Bondfield and J. J. Mallon. In January 1916 an article on 'Drunkenness in Women' attributed the increase in drunkenness in a great measure to poverty, dreariness of bad housing that made public houses all the more attractive, and loneliness caused by the absence of soldier husbands.

Matters prescriptively concerned with the home and the health of mother and child and the welfare of women in industry, were ever to the fore, as well as issues that reflected the whole political spectrum, for Phillips was determined that women should be as well-informed politically as men on matters affecting the nation, and indeed other nations.

Additionally, *The Labour Woman* throughout the dark days of the war contained much that was in lighter vein. People needed to be comforted and uplifted. As well as the book reviews, there were stories — often love stories. Phillips wrote some of them herself. On occasion she wrote serials under her own name. 'A Long Life', a serial in three parts was one of her efforts. Another was 'Friends' in two parts. Sometimes she used a *nom de plume*. Children's stories too, often appeared. Katherine Bruce Glasier wrote some of them.

So during those sombre years *The Labour Woman* succeeded in being as lively and varied as it was instructive, always seeking, in the words of the advertisement for Pelaw polish which appeared so regularly in its pages, to 'improve each shining hour'!

However, so much of Phillips's time during the war years was taken up by her committee work, that for a brief period she relinquished the Secretaryship of the Women's Labour League.

In 1914, she had been nominated to serve on the Queen's Work for Women Fund Committee which later became the Central Committee on Women's Training and Employment. This committee brought her and Mary Macarthur into regular contact with Queen Mary who seemed to like the two Socialist women, according to Marion's nephew A. A. Phillips who often stayed with her while he was at Oxford. Referring to his aunt, he said:

> Strangely enough for a Labour woman, she got on well with Queen Mary. They both had the same interest in housing; they both had the same down-to-earth personalities; they were certainly two of the worst-dressed women in England.[7]

Violet Markham, the Chairman of the Central Committee, in a memorial tribute to her colleague referred to her outstanding intellectual gifts and her warm compassionate heart.[8]

The work of the Central Committee continued for years after the war. It fought hard for equal opportunities for women in education, training and employment throughout its existence.

Yet the most important of all her committees was the Standing Joint Committee of Industrial Women's Organisations. It was set up in February 1916 when Phillips became its Secretary and remained in that office until her death. Susan Lawrence, one-time Chairman of the Standing Joint Committee remarked on her 'energy and drive and close attention to detail and her cool and practical judgement.'[9] while Beverley Kingston concluded, 'Her proven efficiency and capacity for preparing and drafting extremely clear and succinct reports and resolutions made her an obvious choice as Secretary. Her forceful and fearless style on public platforms and her willingness to travel and to speak whenever and wherever it seemed useful, quickly established the voice of the Standing Joint Committee as the legitimate voice of the women of the working classes.'[10]

The Standing Joint Committee itself brought together the Women's Unions, the Railway Women's Guild, the Women's Labour League and the Women's Cooperative Guild. Phillips herself could be regarded as the voice of International women since she had been Chairman of the British Section of the Women's International Council of Socialist and Labour Organisations for many years and was aware of the needs of women at every level and in every sphere.

The establishment of the Standing Joint Committee was a brilliant move. A cohesive body with a structure of researching sub-committees, it produced progressive and pragmatic policies that influenced legislation. It was to become

The Advisory Committee to the Labour women's Annual Conference, drawing up the Agenda and submitting resolutions and discussion topics. Set up primarily to seek full representation for working women on local Pensions Committees, it soon developed as a powerful national body. Describing its function in the Twenties of the last century, *The Book of the Labour Party* Vol. II, refers to it in this way:

> Recognised as representative and authoritative, it is received and consulted by Departments of State and is frequently able to bring pressure in Whitehall, in the interests of women. In addition, working in close co-operation with the International Federation of Working Women (of which Phillips was also Secretary) it is in touch with continental opinion on all questions affecting the welfare of women ... It was consulted during the war by the Ministry of Food, the National Service Ministry, the Local Government Board and the Ministry of Agriculture, and was asked to appoint three representatives to the Consumers' Council set up by the Ministry of Food. In the work of reconstruction since the Armistice it has had members on the Housing Advisory and other Consultative Councils of the Ministry of Health; the Overseas Committee of the Colonial Office; the National Council for the Unmarried Mother and her Child and other national and administrative Committees.

A long list then follows of the questions in which members of the Committee continued to be involved: matters of employment, health, education and the work of women magistrates and penal reform. The Standing Joint Committee was to become useful in advising and supplying information for the Labour Party Executive and Parliamentary Party on certain bills that came before the House, particularly dealing with social and industrial matters.[11]

Other war committees too, claimed her attention. One was the membership of a committee set up to oversee the working of the National Insurance Act. She had, of course for years, been explaining relevant sections of the Act and advising readers in the columns of *The League Leaflet* and *The Labour Woman*.[12]

She was appointed also to serve on various Government enquiries. Then in February 1917, Marion Phillips and Beatrice Webb found themselves as the only women members on Lloyd George's new Reconstruction Committee. Mrs. Webb in her diary entry dated 19th February 1917 is elated that its members were 'young and vigorous persons with the Prime Minister as Chairman and the youngest and ablest of the Ex-Cabinet Ministers as Vice-Chairman'. The Committee did indeed include eminent people drawn from academic, political and business spheres.

Her delight grows as she records in her diary entry of 22nd February 1917, how Tom Jones — Dr. Thomas Jones — Deputy Secretary to Lloyd George's War Cabinet, described to her how the Prime Minister himself had carefully selected the membership of the new Reconstruction Committee. According to her, 'Then apparently without consulting Montagu or Vaughan Nash, he ordered a letter to be written to each of the selected ones, asking them in the name of the War

Cabinet to serve on the New Reconstruction Committee'.[13] Marion Phillips does not seem to have been so impressed as Beatrice by this turn of events, according to her light-hearted remark, twelve years later in the House, that the Reconstruction Committee was 'appointed in a fit of audacity by the Rt. Hon. Member for Caernarvon Boroughs, Mr. Lloyd George.'[14]

Mrs. Webb's euphoria, alas, does not last. The 3rd June entry in her diary, indicates total disenchantment with the committee. They are all clearly out of step. The Vice-Chairman, Edwin Montagu is a 'great disappointment' and the staff are 'incompetent'. Jack Hills is 'without any special reasoning capacity', and Lord Salisbury talks too much. Professor Adams (warden of All Souls and Private Secretary to Lloyd George — 1916–19) is a 'high-browed idealist'. Philip Kerr (later the Marquess of Lothian), is an 'ultra-refined aristocratic dreamer'. The list of offenders continues. Marion Phillips, Mrs. Webb's colleague in the Labour Movement similarly incurs her displeasure. While she concedes that 'Marion Phillips is shrewd and capable', she adds, 'but she is contentious and she tries to oppose anything I propose out of some vague desire not to be considered as a Webb disciple'. The latter part of her complaint merits no comment, but her charge of 'contentiousness' against another committee member carries a rather amusing sequel. The Prime Minister himself in his *War Memoirs* recalls how one of the sub-committees of the Reconstruction Committee 'under the Chairmanship of Rt. Hon. J. H. Whitley, M.P. was charged with the study of Relations between Employers and Employed'. On 8th March, 1917, it produced a report in which it proposed the setting-up of Joint Standing Industrial Councils in the better-organised industries. The report had a mixed reception from the Members of the Reconstruction Committee. Mr. Montagu, the Vice-chairman, was in favour of the proposal. Mrs. Sidney Webb, on the other hand, subjected it to a torrent of destructive criticism and concluded that such councils could only be set up in the railway and postal services; and declared:– 'I cannot imagine that it would be worthwhile the Government committing itself to such a harmless but insignificant project, or that it could be, with any wisdom, separately promulgated apart from other items in the Government Reconstruction Programme on the Relation of Employers and Employed.'

Mr. Whitley's committee made prompt rejoinder to her criticisms, and it was eventually decided by the War Cabinet on 7th June, 1917 to circulate the report to the leading trade unions and employers' federations, and the Commissioners on Industrial Unrest, for their views. On 19th June we took the further decision to publish the Report.'

The Prime Minister's account then went on to state that all three bodies declared in favour of the report, and following its official adoption on 31st December 1917 the first National Whitley Council — for the pottery industry — was announced. Others followed and by the early years of the 1920s, seventy three joint councils had already been established. Since then, they have been a most valuable feature of the mechanism of industrial conciliation.

In her diary entry dated 3rd June, Mrs. Webb referring briefly to the 'animated debate' on the report of the Whitley Committee in the Reconstruction Committee announces that she was the only one to oppose it.[15]

In an entry dated 18th July, she notes the end of the Reconstruction Committee and it is clear that she seeks to minimise any great differences of opinion among the members. Recording that the last meeting of the Committee was 'a cordial one', she adds blandly, 'There has been singularly little friction between the various members of the Committee — the trouble has been between the old office-holders, Montagu and Vaughan Nash ... and the new Committee of outsiders'.[16]

In August 1917, the Reconstruction Committee was replaced by the Ministry of Reconstruction under the chairmanship of Dr. Addison (formerly the Minister of Munitions). The sub-committees set up by the Ministry were of great value paving the way towards new legislation at the end of the war.

Another body set up early in the last year of the war was the Consumer Council, of which Marion Phillips became a hard-working member. In the Autumn of 1916, Lloyd George, worried about the acute problem of food shortages, had stressed that it was imperative to appoint a Food Controller to organise the production, purchase, distribution of supplies and the control of prices. When he became Prime Minister in December 1916, he appointed Lord Devonport as the Food Controller. Frank Owen in his *Tempestuous Journey* describes how Lord Devonport in 1917 appealed to the public to ration themselves voluntarily in bread, meat, sugar and potatoes, and how in response to this there were 'meatless and breadless days in taverns and hotels'.[17]

In May 1917, Lord Devonport was replaced by Lord Rhondda (formerly D. A. Thomas, the Welsh Liberal M.P. and coal-owner). He extended the previous system of food control, immediately setting up a costing department to examine food costs and to fix maximum prices. In June 1917 an Order in Council was passed, giving him full powers of requisitioning food and fixing food prices. The latter was long overdue since by June 1917 retail prices had risen 102% over 1914 prices.[18] In this urgent situation, to check speculation and to cut out the middlemen Lord Rhondda ordered the fixing of bread prices and drew up a scheme for sugar distribution. Further, he requested local authorities to set up Food Control Committees. By August 1917 he laid before the local authorities a scheme of food control that had three aims: to conserve supplies, to ensure that rich and poor shared alike; to keep down prices. He recommended too, that central kitchens should be used as a means of economising food and fuel. Sugar cards were issued and local authorities were notified of the intention to fix a general scale of prices for all important foodstuffs. This was done and on August 10th, six Food Commissioners — four in England and Wales and two in Scotland were appointed to supervise the working of the schemes. In September, Orders were made, fixing maximum prices for meat, butter, flour, potatoes and other commodities. A new scale of voluntary rations of basic foods appeared in

November, and in December a further Order was made by the Food Controller to ensure distribution to try to prevent food queues.

Much had been done but many grave problems remained. There were shortages and there were queues. Early in January 1918, therefore, Lord Rhondda, in conjunction with his successor — J. R. Clynes, set up the Consumer Council 'to enlist the co-operation of the organised working classes and the co-operative movement in the gigantic task that lay before the Ministry' [Ministry of Food, which had been set up in 1916].

Representatives were invited from the Parliamentary Committees of the Co-operative Congress and the T.U.C.; from the War Emergency Workers' National Committee (the W.N.C.) and the S.J.C. Phillips was one of the three representatives from the S.J.C., serving also on the Ministry of Food Central Classification Committee for Supplementary Rations for Heavy Workers — under the Meat Rationing Order of 1918.

Until now, organised Labour had been opposed to compulsory rationing but in the circumstances of 1918, declared itself in favour of it as an alternative to queues. Extensive rationing was now envisaged and on 25th February 1918, a scheme of rationing meat, butter and margarine, came into force in London and the Home Counties and by April 1918 meat was rationed throughout the country.[19]

Ration Books were issued in July and the consequent rationing of the basic commodities ensured a regular and efficient food supply. It was impartial and well organised and while Britain faced shortages it did not experience famine, faring better than most of the other Allied countries.

Among Phillips's Consumer Council files there were many references to National Kitchens. She was extremely impressed with their efficiency and quality and after the war, had high hopes that they might become a part of the life of the overworked housewife in the context of a new approach to housing and town planning. A start had been made in the Government-run canteens of the war-time Munitions Factories, prompting the Prime Minister to go further in providing help to the munition workers, '... by pressing forward the extension of canteens for them where they could be sure of getting good food at reasonable prices. So successful were we in this that we actually had a complaint by a Member of Parliament on 24th October 1917, that in one munitions area, the excellence of the arrangements ... in providing high-class but economical meals to the public is a menace to the existence of privately owned restaurants and cafés!' The objector was informed, in answer, that 'We shall certainly do nothing to interfere with the proper provision of food for our munition workers'.[20]

The proper provision of food, in the form of National Kitchens, became popular in various localities until there were about three hundred and sixty three of them throughout the country by the end of the war.

1918 was a particularly busy year for Phillips on the Consumer Council, at the same time as she was heavily involved with other duties. In March of that year, she was writing to the Ministry of Food about the need for extra meat rations for women workers and a copy of the reply states that 'representations were being put to Mr. Beveridge', on the matter.[21]

In April, there is correspondence with the Belvedere Women's Co-op Guild about extra rations for expectant and nursing mothers. The correspondence includes a letter from Annie Robinson, mid-wife, Belvedere, about the needs of pregnant and nursing mothers and requesting Marion Phillips to come and address the Women Workers' Committee of St. Augustine's Church, Belvedere.[22]

For the rest of the year and much of 1919 she was concerned with a great range of food supplies including soft and dried fruit, jam, meat, sugar and especially milk products. In her files for June 1918, there is a report by the National Clean Milk Society of its investigation into the hygienic quality of milk supplied during 1916 to babies attending certain schools for mothers, and during 1917 to twenty one London hospitals.[23] Then on August 7th 1918, under the heading, 'Milk of Special Quality,' there is a copy of a letter written by Marion Phillips to the Ministry of Food about the higher price of milk; the licences for purchase and sale, and about the Ministry Of Food inspection of farms and score cards.[24]

On November 18th 1918, there is further correspondence between Marion Phillips and the Ministry of Food again regarding milk under the Mother and Children Order, including its application to Scotland.[25] The correspondence about milk continues into 1919.

In March 1919 there is a discussion with the Ministry of Food about dried milk,[26] and in the same month there is correspondence regarding 'Glaxo' (providers of infant and invalid food) between Marion Phillips and Alex Nathan, the Director of Glaxo[27] and in April of the same year, she is still concerned about the quality of milk, as the correspondence about the comparative analysis of milk samples before and after factory processing reveals.[28]

In May 1919, there emerged a gloomy report on the future of the Ministry of Food,[29] and in the same month there followed another report on the lapsing of food controls.[30]

On 13th August 1919, the Consumer Council appointed Phillips to represent it on a deputation to the Prime Minister. But it was all over. The splendid efforts of the Food Controller, the Ministry of Food and the Consumer Council itself, in safeguarding the quantity and quality of available foods — particularly that of milk to infants and nursing mothers, as well as the strict control of prices, came to an end, as part of the post-war economy measures of the Government.

It was a bitter blow. While lamenting that the 'Flower of the Nation' had perished on the Somme, the authorities decreed that protection was to be removed from the most vulnerable of the budding generation. The profiteers were back in business. Marion Phillips in and out of Parliament continued to campaign persistently for free milk for necessitous mothers and infants. How happy she would have been to behold the result of Labour Government policy after the Second World War: the bonny babies that were the pride of Britain and the envy of the world.

Chapter 10: Chief Woman Officer

Since the birth of the Labour Party, its leaders had stressed the paramount need for organisation. Though hampered by lack of money, and hamstrung in so many other ways, Keir Hardie and those close to him had faced the home truth that without organisation the cause was doomed. The fate of women would be similarly sealed, as J. J. Mallon, Secretary of the Anti-Sweating League pointed out in a Foreword to *The Souvenir* to celebrate the first Labour Women's Day in Britain — 17th July 1909. Condemning the drudgery of a woman's life of 'mistreatment and woe' and claiming her right to a 'higher and finer life', he warned that 'the open sesame to that better life is organisation'.

John Galsworthy too, in his article in *The Souvenir* on women working in industry, made the same point: 'Go on' he said, 'putting your forces together, extend your organisation, combine, stick to each other'.[1]

Arthur Henderson saw the need to organise better than anyone. He himself, was a master of the craft. Marion Phillips possessed the same flair. Together, they made a formidable and unassailable team.

The newly-structured Labour Party in 1918 depended on them and they were ready for the fray. Francis Williams was to say of Marion's triumph with the women, 'Under Dr. Marion Phillips, a women's organisation had been created such as no other party possessed.'[2] That organisation rallied the women bringing them into the Party in hundreds of thousands, establishing its own record. *The Book of the Labour Party* refers to the same phenomenon when it describes the setting up of the Women's Organisation:

> The importance of this step cannot be over estimated ... This undoubtedly has been one of the most successful developments in the Party's work. The women were probably more enthusiastic than the men and at the Annual Conference, 1925, Dr. Marion Phillips was able to report that apart from Women's Ward Committees, over one thousand, two hundred Women's Sections of the Party had been formed with a membership of over two hundred thousand.[3]

The machinery of re-organisation had been set in place by the Labour Party's Revised Constitution early in 1918. A section of the Revised Constitution stated its policy: 'To promote the political, social and economic emancipation of the people and more particularly those who depend on their own exertions by 'hand or brain' for the means of life'.

With the focus on 'hand or brain', it was clear that Labour's aim was now to appeal to people of goodwill across the whole span of society, just as the early I.L.P. had done. Henceforth there would be no barriers to joining the Party.

Anyone sympathetic to its purpose could belong merely by enrolling as a member of a local branch. The Women's Labour League from now on, would be brought into the new branch structure of the Party as Women's Sections with their own organisation.

Phillips was installed in her own office quarters on the first floor of the Labour Party Headquarters in Victoria Street, ready to start on her country-wide campaign to appeal for support among the six million new women voters over thirty years of age. She was, from the beginning, a presence and a power, directing operations with authority and confidence. Leah Manning in her autobiography, *A Life for Education*, says that Marion Phillips 'was a woman of great independence of mind. She ran the Women's Department at Transport House without reference to anyone else, indeed so much was the case that on her sad and premature death, it was firmly laid down that her successor would be subject to the controlling guidance of the General Secretary'.[4] If as it seems, that she was a law unto herself, then, judging by results, it paid off handsomely.

But she and Henderson worked well together. 'She was,' he said after her death 'one of the best and most practical women in public life.'[5] Practical, yes, like himself. Both had a clear vision of the future, but first of all they applied themselves to the nuts and bolts of immediate demands with all their might. They both in addition had good judgement, common sense and an intuitive touch in handling sensitive matters of policy. Her appointment itself indicated a mutual trust and liking. Henderson, along the years had stood like a rock in support of complete adult suffrage and the granting of women's rights. Mary Macarthur had found in him a staunch ally in the fight to set up Trade Boards for the protection of women in industry. The combination of Henderson and Phillips in 1918 boded well for the future.

Anticipating a General Election after the cessation of hostilities, the Labour Party convened a National Conference of Women to meet at the Caxton Hall in London, on October 15th and 16th, 1918. Much of the discussion of that conference appeared in Marion's editorial article in the December issue of *The Labour Woman* under the title 'The Policy of the Labour Party'. This was a special election issue of the magazine. In it, she considered 'the matters which are most important in women's minds today. The fundamental necessities of being are food, shelter and dependent on them both, health'. But since social reforms at home depended on peace abroad — which entailed fair and lasting treaties — she set forth Labour's views on the League of Nations. Other matters considered in the article were public health services and the food supply; housing, and the whole question of the emancipation of women.

Under the heading, 'Equal Civic and Political Rights for Men and Women', she explained Labour's policy of complete adult suffrage for men and women at twenty one. Further, Labour would make women eligible for office as judges, magistrates, ministers, members of juries and of all the professions. Labour too, she continued, believed in an equal moral standard for men and women. It would give British women the right to choose British nationality on marriage with an alien, and the widow of a soldier or a civilian would have the right of maintenance for her dependent children and such a provision should also be applied when the breadwinner's health broke down.

As for the 'Health of the Nation', the way forward would be a Ministry of Health as a centralised department, overseeing all aspects of health throughout the community. Chief among these would be maternity and housing. Phillips stressed the need for working women to serve on the special Maternity Committees which were being set up under local health authorities as a result of the efforts of the Co-operative Women's Guild and the Women's Labour League. In order to ensure the welfare of mothers and babies, local hospitals and clinics and a system of trained home helps had been advocated by the Labour women for a long time. In addition, Labour urged that hospital care for everyone should be free from 'any sort of Poor Law interference.'

The importance of working women representatives on health committees was vital, she said, in particular in view of returning soldiers possibly infected with strange diseases. So, she continued, 'the watchword of Labour's health proposals is, you cannot run an A1 nation with a C3 population.'

Referring to the Labour Party's 'Housing Campaign', she said that the Rent Act should be continued until there were sufficient houses. Building programmes should continue rapidly. After the disappearance of the Rent Act, Labour believed it should be replaced by 'Fair Rent Courts'. She maintained that people should no longer be in 'the hands of the landlord and employer owning the houses. We do not want tied cottages for any family.' Good municipal buildings was the answer. Money should be provided to help municipal schemes and working women should be consulted about the plans.

As for food programmes, Labour's plans at the outbreak of war had been ignored with disastrous consequences and it was not until the end of 1917 with the appointment of Lord Rhondda as Food Controller that the situation was reversed. 'Labour's policy,' said Phillips, 'was to insist that there should be more rigid control over the food speculator,' resulting in a reduction of prices. Only Labour demanded that the food supply stayed in the hands of the people. It was totally opposed to any customs duties on food and insisted that it was 'only by nationalisation of the milk supply and its distribution through the municipalities, can a pure, cheap and plentiful milk supply be obtained for babies.' Free milk should be available to babies and nursing mothers, small children, individuals and old people on application through the Public Health Authority with 'no impertinent enquiries to prove necessitous conditions ... No baby, no young child should suffer because it cannot get its necessary food.'

She praised the Local Food Control Committees for helping to 'bring the fresh air of democracy into the administration of local food supplies.' Praise was due too, to the work of the Consumer Council. Labour believed that both bodies should continue. She concluded, 'we do not believe that the food speculator who could not be a patriot in wartime will be a patriot when peace comes. We have no reason to trust him in the past and we propose to control him in the future.'[6]

Unfortunately, there was little opportunity to inform the electorate of Labour's policy. The Prime Minister rushed the country into the 'Khaki' Election in December and nearly all the Labour leaders including Henderson were defeated. Dark days were to follow. In 1921 the jobless reached two million.

However the Labour Party reorganisation was under way to prepare for the next election whenever it came. The individual membership drives started first where there was Labour Party representation on trade councils, since these had already acquired experience in practical matters. By the end of 1919, there were six thousand Labour representatives on local bodies. The numbers increased with each election, and on public committees and magistrates' benches, large numbers of women were now taking their place.

Gradually, a network of local Labour parties was formed, covering the whole country, which in its turn was divided into nine areas. Each area was in the hands of two organisers, one man and one woman. The scheme was co-ordinated under the Chief Agent.

The women organisers each worked to Marion Phillips — their 'Chief'. At the local level were the Women's District Committees. Membership of Women's Section carried with it the right of individual membership of the local branch and special provision was made in the Constitution to ensure that they had adequate representation on local committees. Almost immediately the all-important 'grass-roots' activity sprung into action. Local members were responsible for recruitment and for running committee rooms. Women acquired organisational experience and many acted as Party agents. At least four seats were allocated to women on the Central Executive of the Party in London and more could be elected if they were successful in any of the group ballots.

Representatives of the Women's District Committees formed the Area Advisory Councils. There were forty-two of these in the 1920s, arranging conferences, summer schools, galas and Women's Day celebrations. They had bands and banners and as many as ten thousand would assemble, particularly in the north of England at some of these gatherings, to take part in huge processions and to listen to an address by some well-known Labour politician.

There was also a Women's Annual Conference where women's interests at home and abroad were discussed in a well-informed and constructive way, as well as matters of general import. Often they would consider reports and recommendations submitted by the Standing Joint Committee of Industrial Women's Organisations — of which Marion Phillips was the Secretary — on matters ranging from education and employment, pensions and maternity care to penal reform and disarmament. Housing and rents concerned them too and of course, the still-burning issue of full voting rights for women.

The purpose of the Women's Section remained the same as that of the earlier Women's Labour League: to involve women — particularly housewives — in politics and social affairs; to educate and inform them of widely-ranging issues concerning their lives and to develop their own skills in public work.

Thus the shy housewife would gradually become a confident speaker and competent committee member, her enthusiasm growing with her new-found ability and above all, the realisation that she herself existed as an independent personality. This enthusiasm poured out of homes and committee rooms into the streets of the industrial towns in the Twenties. Whole households were infected, including children. Children particularly! How excited they became when there was an election in the air. It was a breath of life to youngsters who knew nothing of pantomimes and circuses. Who needed them? This was the real thing, providing colour and gaiety and the clash of a contest. Election day meant a school holiday. It meant too, cars decorated with red and yellow ribbons from which whippers-in in dark suits, clutching lists of names would emerge to knock urgently on doors, to hurry people to come to vote. They kindly allowed little boys with Party badges on their jerseys to come for short rides on the running-boards of the cars. Sometimes their little sisters, their hair tied in Party-colour bows came too. Photographs of candidates were displayed in parlour windows; groups of people talked excitedly here and there in an electric atmosphere. The children sensed it and understood much of the conversation of their elders. Indeed they were probably more politically literate than most adults today. A paragraph in *The Book of the Labour Party* (Vol.I) captures the spirit of the times: 'Nothing could be more inspiring than to see the womenfolk from every house in certain streets form processions to march to the ballot box and vote Labour, and nothing did more to make a Labour Government possible than the women's vote'.[7]

Marion Phillips was well-known and held in great affection and admiration in these towns. Throughout the years she had been coming and talking to the women about health and nutrition, about the need for baby clinics and better housing, about education and women's rights. Warm, reliable and inspiring, she stirred their hearts and minds. Women at all levels knew and trusted her and followed her brisk advice. Little wonder that her photograph appeared on so many mantelpieces in Labour houses across the country in those days.

Since women over thirty now had the vote, it was more important than ever that the women themselves should seek new recruits. In 1921 she issued a handbook for officers and members of Women's Sections, called *Organisation of Women within the Labour Party*. Two years later, notes for speakers and workers' classes appeared in the form of a booklet called *Women's Work in the Labour Party* which was essentially a re-issue of the excellent *How to do the work of the League* which she had compiled and published in 1914. An article by A. D. Sanderson-Furniss — 'The Citizenship of Women', says, 'The work of organising women within the Labour Party has been so successful that apparently one opposition party at least thought it could not be bettered. Recently the Conservative Party in a booklet issued to its own associations, paid the Labour Party the compliment of quoting almost verbatim and without acknowledgement large slices of the Party's publication on the subject. And although the booklet was withdrawn after protest had been made, the compliment remains and deserves to be placed on record'.[8] The Women's Movement was now reaching massive proportions and in the December 1923 General Election, the intense activity up and down the country bore fruit. Though the Conservatives were returned as the largest party with two hundred and fifty-eight seats, they had no overall majority. Labour won one hundred and ninety-one seats and the Liberals one hundred and fifty- nine, and when the new Parliament met in January, the Conservatives were defeated by the combined might of the Labour and Liberal vote and consequently Ramsay MacDonald was invited to form a minority Government. In an article in *The Labour Magazine*, Marion Phillips jubilantly declared: 'As soon as the Election was over, Lord Younger told us that it was women voters who were mainly responsible for the downfall of the Conservative Party. I think he is right about it and if women between twenty-one and thirty had been enfranchised as well, the defeat would have been even more signal'.[9]

Regretting however, that it was 'more difficult to get an organisation in full swing in the rural areas', so placing the Labour woman in the village at a disadvantage with her urban sisters, she promised that the problem would be tackled urgently. 'A more direct personal tyranny presses down upon her than upon the townswoman', she added, clearly aware of the vestiges of feudalism still lingering in the British countryside.

She spoke of five years of 'tremendous progress' praising Labour women for their part in the electoral machinery of the Party. 'By 1923', she added, 'there was an army of voluntary canvassers, speakers, committee-room workers — all ready to enter the fray'. Her training programmes had clearly been effective. The 'steady educational work' in the Women's Sections, in the conferences held by the Women's Advisory Councils and in the 'Speakers and Workers classes', all under the direction of the regional organisers, had developed their political knowledge to a high degree and provided them with the tools for the job in hand.

The housewife herself, in her own right, who was always at the heart of Marion Phillips's attention, is praised by her for her quiet determination. She says: 'There is in women a certain dogged persistence and patience which comes from the very nature of their work in their own homes and which has created a psychology invaluable, from the point of view of electoral work. They apply to politics the same patience with which they deal with the daily problems of the household'.

After emphasising the importance of the campaign to enfranchise the four million women in the twenty-one to thirty age group, Marion Phillips ends her article with a hopeful eye to a future in which women politically dominate their menfolk. She quotes the comment made by a Labour Party woman worker: "As I say to my husband, 'Whatever way you vote, I will always vote the same,' but I will always see that he votes as I want".

Marion Phillips concludes contentedly, 'After all, this has been the way in which women have managed men throughout the ages'.

Her unflagging energy and capacity for hard work was recognised by everyone. Len Fox tells us that A. A. Phillips recollected that she was 'a terrific worker ... very good to young people ... and liked the rank and file women she worked with ...'[10] As a 'terrific worker' herself, she expected a similar performance from others. 'Critical' was the word used most often to describe her by her niece, Frances Levy. Frances — well over eighty at the time of our correspondence, had in her young days been converted to socialism by her aunt and at one time was the Secretary of the local Labour Party in Welwyn Garden City, 'but she was always very critical of my efforts,' she recalled.

While it is not unusual for members of a family to be mutually intolerant, it is quite conceivable that Marion Phillips could be impatient with colleagues too if their work fell below the expected standard. There is no doubt either, that on occasion, she would become rather 'phillipsy', but had these traits been seen as anything but fleeting lapses, it would have been astonishing to find that she was held in such deep respect and affection not only by the rank and file section members throughout the land but also by the regional women organisers, directly answerable to her, who worked most closely with her in all weathers and who knew her best.

But Mrs. Webb in an entry dated March 1920 in her diary, describing a visit to the Labour Party Headquarters at 1 Victoria Street, remarks, 'Upstairs, superintending the Women's Section, sits the redoubtable Marion Phillips', adding rather curiously, 'hardly an element of solidarity in an office'.[11] What prompted the latter comment, one wonders? Perhaps it was because Marion Phillips was not 'a disciple of the Webbs', as Beatrice had once suggested, or a member of Beatrice's 'Half Circle Club'. Or was it the memory of a temporary disagreement on policy in the Fabian Society, some dozen years before, that still rankled?

On this occasion however, Phillips fared far better than the rest of the staff. Mrs. Webb cannot bring herself to say a single kindly word about any of them. She describes 'two seedy male clerks' and 'somewhat inferior female types'. She is even less charitable about the Parliamentary Agents, referring to them as 'old men, unkempt men, half-educated men — an inferior brand of the old Trade Union branch official'.

A contemporary photograph shows that she is inaccurate on all counts. The 'old men' referred to, incidentally were probably a good deal younger than Mrs. Webb herself, while Marion Phillips was just thirty-nine.

The two women could not have been more different in personality. Marion hated snobbery and while Beatrice was vain and humourless, Marion, according to Margaret Gibb, was a 'hard working happy woman' who 'became a friend to all ...' and 'had time for everyone ...' Indeed, 'considerate', 'understanding', 'appreciative' were the adjectives most often used to described her by those who worked with her, and Margaret Gibb again reinforces the evidence of the excellent relationship between her and her colleagues in her comment: 'One always looked forward to Dr. Phillips coming into the area; she so readily grasped difficulties and was so appreciative of one's work.'[12]

But it was of Marion's warmth and personal kindness that Mrs. Gibb wrote to me, shortly before her death. She said that she had lost her husband in 1927, and still remembered over half a century later how Marion had invited her to spend that Christmas with her at her home in London. Others too, experienced her kindness and compassion in trying times. The genuine grief expressed in the memorial tributes of those who knew her well, bear witness to this. The main tribute in ,*The Labour Woman*, of March 1932 contains these moving words: '... it is for what she was, as well as what she did, that she is remembered with misty eyes today, wherever a little band of Labour women meet to carry on the work she loved. Marion was a great leader and a great soul.'[13]

Chapter 11: Much Work and Little Leisure

At the same time as the re-structuring of the Labour Party was in progress, there was some reorganisation of Marion Phillips's domestic arrangements. A few years previously, after Dr. Bentham had moved from her home — 74 Lansdowne Road — to another area, Phillips and Mary Longman, who had shared it with her, found new accommodation at a house nearby. In 1919, however, Mary Longman married and went to live in Sweden, while Marion found herself a flat at 14 New Street Square, Fetter Lane.

This was the first home of her own Phillips had known since she had arrived in this country and here she remained until her death. According to Frances Levy, who often spent week-ends with her, Phillips had no time nor inclination for housework. It is, therefore not surprising that she so fiercely resented the time that working-class housewives were forced to waste in daily drudgery. Little wonder too, that she championed so long and vigorously underpaid and underprivileged domestic servants. She saw housing reform as one of the country's paramount priorities. Sensible planning, bathrooms, convenient kitchens, plenty of labour-saving devices would make housekeeping pleasurable and provide the housewife with opportunities to develop her mind.

Phillips herself found an excellent housekeeper to take charge of her home, in Mrs. Deacon who stayed with her for fourteen years and who paid tribute to her kindness, advice, and encouragement during that time. Although her financial position had improved with her appointment as Chief Woman Officer, according to Mrs. Deacon, Phillips's 'way of living was very simple'. and she continued to supplement her income with occasional lecturing between 1918 and 1920 at the London School of Economics.[1]

In 1919 Phillips ceased to be a councillor of the Royal Borough of Kensington, where she had sat with Dr. Bentham since 1912, representing the Golborne ward. However, in the same year, she became one of the first women magistrates in the country, sitting in the Children's Court of the Finsbury and Holborn Bench. She was, too, among the first group of women magistrates appointed to the Lord Chancellor's Advisory Committee for the County of London. This latter appointment gave her the opportunity to nominate magistrates who were down-to-earth and familiar with the background of the lives of those ordinary working people who so often appeared in the courts. As Gertrude Tuckwell, a fellow magistrate and colleague on the Advisory Committee remarked, Phillips always refuted 'the idea that the title of J.P. is a sort of *Legion d'Honneur*.'[2] To some extent, even today, as the century stumbles towards its close, this misconception, unfortunately, still survives. In spite of the improvement in the level of competence of magistrates, largely due to the compulsory training programmes, and the emphasis laid by the Lord Chancellor's Department on the desirability of obtaining a 'good mix' of professions, occupations and background on benches, this problem has not been entirely resolved. Far too often, members of Advisory Committees make recommendations partially on the grounds of availability. This is not their fault. It is easier for the self-employed to accede to the ever-growing demands on a magistrate's time than the salaried worker. In some counties, teachers, for instance, find difficulty in being released from duty to perform this important public service.

As a magistrate Phillips was much concerned with penal reform. Sitting in the Children's Court, she often felt that offenders should be dealt with outside the court system, and that the age of criminal responsibility should be raised from seven years. Her beliefs, based upon experience, anticipated reforms of a later time. In Britain we have seen the use of cautioning of juveniles for some years, while in America, progressive states like Wisconsin have for a very long time successfully applied the practice of 'diversion', that operates outside the courts.

The Probation of Offenders Act had been passed in Britain in 1907 and Phillips saw the value of Probation Committees, urging that 'good magistrates' should be appointed to serve on them. She announced that the Labour Party was keen to ensure that a young person, who was a first offender, was not sent to prison.

Penal reform was, quite naturally, one of the major concerns of that powerhouse of progressive policies — the Standing Joint Committee of Industrial Women's Organisations. On its behalf, Phillips in the September 1919 issue of *The Labour Woman* voiced her concern that a magistrate had ordered a Woman Police Officer out of court while 'painful evidence' was being given by a woman.[3] Referring to the Summary Jurisdiction Act of 1820, she stated that a magistrate had no right to clear a court in that way. She added that it was disgraceful that women and children had to give such evidence when only men were present and that, indeed, a woman police constable should always be present on such an occasion. In the November issue of the magazine, a letter from a woman probation officer supported Phillips's view and she related how she had been turned out of the Westminster Court to prevent her hearing evidence concerning a woman. The Standing Joint Committee strongly pressed for more women to be employed in the Police force, emphasising that a woman police officer should always be present when a woman was remanded in a police station.

Resolutions on these matters were introduced at the Annual Conference of Labour Women in 1924.[4] One declared the Labour Party's support for the Probation Service, and deplored that one hundred and eighty Courts of Summary Jurisdiction were without Probation Officers whilst, in many others, they were inadequately trained and badly paid. In addition, the service was totally funded from the rates, resulting in unevenness of representation throughout the country. Responding to the resolutions, the Conference not only urged the institution of a National Probation System supported by Treasury grants but also, the appointment of three Probation Commissioners, one of whom should be a woman. It was apparent, therefore, that since the early days of its existence, the Standing Joint Committee anticipated the development of the Probation Service as an effective, economical means of dealing non-custodially, with offenders, although nearly half a century was to elapse before Community Service Orders, Day Centres, Training Courses, Probation and Bail Hostels came into being.

Conference members also pressed for improvements in the running of courts.[5] There should be more working women magistrates; the provision of legal aid in the lower courts, and all Maintenance and Affiliation Orders should be implemented through the Clerk of the Court or an officer nominated by him.

The resolution on prison reform stressed that no young person under seventeen years of age should be detained in an adult prison, nor should mentally defective people be housed with other prisoners, whilst women prisoners should be found 'open-air employment' and 'the means of exercise'. In addition, police stations should not be used for short-stay remands.

As for prison administration, the Conference called for the appointment of a woman Commissioner, a woman Prison Inspector and a woman Medical Officer.

Finally, the Conference deplored that capital punishment —'that relic of barbarism' — had still not been abolished.

Since these radical resolutions were passed at the Annual Conference of Labour Women in 1924, most of these reforms have been implemented. A great deal has been done to humanise the penal system but much that is a blot upon a civilised society still remains, seventy years after these forward-looking women formulated their sane and enlightened policies.

Phillips performed all her wide-ranging activities with energy, enthusiasm and great thoroughness. The years immediately following the First World War saw the widening of the Standing Joint Committee's constitution so that the Executive Committee of the Labour Party, the Parliamentary Committee of the Trade Union Congress and Labour Organisations would be represented.[6] The Standing Joint Committee itself was already represented on a number of important bodies and had, in turn, successfully obtained the representation of working women on a number of local committees such as Food Control, Maternity, Insurance, Pensions, Agricultural Wages Boards and Local Advisory Committees of Employment Exchanges. Additionally, its representatives had taken part in a number of deputations to various Government departments, resulting in many Government circulars bearing mention and, thereby recognising the work of the Standing Joint Committee.

Phillips herself was continuing as hitherto to give evidence before Government commissions and committees. Sometimes she acted as a member of them. In 1918 she was a member of the Ministry of Reconstruction Women's

Advisory Committee on the Domestic Service Problem which reported to the Minister in 1919. In 1919 she gave evidence before the Royal Commission on Income Tax. In 1920 she gave evidence before the Departmental Committee on the Employment of Women and Young Persons on the Two-Shift System, which gave rise to a pamphlet on the subject, stating the Standing Joint Committee's objections to it. These comprised of: bad meal times; late work on the second shift; factory and work-shop difficulties; artificial lighting; inspection, educational difficulties; married women's long hours; and unsettled conditions.

Phillips also produced seven other pamphlets dealing with widely differing topics. One concentrated on *The Distribution of Work and Goods;* another posed the question *Can Great Britain Save Europe?;* whilst the other five dealt with various complex branches of taxation.[7] She also supplied, in The *Labour Woman,* reading lists of books, pamphlets and Government publications for discussion in the Women's Sections. In addition to suggesting other topics for discussion such as: the work of the Standing Joint Committee; the Annual Report of the Chief Medical Officer of the Board of Education; maternity and housing matters; and pensions, she often published reports on conferences in the magazine. There was so much dynamism that the May 1920 Conference was described by Phillips as 'The Labour Women's Parliament'.

In the June 1920 issue of *The Labour Woman* there appeared an item of news close to Phillips's heart. It was a report of the opening of a small babies' hospital as a development of the Margaret MacDonald and Mary Middleton Memorial Clinic at Ladbroke Road. The hospital was established specifically for children under the age of five years and was described as a place 'where ailing children can be nursed and fed and sunned back to health and strength'. It was estimated that the hospital would cost £2,000 a year to maintain and Phillips appealed for help to all the Women's Sections to support this worthwhile venture.[8]

At every opportunity, Phillips provided reasons, scrupulously endorsed with facts and her own particular vision, why every working woman should vote for the Labour Party. In *The Labour Woman* of April 1920, with reference to the by-elections of that year, she discussed the two matters which made the life of a wife and a mother 'one continual round of toil and anxiety'. First there was the constant rise in prices and second there was the chronic lack of decent housing. The first was due, she said, to the evils of profiteering, while the second could be allayed by Labour's demand for a publicly-founded national housing scheme. She reminded her readers that Mr. Lloyd George had emphasised the need for houses, and that one of his own committees had stated that three hundred thousand were needed in the first post-war year. Labour's estimate was one million. In the event, she said scathingly, 'the Coalition Governments total achievement after one year was one hundred and twenty four'.

Phillips's abiding concern with housing led her in 1920 to Norway, to address a women's Conference on the subject and later visiting Sweden and Finland.[9] She was to spend much of the next decade making an invaluable contribution to

International Socialist Women's gatherings. In the November 1922 issue of *The Labour Woman*, she described the meeting of the second International Congress of Working Women held at Geneva, from which the International Federation of Working Women was founded. Marion became the first International Secretary of the Federation and remained in that office for the following six years.

While deploring the lack of organisation among working women in the individual countries at the time, she was nevertheless, impressed by the representation that came from the United States, France, Belgium, Switzerland, Italy, Czechoslovakia, Poland, Norway, Cuba, South Africa and Great Britain. There were too, fraternal delegates from China and Japan. Marion commented, 'Miss Zung, with her voice like the tinkling of the finest porcelain, was the most interesting figure present. She spoke with great care and delicacy in excellent English.' Phillips continued by giving a lively description of some of the other delegates, including the 'two Italians — Madame Casartelli and Madame Altobelli — with their inexhaustible enthusiasm and vivacity.' How she must have enjoyed their company. Many lasting friendships were forged with people from all over the world at these meetings. Indeed, when Phillips stood for Parliament in Sunderland in 1929, a telegram of good wishes reached her from Kobe, Japan.

The following month, December 1922, Phillips returned to the Continent to attend the International Peace Congress at the Hague, called by the International Federation of Trade Unions. Both she and Mlle. Bouvier of France, represented the International Federation of Women Workers. On the last morning of the Congress there was an 'informal conference' arranged by the International Federation of Women Workers under Marion's Presidency, which recommended a 'new Triple Alliance' of mothers, teachers and young workers throughout the world in order to carry out the educational programme of the Congress.

With few to equal her ability, energy and drive, Phillips may have felt that the Congress was moving too slowly. Always anxious to 'get things done' she, inevitably, had a plan of action at hand. Writing in *The Labour Woman* the next month, she stated that 'practical measures' recommended by her conference were 'that the secretaries of the International Federation of Women Workers, the International Committee of Co-operative Women, the Young Workers International, the Organisations of Socialist Women and of teachers, shall keep the Bureau of the International Federation of Trade Unions informed of any interesting work on these lines and the Bureau will communicate it to the other organisations. The Bureau also be asked to convene annually a joint meeting of the Secretaries of these international organisations to discuss the quest for peace'.[10]

Phillips's life during these post-war years was clearly one of non-stop work. Yet, it is unlikely that some corner of it would not have been devoted to those 'joys of fruitful leisure' by which she herself set such store. She was, like other members of her gifted family interested in art and literature. She loved beautiful things and felt that the ordinary object of everyday life should be pleasing to the eye as well as useful. After she went into Parliament she served on a Parliamentary Committee on Art and Design in Industry.

Phillips enjoyed travelling abroad and walking, whether in the mountains of Europe or in the English countryside. Frances, her niece, talks of accompanying her aunt on a walking tour in Devon but there is no knowledge as to who accompanied her on her brief holidays that often followed those International Conferences in Europe. According to her nephew, A. A. Phillips, in her younger days she had been 'a handsome girl with dark flashing eyes.' He added that though she had put on much weight in the twenties, she was still 'an attractive person'.[10]   One of her colleagues too, referred to her 'clear and humourously critical eyes' in a memorial tribute to her.[11]

Little, however, is known about Phillips's private life. Beatrice Webb does not speculate about her in her diaries as she does about the personal lives of other prominent Labour women.[12] She writes mockingly, 'How eminently respectable are these three women M.P.s — Susan Lawrence, Margaret Bondfield and Ellen Wilkinson. You can barely think of any one of them having an 'intrigue' or even a flirtation. They lack all the temperament of a lover — they are distinctly celibates.' But Ellen Wilkinson does receive a compliment — albeit a double-edged one. Webb proclaims, 'she is attractive to men', then adding with *soi-disant* expertise, 'but not attracted to them and therefore not seductive.' She continues 'Margaret has her religion for relaxation. Susan and Ellen have their travels, their gossips and their smokes; not one of them seems to need emotional companionship … I doubt whether one of the three had had a lover.' It is puzzling how Beatrice Webb could have reached these firm conclusions based on such superficial observations.[12]

Beverly Kingston rightly says that it was the availability of Marion Phillips and these other able women to shoulder such a heavy burden of duties that turned them into 'invaluable work-horses'.[13] That may be so. On the other hand, there may be a tendency to assume, because of a lack of concrete evidence, that none of these women had 'a private life.' Sixty or seventy years ago the details of the private life of public, or even less public individuals, were not customarily bruited abroad. No papers relating to Phillips's personal life have come to light. This part of her existence seems to have been closely guarded and remains so.

What is known is that Phillips had her own close circle of friends, preferring, as her niece said, 'male society as a rule,' adding that her aunt could be 'very charming.' Other members of her family suggest that she had an especially close relationship with one man. He was Charles Wye Kendall , the sole beneficiary and executor of her will.[14]

Kendall, a barrister, unsuccessfully contested the Stroud Division of Gloucestershire as the Labour Party candidate in the December 1918 election. He was listed as Captain Charles Wye Kendall of the reserve unit Tank Corps, Swanage and resident at 9 Lordship Park, London. He further contested the

Suffolk East (Eye) seat for Labour in the 1923 and 1924 elections, again without success. His final bid to enter Parliament was in 1935 — three years after Phillips's death — when he stood unsuccessfully in Bromley, Kent.

Kendall founded the Guild of Arts for Youth and lectured to the Workers' Travel Association (now Galleon Travel) and other organisations. Phillips was, in the post-war years, a member of the Council of the Workers Travel Association and she and Kendall would certainly have met in that connection. However, it is not unlikely that they would have been acquainted long before that time, moving as they did in the same political circles.

He died five years later than Phillips, on 15th September 1937.

Chapter 12: Women and the Labour Party

In 1918, Marion Phillips, with the aid of Gertrude Tuckwell[1] and Susan Lawrence,[2] edited and published a remarkable collection of short essays by prominent Labour women — each an expert on the subject of her choice. The title of this little volume was *Women and the Labour Party*. Not content merely to condemn the ravages of poverty and injustice, these women, having identified the causes of deprivation, battled to eliminate them and to build a better future. In that struggle they believed that men and women should fight together on an equal footing. Arthur Henderson, the doughty champion of women's rights, wrote the Preface and Phillips wrote the Introduction.

She explained that the purpose of the book was to make a special appeal to women who henceforth would be able to vote. 'The object is to bring before them the contribution which the Labour Party has to make upon questions that are peculiarly the concern of women.'

She regretted that because of matters of costs, it had been necessary to curtail the size of the volume and that meant the omission of the treatment of many important issues. While, she continued, the interests of both men and women were basically the same there were certain matters that related more closely to women, like the planning and running of a house, the upbringing of children, the care for the whole family in times of sickness. It was the special experience of women in such matters that could produce the right solutions.

But there was a second role for women which involved working side by side with men in the post-war reconstruction of society, if 'a repetition of the old social confusion and misery' was to be avoided. She went on: 'Thus from two points of view the Labour Party has recognised the importance of women's participation in its work; women must give their best thinking power to the solution of the problems which lie nearest to them, which grow out of the very centre of their existence in the family group, and they must also play their part as human beings in the great task of democracy... of developing a finer citizenship and raising the level of national existence.'

With that in mind, she urged that the campaign to enfranchise all women over twenty-one years of age should be waged without respite. A Labour government, she pledged, would 'secure voting rights for all on absolutely equal terms as human beings.'

She then briefly explained that machinery of that part of the new constitution affecting women, adding that behind the eminent contributors to the volume, there was a great mass of working women who through their support of Labour, would help to solve the problems of democratic government and build a new social fabric.

Then there followed what may well be described as a declaration of Marion Phillips's political philosophy. She stated, 'The Labour Party will fail to be a People's Party if it leaves its thinking to a few. It must not become a caucus of superior persons but must in truth be broad-based upon the people's will. Essentially, it deals with the simple, primary needs of life — desire for home and shelter, security and sufficiency of material needs, control over the framework of life, in order that nobility of action and thought, joy, beauty and the gift of service may be the rule for all. Love of the cheery humanity of common things makes the background of its political work.'[3]

These simple words echo the message of Robert Blatchford. His abiding concern was that happiness and laughter arising from the provision of the common decencies of life, should become the lot of the 'jolly nobodies' for whom he felt such affection.

The word 'cheery' constantly recurred in Phillips's writings, and her faith in the experience of ordinary people who provided the 'common facts' for those more clever than they to 'interpret and transform' always shone undimmed throughout her life. In this Introduction she pressed home her point:

> We are too apt to think of politics as though its whole subject matter was abstract ideas. In reality, it is only another side of our everyday human activities and the provision of bathrooms may become a political issue of real importance in creating a finer race, just as the League of Nations has a distinct bearing on the individual home where a mother today mourns for her conscript son. It is for this reason that every woman should take her place in the ranks, ready to give her thoughts as well as her vote for the representatives in whose policy she believes.

Referring to the Great War, she made the point noted elsewhere: 'Politically women have a clean slate. They cannot bear any direct responsibility for the catastrophe which has overwhelmed Europe and drawn the whole world towards disaster.' On the contrary there were certain women, including those who contributed to the book, who had 'borne a prominent part in seeking to humanise our civilisation.' She went on to appeal for the support of others, urging them to come forward for public service as opportunities arose.

Phillips ended with a characteristic protest against the tyranny of drudgery that killed any chance of leading a civilised life. The eloquent final sentence is the best-known of all her words:

> The nation has not yet attempted to repay the debt it owes to the patient toil of tired women, a toil that could with thought and determination be replaced by lives in which happy hours of work alternated with the joys of fruitful leisure.

The title of Rebecca West's article, 'Women as Brainworkers', refers to a phrase in the New Labour Manifesto of 1918 — *Labour and the New Social Order*: that all workers 'by hand and by brain' could henceforth claim membership of the Labour Party. She made a sparkling contribution, setting the pace with a typically Shavian onslaught: 'Now that the State has admitted that women are citizens, we are relieved of the tiresome necessity of proving that we exist.'

After a passage of withering irony she directed her attention to the consequences of the enfranchisement of women, emphasising that it was not enough for them to have the vote. It was now vital that they used it for the right purpose because 'the arguments of oppression are not less dangerous from the lips of women than they are from men. It is a test that we must apply to all the activities of women now.' She developed the theme by being severely critical of the appointment of a woman member of the Anti-Suffrage League to a diplomatic post, maintaining that with her antecedents, she would be merely the female counterpart of her right-wing male predecessors.

She proceeded passionately,

> We want women to represent a love of life that will let no child starve, no sick person suffer for lack of any help that human hands can bring, no old man die except in ease, and that will fight for conditions which make health and serenity the common lot, with the same obstinate fervour with which the protection of privilege and the rights of Capitalism are fought for today.
>
> The only Party that guarantees that women shall perform this function is the Labour Party.

Like Marion Phillips in the Introduction to the book, she stressed the necessity to nurture the growth of well-informed public opinion throughout the land. Failing this she warned mischievously, that the women's vote might yet produce 'a female Sir Edward Carson, a female Lord Milner, or to look at the funny side of things, a female Lord Curzon.'[4]

Then, moving hurriedly away from the contemplation of this bizarre possibility, she urged the Labour Party as its second duty 'to form an army of brainworkers,' by offering them an acceptable standard of life. She insisted that women should be given a good general education to develop their individual capacity. Teaching, she regarded as a 'sweated industry' and she emphasised the need to pay teachers better salaries. It is a tragic comment that seventy years later, teachers are still underpaid and underrated.

She was particularly scathing about the wastage of women's ability after marriage. 'We murder the brains of married women not of the prosperous classes' and she continued in a highly entertaining vein:

> ...there is no inherent reason why the adoption of the career of wife and mother should prevent a woman in middle-age taking whatever place in public life her brains entitle her to, any more than a middle-aged man is prevented from entering Parliament by the years he has spent in law or commerce. Indeed ... fifteen years spent in rearing children ought to be a better preparation for the business of governing one's fellow-creatures than an equal space of time spent in cross-examining scoundrels.

Amen to that, but what does inhibit women today from seeking parliamentary careers is the absurd system of hours which governs the work of the House. West, with paradox and passion proceeded to condemn the social ills of the time, that threatened to overwhelm the working-class mother. It was, she wrote, a truly appalling indictment of the state which while paying lip service to 'the sacred duty of motherhood' still said, 'we will not intervene between you and the capitalist system which will perpetually make war on you and your children'. Sadly she reflected, that the 'end of this *mater contra mundum* controversy is frequently the survival of the children at the cost of the mental death of the mother'.

However on a more hopeful note, she looked to a future in which the endowment of motherhood, good medical service, decent housing and a good education would change the status quo.

In the remaining pages of the book, other Labour Party women dealt with specific aspects of the reforms that Rebecca West so fervently advocated in her exhilarating, hard-hitting essay.

The theme of *mater contra mundum* was further pursued in the article, 'The Claims of Women and Children', by Margaret Llewelyn Davies whose name is chiefly associated with the growth of the Co-operative Women's Guild and the campaign for adult suffrage. Within these pages she outlined the means by which the burdens of the mothers of her day could be lightened.

The war years in many ways, had had an unprecedented effect on the lives of married women. Strains and stresses of marriage, separation from husbands, the high infant mortality rate, the growing disregard of marriage vows, the increase in the incidence of venereal disease all contributed to a change in public opinion about the relationship between men and women. Women, said the author, were becoming aware of themselves as a 'national force' and their enfranchisement in 1918 strengthened a feeling of new-found independence. She stated crisply that enfranchisement had 'come none too soon.' Mothers determined on sex equality were concerned with two main matters: the welfare of their children, and the attainment of their own individual freedom. The latter involved relief from household drudgery coupled with monetary independence.

It was poverty, she maintained, that hindered progress in that direction, but it could be overcome in two ways: the first remedy — that of safeguarding the health of mothers and infants, depended on the provision of common services and institutional treatment. She insisted that the Poor Law methods — infirmaries, rescue homes, lying-in hospitals — all tainted with charity, should all be swept away and replaced by maternity and infant provision, with emphasis on prevention and run by the public health authorities. As for the Maternity and Separation Allowances — welcome as they were as being the mother's own property, there should be improvement, as the Maternity Benefit itself was inadequate for a number of reasons. There was also need for new maternity homes and maternity centres where dinners and free milk would be provided as treatment, and a system of home helps during confinement.

The second way to help the mother, wrote Miss Llewelyn Davies, would be the implementation of a new 'Endowment of Motherhood' scheme without delay.

She praised the new Local Government Board for recommending that working women be placed on Public Health Maternity Committees. She commended the Board too, for its support of the principle that no distinction should be made in the treatment of married and unmarried mothers. Indeed, she stressed that the need for help was greater in the case of the latter category, pointing out that the death rate of illegitimate children was 'peculiarly high.' Urging the need to remove the stigma from the child, she praised the good example set in Norway in 1916 and 1917.

The author advocated too the need for marriage law reform, since the law as it stood caused 'great suffering and injustice, ill-health and death.' These were early days, too, for the following brave words:

> When a marriage has become an unhappy one from whatsoever cause and mutual love is dead, there is nothing gained by refusing the possibility of retrieving a tragic mistake.

Labour M.P.s she said, supported reform, adding that large numbers of separation orders were in existence during the war years, and in her opinion, a legal or voluntary separation after a period of time was a ground for divorce.

She saw too that the Endowment of Motherhood would be a great advantage in this respect 'in giving working mothers a possibility of escape from degrading conditions of life, for they have been more at the mercy of bad marriage relations than rich women through having no money of their own.'

This essay dealt perceptively with human problems and social injustices at the time of the First World War. The practical means of meeting the claims of the most defenceless members of society are set out with clarity and compassion. Margaret Llewelyn Davies, the daughter of a Welsh Nonconformist minister was indeed a doughty fighter for women's freedom from misery and injustice. She has not yet been awarded the place she deserves in the annals of the great emancipators. She was a woman before her time.[5]

The essay on 'The End of the Poor Law' was written by an expert in the field: Beatrice Webb, the author of the Minority Report of the Royal Commission on the Poor Law. It is a clear, simply-written, concise charter for social reform.

She began her essay with a statement: 'Parliament may pass laws, but it is the local authority that executes them.' It was then, important that women having been enfranchised, should take on the responsibility for good, local government. Local government, she explained, was concerned with a wide range of matters — health, housing, education and the environment.

Most important was the proposed abolition of the Poor Law and the Board of Guardians. Labour, she wrote, had been pressing for years for their powers to be transferred to committees of the town council and other local authorities, and she hoped that the government of the day would act to do so. She found the existing system of labelling as 'destitute' infants, children, sick and mentally afflicted people and the unemployed, degrading and deplorable. Because of the degredations, she went on, those in dire necessity were deterred from seeking help. The Board of Guardians, she further explained, was a body restricted to one function: to deal only with destitute people while they were destitute.

Mrs. Webb, anxious to be rid of this cruel folly, set out a 'simple alternative'. First it was necessary to abolish the Destitution Authority. Then, beginning with education, the Local Education Authority could provide education for destitute children just as it did for the majority of other children, and subsistence could be added.

Second, the Public Health Authority which was bound to provide medical treatment for infectious diseases and other treatment for some mothers and infants, could provide health care plus subsistence for destitute children too.

Third, there was the question of unemployment. How, asked Mrs. Webb, would the post-war ranks of the unemployed be treated, always remembering that among them would be ex-servicemen and ex-munitions workers. Would they be subjected to the 'able-bodied work house test'? Reminding her readers that the Labour Party, resentful of this infamous treatment of the unemployed, had successfully pressed for the passage of the Unemployed Workmen Act in 1905, appointing a Distress Committee of the town council with limited powers. Mrs. Webb suggested that a new committee of the town council now be set up for the prevention of unemployment and the provision of training. Distress Committees, she believed, were no longer necessary. Either work should be found for the unemployed by the committee of the town council or full subsistence should be granted while they were involved in training. She urged women to study the Report of the Local Government Committee of the Ministry of Reconstruction.

An additional committee of the town council she announced, was also proposed. To prevent the break-up of a family, the Home Assistance Committee would take over the duty of the Poor Law to see that no one died of starvation. The new committee too, would be responsible for the maintenance of the home and would award allowances and pensions for this purpose. When necessary, this committee alone would make inquiries about financial means, thus curtailing much of the interference of officialdom.

What a sane, straight forward substitution for the cruel indignity of the past. Mrs. Webb ended her splendidly clear article as she had begun it, by urging members of Women's Sections up and down the country to become involved in these matters, so that they could exercise their influence on local bodies in order to right old wrongs. Her own Minority Report had outlined the 'simple alternative' to the Poor Law, ten years earlier. Unfortunately, the Poor Law was to remain as a hated feature of the British social system for many long years after the publication of this essay.[6]

The article 'Women and Internationalism' which Mary Longman contributed to the Series, briefly traced the growth of the Women's International Socialist Movement and the involvement of British Labour women with it.

The bond between these women had held firm in spite of the war, and although it had not been possible to arrange another war-time meeting after the historic women's conference in 1915 at Berne, Longman rejoiced that the Peace Policy adopted at Berne had been accepted by all the Socialist and Labour movements in the Allied countries, and that its peace demands were 'also re-echoed in the Memorandum recently adopted by the Allied Socialist and Labour Conference in London'. She further quoted a passage to show how the ideas announced by the women had 'after two years, been reiterated by the whole of the democratic forces of Allied Countries'.

Longman concluded by looking forward to the next conference after the cessation of hostilities. The Council (the British Section), she assured her readers, was already preparing for it. Women from all the countries, she promised, would together be involved in building a new and better society. Similar problems in the various countries would call for common solutions and the women would be there willing and ready to take responsibility for them.[7]

Immediately after the war, Marion Phillips and her colleagues resumed contact with the women overseas and the next twelve years saw a remarkable development in international activity. The co-operation, goodwill and understanding that had grown in pre-war days, burgeoned into a network of regular conferences, visits and committee meetings in various European cities. The discussions and resolutions passed at these conferences not only produced a feeling of solidarity and confidence among its participants; it also influenced progressive legislation in the constituent countries and at the League of Nations on a great number of concerns affecting the lives of women everywhere.

The essay written by Margaret McMillan struck a totally different note from its predecessor.

McMillan was one of the great pioneers of infant education in this country. Applying her faith — that the mind and body of a child need to be educated together — to conditions in her native Bradford, she soon convinced the local authorities of the need for school baths, school meals, school clinics, school doctors, open-air education and ultimately nursery schools. That was the beginning. Legislation was to follow later.

'Educate every child as if she were your own' said Rachel McMillan, who with her sister Margaret, the author of the essay 'The Nursery of Tomorrow', blazed the trail.

Having explained here the need for nurseries for little children, she described in some detail how they were run. She expressed satisfaction that 'the Bill now before the House of Commons asks in its first line for a System of Nurseries or Nursery Schools preferably open-air.'

I have tried to convey elsewhere in the book, the importance that the

McMillans, Marion Phillips, Ethel Bentham and other prominent members of the Women's Labour League attached to the setting up of these nurseries, which should, in McMillan's words always be planned as 'outdoor places' surrounded by flowers and trees, birds, music and happy voices. A good diet, sleep and regular hours of play should start little lives on the right track.

The quality of staff was always important she insisted, with a well-trained woman, possibly a graduate in charge, and helped by young practitioners. McMillan's nursery school at Deptford adopted the practice of payment for their small charges but Labour opinion as expressed in Women's Conference resolutions was generally in favour of free provision for all children.

The author of the essay felt, that the nursery and the nursery school should be linked together and be under one head. The leaving age, she believed, should be seven.

Again we are struck by the foresight and enthusiasm of these early pioneers who anticipated modern thinking about the development of infants and the need of adequate provision for them, by the better part of a century.[8]

Mary Macarthur — one of the brightest stars in the history of women trade unionists in this country, contributed the article 'The Women Trade Unionists' Point of View'. Commenting on the change in public opinion during the war years about the role of women in society, she remarked drily,

> ...no longer are we told that 'the hand that rocks the cradle rules the world'. Today it is the hand that drills the shell that determines the destiny of the world; and those who did not hesitate to refuse the rights of citizenship to the mothers of men, are ready and anxious to concede these rights to the makers of machine-guns.

Mary never minced her words. Having stated that the number of women employed in industry and commerce had increased by over forty per cent since the outbreak of war, and after listing the advantages and disadvantages to women, resulting from this, she looked to the future, insisting that they should be paid wages that would ensure their health and comfort, and be equal to those paid to men for equal work. It was important too, she stressed, that conditions of work should promote and not retard their physical and mental development.

Two methods she claimed would ensure these results: effective trade union organisation and state action.

First, the unions. She urged that men and women should join the same union, and that women should be involved in the administration and formulation of policy and be a strong voice on the governing bodies of unions. In this context, she sharply criticised male hostility to women in some trade unions. She proclaimed further that the 'greatest function of the Trade Union Movement is the function of education, a function more important than ever now, when women at last are to be given the rights and duties of citizenship.'

She then dealt with the need for new legislation to safeguard the position of women workers. She insisted that:

... organised women are clear that Trade Unionism must be supplemented by State regulations of industrial conditions, and they are not content to urge ... merely the restoration of the status quo ante bellum ... They want in addition, a new and improved Consolidating Factory Act — legislation long overdue, for the last Consolidating Act was passed in 1901.

A long list of vital requirements then followed. She added too, that a new Factory Act would need to be accompanied by an 'improved Trade Boards Act and a legal minimum wage ... must be fixed in all trades and industries.'

Departing from the industrial provision for women, she then directed her attention to the social welfare of women workers. She insisted on 'adequate provision ... for motherhood,' spelling out the details carefully. Working women, she wrote, were demanding a Ministry of Health. She went on, 'The present system of unemployment insurance should be replaced by a new and comprehensive non-contributory scheme. Women should not be allowed to deteriorate during periods of idleness.' Like Bondfield, Phillips and many others, she advocated courses of training at such times.

She pleaded too for educational reform that would include raising the school age to sixteen, and the provision of part-time general education to eighteen.

Finally, while Macarthur stated that she did not think that giving women the vote would mean 'a new heaven or a new earth,' it would produce a change mirrored mostly in domestic reforms, affecting the welfare of children, housing and public health. She was right, of course, but that road to reform was also very long and uphill all the way.

Mary Macarthur had spent her life fighting for oppressed women in sweated industries. Her last message in this essay, however, concerned motherhood. 'Women,' she wrote, 'desire above all else, to conserve the race.' The detection of a sad note is perhaps imaginary. Soon after the end of the war, Wil Anderson, Mary's husband lost his life in the influenza epidemic that swept the country and in 1921, she herself — barely forty — died. They left a small daughter.[9]

Susan Lawrence, later to become Parliamentary Secretary at the Ministry of Health in a Labour government, was one of three women who compiled and published *Women and the Labour Party*. In addition, she made a most valuable contribution to the book in her article 'The Woman as Wage Earner'.[10 [see Note 2]]

Lawrence was an outstanding personality among the Labour women of her time. Coming from a family of eminent lawyers, she herself was a distinguished academic with an honours degree in mathematics taken at Newnham College, Cambridge. She first sat as a Conservative on the L.C.C., but after her experience of serving on a committee dealing with charwomen's wages, her gradual conversion to Labour politics was completed, and she joined the Party in 1912. Her fight to secure justice for the underprivileged in Poplar, resulted in a six-week period of imprisonment. The tall dignified woman wearing a monocle, soon became recognised as a champion of the poor. Later she became an Alderman of Poplar.

Among her interests were education, finance and the problems of unemployment. For a time she worked with Mary Macarthur as assistant secretary of the Women's Trade Union League and then as organiser of the National Federation of Women Workers which later merged with the National Union of General Workers. She served on a host of committees, among them the Labour Party Advisory Committee on Local Government, Trade Policy and Finance — representing it on Trade Boards, and on the Committee on Relations between Employers and Employed. She was also the Secretary of the Working Women's Legal Advice Bureau. In 1923 Lawrence entered Parliament as the Member of East Ham North.

In the article 'The Woman as Wage Earner', she expressed her concern about the fate of women munition workers at the end of the war when demand for their labour would cease. Unemployment, insecurity and a drop in their living standards was inevitable.

However, she maintained that just as the Munitions Act offered temporary protection of women's wages during the war, it was the Trade Board Acts — passed under pressure from the Labour Party that would offer permanent protection of wages when the war was over. Like Mary Macarthur, she pinned her faith on the amending of the Trade Boards Acts. Already about three hundred thousand women came under the operation of these acts. She provided a list of tables relating to various types of work to show the improvement in wage levels gained by the Orders of both Acts.

She insisted that wages legislation was therefore necessary. 'War conditions,' she said, 'have resulted in lifting whole trades from sweated conditions, to a position where a reasonable minimum is paid. If these are not to revert to their previous states, and if all the remaining poorly paid women's trades are to be raised, we shall want Trade Boards on an altogether unprecedented scale.' She warned that there would be much opposition to this, but she went on:

> The Labour Party Policy is to amend the Trade Board Act and to secure its extension to all employments where any considerable number employed receive less than thirty shillings a week.

She concluded her article by referring to the distress of the unemployed workers who could not benefit from this legislation. The Labour Party however, she said, was committed to the maintenance of the unemployed at the cessation of hostilities. In support of this, she announced: 'The Labour Party stands for two great principles: first that it is the duty of the government to find suitable work for all, and secondly, that wherever it is unable to fulfil this obligation, it must provide the worker with maintenance'.

Margaret Bondfield, the first woman cabinet minister in Britain was the author of the article, 'Women as Domestic Workers'.

In her introduction, she said that there were two kinds of domestic workers: the paid and the unpaid. Housewives and home-makers fell into the second category. Both sections were disillusioned and angry that no attempt had ever been made to remove drudgery and prevent time-wasting and pointless expenditure of energy in their lives. They were now however, bent on seeking redress of these injustices.

Dealing first with the discontent among paid domestic workers Bondfield recalled a conversation between unemployed women munition workers and a number of Members of Parliament.

'My wife says she cannot get servants', urged an elderly M.P. 'Would you like to go back to domestic service?'

'No', was the prompt reply, 'Would you?'

The woman who had so replied gave Bondfield a description of 'pre-war servitude' — dark, inadequate kitchen and sleeping quarters, miserable pay and in Bondfield's words, 'the petty tyranny of little minds and, above all, the consciousness of inferior status ... which had become intolerable after the experience of the greater freedom of factory life.'

That these ex-domestic workers actually preferred the dangerous work of munition factories with all the attendant hazards: night shifts, and journeying to work in all weathers at all hours — all that — to living in the safety of their employers' homes was indeed a damning indictment of domestic service in those days. It was, said the writer, an 'unregulated, sweated industry' in which badly-trained employers could at any time draw upon a pool of cheap young labour. She conceded that there were exceptions to the rule. There were, of course, a body of domestic workers, who because they worked for civilised employers, found satisfaction and happiness in an atmosphere of mutual respect and appreciation.

But to return to the misery of the others, Bondfield remarked that 'because domestic service has borne the mark of servitude, lack of education had always been regarded as the sign of the good servant.' (And, one might add, the hallmark of the bad employer.)

She continued, that Labour women were convinced of the urgent necessity for training in domestic service in order to turn it into a 'well-regulated industry in which the social status of its workers will be equal to that of any other section of labour.' The need for education therefore was paramount.

In the meantime, Bondfield maintained, urgent reforms should be enacted. First, there should be a regulation of hours of work to a minimum of eight hours a day; second, there should be an abolition of living-in as a condition of employment. Third, a worker's right to privacy in her own time should be observed. Most importantly, she insisted ... 'the bell-ringing habit must be broken ... Human energy must not be wasted in running up and downstairs in obedience to the whims and fancies of idlers.'

Instead of this particular form of human servitude, Margaret Bondfield suggested that the system of a non- residential daily service was 'a great safeguard of the liberties and independence of the paid domestic.' She also praised the Memorandum issued by the Women's Industrial Council in January 1918 that proposed setting up 'domestic centres' that would act as agencies supplying help by the hour and providing training courses as well. Much would be made of these ideas in the coming years but because of the economic climate of the Twenties, the problem would, alas remain. She pressed too, in the article, the need for sound trade union organisation in the future for the protection of these vulnerable workers.

Marion Phillips — a member of the Ministry of Reconstruction Women's Advisory Committee on the Domestic Service Problem, set up in 1919 was to take up the cudgels on behalf of these disadvantaged women in a long campaign that lasted throughout the Twenties. It culminated in the presentation of 'the Domestic Workers Charter' to the National Annual Conference of Labour Women in 1931. Many of the suggestions for reform in Margaret Bondfield's article in this Book, were embodied in the Charter.

The remainder of Bondfield's essay was devoted to ways in which housewives and mothers — the unpaid domestic workers — might find useful in saving time and energy.

The genuine concern about the 'mental death' of a working-class mother — the paralysing of a personality through domestic drudgery — was a continuing theme in the writings of these early women politicians.[11]

If the remarkable woman who wrote 'The Labour Woman's Battle With Dirt' were alive today, she would surely be hailed as a heroine in the struggle to protect the environment.

Katherine St. John Conway married to John Bruce Glasier, Labour Politician and disciple of William Morris, gave long years of her life campaigning steadfastly against the pollution of the atmosphere.

In this article, she pleaded that men and women of the Labour Party 'pledge themselves to war to the death with dirt in the sky, in the river, in the street, on the human body, in the home. For dirt has been rightly defined as 'matter in the wrong place'. It is always an inward and spiritual disgrace either in the individual or in our social system.'

She found too, much hypocrisy in the comfortable Victorian adage that 'cleanliness is next to Godliness', remarking cuttingly, '... more and more, it is being recognised that to be willing to live clean oneself in airy, spacious dwellings and do nothing to help cleanse the world for others is simply to be 'unclean' in soul.'

It is interesting that the verb 'pollute' in Milton's *Paradise Lost* has a spiritual connotation and much affinity with the philosophy of Mrs. Bruce Glasier.

She described the housewife's daily battle with dirt in the 'smoke-belt' as hopeless, and while all efforts at smoke abatement and the provision of sanitary and cleansing arrangements by municipal services were strongly supported by Labour women, the abuses persisted, and she suggested ways in which working -class homes could combat them.

In tackling problems of 'Industrial Dirt', she deplored the fact that Great Britain lagged far behind the United States, the Dominions and the countries of Western Europe. She referred to the cities of New York, Montreal and Sydney that had long decided that industrial grime and dirt should be outlawed from transport systems and people's homes.

This brought the writer to consider the plight of homes in mining areas in this country. She spoke of the 'black slavery' of miners' wives and mothers for whose emancipation she herself fought such a long, gallant, and eventually successful battle. Providing details of appalling conditions, she wrote, 'All over the country, there were not three miners' homes in a hundred, fitted even with a hot and cold water tap over a sink' and 'the coming in daily of a black abominable burden of coaldust on the muddy and often foully-smelling clothing of several miners (the clothes also needing to be washed by women at home), involved a battle with the intruding pit dust that ought never to have been.'

Of course, she re-emphasised, all this pit dust should be left at the pit head and a legal duty should be enforced upon the employers to provide facilities for the cleansing of miners' persons and clothing.

Such a reform was long overdue. The invasion of a miner's spotless home by the filth of his workplace was indeed degrading and an affront to the dignity of men and women. For the housewife it presented a daily hell — deprived as she was, of a bathroom with constant hot water — to have to provide bathing facilities for her husband (and sometimes sons as well) and then somehow, try to dry their wet, stinking apparel before the kitchen fire for the next day's shift. Consequently, the health of children as well as adults would frequently be affected by this obscene misery.

Katharine paid tribute to Robert Smillie,[12] the miners' leader for his support in the campaign for pit-head baths. She recalled how he had written in a Women's Labour League pamphlet that, 'Medical men had told him that in many of our miners' houses... serious and even minor operations which had to be performed on the spot became a very difficult matter, because of the poisonous fumes from germ-laden pit clothes dried in the house. Wounds could not be kept clean in such an atmosphere.'

She then moved on to deal with an even worse abuse existing in homes where the drying of the working clothes of open ash-pit miners or 'artificial manure' workers took place. It was the national disgrace of this spreading of pestilence among the families of workers that led Katharine Bruce Glasier to campaign across the country so tirelessly for 'Baths at the Pit-Head and the Works.' As part of her campaign, a series of illustrated pamphlets under that heading was issued by the Women's Labour League, describing the installation of baths and wash houses.

Continuing her article, she praised Belgium and the United States for being ahead with these hygienic provisions, even in pre-war days, adding that it was not until 1915 that the Atherton collieries in Lancashire set up the first 'fully-equipped establishment for four hundred men'. Gradually however, the number of installations was increasing as was the adoption of the custom of providing overalls for those engaged in dirty and dangerous tasks. She took heart that though Britain still lagged behind other countries, with the support of welfare officers, trade unions, legislators and enlightened public opinion, this appalling problem would soon disappear for ever.

On this optimistic note, Katharine Bruce Glasier ended her account of how families and communities could be rid of pollution at its most evil, in a common-sense and practical way.[13]

The content of the final article in the book: 'The Working Woman's House' is closely linked with the preceding one. The author was Mrs. Averil Sanderson-Furniss, the Secretary of the Housing Committee of the Labour Party and formerly a member of the Housing Council of the Ministry of Health. Mrs. Sanderson-Furniss and Dr. Marion Phillips collaborated in producing a comprehensive booklet on this theme, and that will be discussed in the next chapter.

Chapter 13: Homes for the Future

'Great Scott, if we leave it any longer to the men, what an unholy muddle they will make of 'housing reform''. What promoted this outburst by Phillips in January 1913 was that a Labour member of the London County Council, and author of the 'Campaign' pamphlet on housing, Mr. R. C. K. Ensor, had told a conference that he doubted whether a bathroom was a 'first necessity'. Was there really a need for a 'fixed bath' or a bathroom, he questioned.

Phillips was indignant that such a doubt should exist at all, and her article in *The League Leaflet* described the toil that a bath night involved for a working-class wife and mother: '... it is women who heat the water and prepare the bath and empty it afterwards ... to take a bath means that the hour must be carefully chosen, since no room is set apart for bathing, and all the heavy work of preparation and clearing up must be gone through.' She imagined the plight of women with five or six children 'with the thought of that Saturday night's tubbing' before them.

Her solution therefore was: 'If Labour Councillors will not support us in this demand as one of the first necessities, we shall have to cry a halt on all municipal housing, until we have replaced all Labour men by Labour women.'[1]

Labour women indeed since the early years of the century at their meetings and conferences had emphasised the need to replace the woefully inadequate dwellings of the working class, with cheerful, well-planned houses in which drudgery would be a thing of the past. They maintained that since homes were the centre of women's lives, they should be a source of pride and pleasure and not the scene of a hopeless war against dirt and infection — daily waged by generation after generation of prematurely ageing wives and mothers.

Marion Phillips herself — a vice-chairman of the Garden Cities' Association, on platforms up and down the country, in conferences and in her prolific writings, vigorously condemned the parlous state of working-class houses as being cramped, damp and insanitary, and lacking all the basic elements of a home decent enough to live in and bring up children. The Women's Labour League strongly felt that if well-built, well-furnished, pleasant houses were to become a reality, it was of paramount importance that housewives themselves should have a say in their design and construction. Phillips and Bentham took a hand in this task as councillors in Kensington, and in the spring of 1913 a conference on 'Houses Utopian and how to get them' was held by working women with Marion Phillips in the Chair, and the topics raised were fully discussed in the July issue of *The Labour Woman*, of that year.[2]

At the end of the war in 1918, Marion Phillips with Mrs. Averil Sanderson-Furniss, Secretary of the Women's Housing Committee of the Labour Party and a Member of the Housing Advisory Committee of the Ministry of Reconstruction, sent out a four-page leaflet containing a questionnaire to all Labour Party women's organisations throughout the country, with architects' plans, asking them to consider two questions.

(a) What is wrong with your house now?

(b) What sort of house do you want in the future?

The leaflet added, 'This is not the time for making the best of a bad job. Let us make up our minds exactly what we want in an ideal house'. After stating the post- war need for a million new homes and the equally urgent need for remodelling existing ones, the leaflet continued, 'The working woman with a home of her own, will be a voter. Let her first effort at citizenship be to improve the home'. A crisp warning to the housewife then followed: '...she alone has the necessary knowledge and experience, and if she can do nothing, her cause is hopeless'.

A list of eighteen questions was set out with a request for additional comments, and the leaflet ended with the words,

> Do not consider the question of rents. We must make up our minds as to the sort of house we want and see if we can get it at the price we can pay. That is where the *building* expert comes in. Women ought to be the *housing* experts and consider what they want and leave compromises on one side. Do not carry your flag too low. Is there any reason why all children should not have the best houses that the nation can provide?

This question of preliminary consultation between architects and builders on the one hand and the inhabitants of dwellings created by them on the other, was a far-seeing and original concept. These women were well ahead of their time, for it is only in the last thirty years or so, after an intermediate period of housing errors and desecrated landscapes that there has been talk of 'community architecture' — a process involving the participators of those who will inhabit proposed buildings. Charles Knevitt the architecture correspondent of *The Times*, in an article, 'Making Community Architecture Work' refers to Professor Alice Coleman's book *Utopia on Trial*, in which she points out to the high degree of crime and 'stress-related illness' on certain housing estates built without reference to their tenants. Knevitt refers too, to the findings of Professor Hugh Freeman, Senior Consultant Psychiatrist to Salford Health Authority and editor of *The British Journal of Psychiatry*. Professor Freeman maintains that links exist between the worst post-war housing and suicide in the area in which he works. According to the article, even more telling is the study by John Murtagh of King's College, London: *The Health Implications of Building Design*, which includes a comparison of two estates: one built with the tenants participation the other without. Knevitt concludes, 'Murtagh's account is only the first, one hopes, of such case studies which might go to prove conclusively that not only does user-involvement result in better 'architecture' but also a physically, socially and mentally better environment.'[3]

These words echo distinctly the sentiments found in *The Working Woman's House*, written by Marion Phillips and Averil Sanderson-Furniss, published in 1920, and embodying the results of the questionnaire sent out by them two years earlier.

It is interesting too that the plea made by the present Prince of Wales for humanity in housing repeats the concern felt by his great-grandmother, Queen Mary, about the need for proper housing in her day.

The Working Woman's House, written clearly and simply is divided into four parts. The first part begins by explaining the nature of the inquiry and dealing with the response to it. A large number of replies were received, mostly from women's organisations: The Women's Co-operative Guild, Women's Citizens' Associations, The National Council of Women, The Federation of Girls' Clubs, Women's Institutes, Local Labour Parties and many others. Twenty-four conferences and forty meetings were centrally arranged with many others at local level to discuss the findings.

It appeared from the replies that the housing requirements of the women largely followed the same pattern. Similarly, suggestions regarding the location of new housing estates all stressed the need to incorporate social and educational facilities in every new development. Plans for new towns were discussed as well as extensions of older ones. The replies from town and country implied that beauty and utility should be combined in any plan for future homes.

As for the internal arrangement of the house, it seemed that women had looked at it from three points of view: the matter of health and decency; the need to curtail housework through the use of labour-saving devices; and the provision in a home for social amenities such as a parlour or a quiet room for study, and a recreational room.

This section concluded with the words,

> As this inquiry proceeded, working women have been found more and more eager to take a place in solving housing problems. Bad housing means constant ill-health, the occurrence of dangerous epidemics, a low level of morale and a continuous waste of national force, and no one suffers from that loss so much as the woman whose work lies within the home.
>
> The reconstruction of society must depend largely upon the energy and wisdom with which the housing problem is met, and in putting forward the results of this inquiry, the women of the Labour Party feel sure that they are contributing to the welfare not only of the present but of future generations.

The remainder of the book fell into three divisions. The first of these concentrated on the inside of the house, dealing in detail with the defects in workers' houses of the time. Many of these houses are still with us. Unmodernised, the narrow, steep staircases, the gloomy, badly ventilated little rooms, the draughty, miserable scullery-kitchens with the larder comprising of a few shelves in the dark cupboard under the stairs, all tell their own story. Defects in rural housing were similar to these and additionally, stone-built cottages in the country-side were notoriously damp and lacking an indoor water supply.

The inquiry revealed that vital need for upstairs bathrooms and a hot water supply and the desirability of central heating in all new properties. Interestingly enough there was too the strong advocacy of the production of power for central heating from the waste heat of factories, providing indeed, heating for a whole village. This alas is still a neglected area as we move towards the end of the twentieth century.

Various examples of house designs were provided on the inquiry sheet and close attention was given to the application of good planning to each part of the house: even the hall and staircase were scrutinised. It was suggested that the old-fashioned scullery should be replaced by a bright, well-planned kitchen and that bedrooms should either have fitted furniture or attractive, well-made furniture of the 'Dawson-Heal type'. Various means of cooking and laundry were discussed and women were encouraged to seek out all labour-saving devices including electrical equipment such as vacuum cleaners, dishwashers, vegetable cleaners, food mixers — all those in 1920!

Every detail in the home was examined! The available types of composition floors; the problems of conversion; the advantages of tiled and painted walls; even the necessity to concrete the yard where the housewife hung out her washing — to ensure dry feet, was noted. To encourage a brightening of the spirit it was suggested too that trellis work be erected in the yard to support climbing flowers. That was sound commonsense: bringing a lily as well as a loaf, as it were, into one's daily round! Today it is taken for granted. Eighty years ago, it must have come as a fresh breeze to so many, conditioned to live in the shadow of the dark satanic mills.

This section of the book concluded with a comment on 'Women as the Home-maker' which might well be re-titled 'Women as the Emancipated Home-Maker' as it insisted that home should be the place that afforded to a wife and mother the freedom to develop her own personality. It was necessary that she

> ... in short be given every opportunity to develop a wider life. Then, and not till then, will she be enabled to take her rightful place in the community as well as to become a true home-maker. It is for these reasons that working women from all over the country have responded to the invitation of the Labour Party by giving expression to their views.

It is not surprising then, that the third part of the book was devoted to indicating the means of acquiring more freedom for the housewife. The thinking in this section was decades ahead of its time although its rather unimaginative title, 'Co-operative House Management' belonged to an earlier age. Briefly it suggested that the housewife might care to make use of external, fully-equipped establishments set up through the co-operation of householders, to save time, effort and money and at the same time improve the general quality of life. Highly skilled people would be employed to provide amenities which were listed as follows: the provision of meals, laundry and heating; child care; home helps, and other social arrangements.

First, the provision of 'take-away meals'. It was argued that since so much of the housewife's time was spent in shopping for food and the preparation of meals that she herself was often too tired to eat, there should be the provision in every housing scheme, of kitchens and restaurants on the lines of the National Kitchens established by the Ministry of Food and Local Authorities during the First World War. These would lighten the housewife's burden by supplying cheap nourishing meals taken at the restaurant by the family or brought home for consumption. The purchase of these meals at cost price — a price that would cover the cost of materials, fuel, management and labour, would be a boon to the working mother. In fact there were three hundred and sixty three National Kitchens in Britain at the time of the Armistice in 1918 but economy measures later forced them into closure.

Examples of menus provided at two of London's National Restaurants make truly impressive reading, the wholesome fare comparing favourably with much of the acceptable food offered today, and certainly far superior to the popular 'junk food'. At Sunderland, for instance, it was possible to obtain a two-course meal for eleven pence, with one penny charged for table services. Prices in those National Restaurants were always reasonable as they were municipally run.

The authors then moved on from prepared meals to launderettes 1920 style. A dual system of laundering clothes was advocated: a home arrangement with copper and wringing for light articles, and a public laundry for heavier ones. A bag-wash service also found favour. How these women planners would have welcomed the automatic washing machine in every home today and the launderette in almost every high street in the land.

Another of Phillips's favourite projects — the nursery school — was advocated as a necessary part of co-operative house management. In such schools, housed in light airy buildings, with attached gardens close to home and run by properly trained staff, little children would eat and sleep and play and learn.

Nor were older children neglected in this management scheme. The hideous asphalt school yard, responsible for countless cut knees and other injuries, would be replaced by something better, and the dangerous narrow streets outside working people's homes where children played after school hours, would give way to green open spaces made available by slum clearance schemes. Connected with schools, there would be children's centres where libraries and recreational rooms would provide an extension of the young folks' social life.

Having suggested these improvements in the care and education of children, the book then proceeded to discuss their mothers' welfare. A modern note is again struck with the plea for home helps. It was stressed that this particular service was essential to every mother during and after the birth of a child. Each Public Health Authority it suggested, should arrange for the provision of capable women, to be paid either by the families or from public funds in the same way as the services of the midwife scheme, advocated especially by the Women's Co-operative Guild and the Women's Labour League and supported by the Ministry of Health circulars on maternity and child welfare. One of these circulars indicated the advisability of special training of home helps at maternity and day nurseries, to include practical instruction in cooking, laundry, mending, infant care and hygiene. A further development of the scheme was here recommended so that home helps would be available at a time of illness and at all times to the overworked mothers of large families.

This section ended with the advocacy of a social centre in every housing scheme to meet recreational and educational needs, replacing inadequate and depressing halls and anticipating the community and leisure centres of the last twenty-five years that embody the earlier ideal.

The final part of the book, bearing the heading 'The Healthy Town' dealt with town planning. It indicated the need for deep and radical changes in social attitudes. It opened with a vigorous attack on 'monstrous and dingy dwellings' and rural cottages 'dumped down' haphazardly simply for monetary gain, and tribute was paid to the Housing and Town Planning Acts of 1909 and 1919 which recognised the need to prepare planning schemes to provide amenity, sanitation and proper siting in areas allocated for building homes.

The Labour movement was constantly urging the establishments of new towns to relieve overcrowding in large conurbations, and the reconstruction of smaller existing towns on garden-city principles emphasising the need for allotments, small holdings, gardens and the installation of the most modern power plants and labour- saving industrial facilities. There was mention of a 'real revolt among women against the long rows of cottages and treeless streets and the general aspect of slumdom'. The free open spaces following slum demolition were welcomed as the 'lung space' of a town. Suggestion was made that these green areas should be kept inviolate and that new houses should be built around the periphery of towns with new transport arrangements being made accordingly.

The authors of the book went on to say, 'the development of new areas ... also gives the opportunity for ending the old custom of segregating the working classes in streets of their own. Why not build new areas of houses of many different kinds, so that the manager of a factory may live side by side with the worker in it, the only difference being the number of rooms in a house and not the address which is given? By such methods there would not only be greater equality in securing pleasant surroundings for all, but much would be done towards reducing some of the worst forms of snobbery in the community'.

This concept is in line with the thinking of some of our most notable modern architects. Ralph Erskine, who was the 1987 R.I.B.A. Gold Medallist and one of the best- known architects in Scandinavia, favours the mixing of homes and work places, insisting too that differing incomes should not be starkly apparent. Additionally it is particularly relevant to the thesis of this book that Erskine was one of the first architects in Europe to consult the users of their end-products.[4]

The question of 'mixed dwellings' incidentally was given a further twist when Aneurin Bevan as Housing Minister once declared that houses for old people should be built in areas where there were young families as well. There should be no segregation according to age, he once said, adding, 'people want to see prams as well as hearses.' But we do not seem to learn. The organisation of sheltered housing for the elderly and infirm, with a warden and staff within the hearing range of an individual emergency bell, must be seen as an excellent provision. Yet how sad and isolated are these silent groves. How melancholy too is the atmosphere of so many coastal areas to which some of the more affluent in our community have retired to live privately or to go into nursing homes. The challenge of bringing a little gaiety and colour into these areas remains unanswered.

Two interesting housing schemes with plans were reproduced in the book: the Kings' Weston scheme and the Reading scheme. Both were discussed in detail and gained the approval of the authors because of their vision and practicality. They embodied many of the features discussed in earlier parts of the book: pleasantly situated homes connected to urban amenities like schools, community restaurants, laundries, social centres and libraries. An interesting feature of both schemes was the central boiler-house providing ample hot water for the houses.

Today, the Duchy of Cornwall's Poundbury scheme in Dorset, which plans to build up to four model villages that will house 8,000 inhabitants, has embarked on its first stage — that of public participation. There will be public meetings and exhibitions and consultations before the building begins. The impact of the Poundbury enterprise in town and rural planning in Britain in the near future may be considerable — and not without a certain nostalgia.

In conclusion, the book dealt with the relevance of the 1919 Housing Act to women's needs. Women were strongly urged to become involved locally with housing plans. Dealing with the recommendations of the Ministry of Health that 'it would be usually desirable that some members of the Housing Committees to be set up by local bodies should be women', the authors of the book sharply insisted that some of these members should *always* be women and these, wherever possible should be representatives of working women's organisations since they themselves would be housewives living in working-class homes.

It was urged too, that full use should be made of the advisory board known as the Housing Council of the Ministry of Health. On a local level, working women should be involved, not only on local authorities, but they should go further and form their own committees to study local housing plans. These plans, it was suggested, should be posted up publicly, and public meetings and conferences should be convened to discuss them. The final message was, that always, at every level, working housewives should be consulted on housing matters.

This bright, far-seeing little book, packed with down-to-earth plans for securing decent homes in pleasant surrounding, inspired new hope that this basic right of ordinary families might become a reality.

Unfortunately, the vision, in those troubled times did not materialise, and it is only lately that it is re-emerging from the mists of the past. Now, 'community architecture' and the importance of blending human need with natural amenity have again become matters of primary concern. In the sensitive hands of architects like Hunt Thompson Associates and Leon Krier, habitations set in well-planned comprehensive developments, will provide that sense of pride and dignity and beauty, sought so eagerly by these remarkable women, so many years ago.

Chapter 14: Letter to a Royal Bride

Marion Phillips throughout the Twenties continued as hitherto, to edit and write much of *The Labour Woman*. Its format had changed for the better over the years and it had become an attractive publication. Often the cover bore a reproduction of some charming picture like J. E. Christie's 'Pied Piper of Hamelin', or Hopner's famous portrait of a little girl, or a jolly scene like 'May Day' 1924. On the cover of the January 1925 issue was a cartoon from a woodblock, drawn specially for *The Labour Woman*, by Eric Gill, accompanied by the artist's comments. Paul Nash was another favourite artist. In 1926 — the year of the Miners' Lock-out, the covers bore some stark designs like Jerome Myers's lithograph reprinted from *The Survey*, bearing the legend, "Back to the Doorsteps' by Order of the Ministry of Health'. In the same year too, the cartoonist J. F. Horrabin provided a clever creation for one of the issue covers.

The publication appeared monthly as before and while its main purpose was always to supply information and to explain its relevance to its readers, at no time did the educating process include picking over the dry bones of dogma. Phillips was an expert propagandist and never missed an opportunity to make a point. At the same time, as a journalist she realised that simply thrusting propaganda relentlessly down people's throats, would kill any publication of this sort, stone dead. *The Labour Woman* was written for housewives, and wisely, unfamiliar facts and figures were interspersed with references to homely matters: news items from the women's sections; hints on good production and recipés — including on one occasion ingredients for a cough mixture — useful perhaps during an election campaign? There was too, a dress-making column that proved popular throughout two decades, and a 'Good Home-maker Column' that offered all kinds of useful tips, among them the way to frame pictures successfully. Book reviews and children's stories always made an appearance, and throughout, the magazine retained its warm 'family' atmosphere, while avoiding sentimentality and meaningless trivia.

As for the serious, solid, informative comment, it ranged from conference reports to proceedings in Parliament. Readers were regularly informed on all national issues: housing, citizenship, trade unionism, education in the form of articles by well-known Labour women, and additionally, items of general interest were always recorded. One of these noted, that the twenty-six year old Barbara Wootton had been selected by the Chancellor of the Exchequer in March 1924 to serve on the 'Committee to consider the best way of dealing with the National Debt'. She would, the comment continued ironically, '... have the unique honour of helping to pull the country out of its financial morass before she is of an age which is considered fit to vote!' Mrs. Wootton had also become a member of the staff of the Joint Department of Information and Research of the Trades Union Congress and the Labour Party.

Finally, in every issue of the magazine, accompanying 'The Editor's Monthly Letter' there would be the familiar photograph of Marion Phillips, confident and reassuring, wearing her favourite lapis lazuli and crystal necklace. Reading her editorials today, one is always struck by her straightforward approach and lack of patronage as she addressed her readers. Here was a formidable academic, an unmarried professional politician talking to housewives and mothers in a 'tone of voice' that was exactly right. She explained the issues carefully and thoroughly in much the same way as an experienced W.E.A. tutor addresses her class. She neither lectured to them as though they were a finals group at a university nor did she 'talk down' to them as though they were grown-up children. Her way was to chat to them, giving them the impression that she assumed that they were bright enough to follow her reasoning. And follow it they did, because one of Phillips's greatest triumphs was her ability to deal with complex issues in simple lucid language. The same clarity of thought and expression that made her the natural choice at international conferences to draft reports, served her well in her task of educating housewives. It was for her a joyful mission that lasted throughout her working life. In her capable hands an abstract concept became a warm reality that touched everyday lives in working-class homes up and down the country. Issues that concerned women at home and abroad were brought to the fireside in the columns of *The Labour Woman*.

In her appeal to women to vote Labour in the 1923 General Election, she warned that they would be told that women, irrespective of Party, were needed to represent women in the House of Commons. 'Do not accept this,' she urged, stressing that it was the Labour Party that had the welfare of women at heart. Like Rebecca West, Phillips insisted, 'It is not the sex of the candidates but their principles for which we should vote.'

The Labour Manifesto which included 'Health, Security, Education — within the reach of all' was then set out by her in a brief and compelling manner.

1923-24 was to be the turning-point in the early Twenties. Immediately after the war, there was hope in the air, a new level of expectation, a feeling of a fresh start. Those who had sacrificed and had worked hard during the war years, now believed that a better life awaited them. Wage-earners were now more aware of their position *vis a vis* the better off. C. F. G. Masterman in *England After the War* summed up the climate of the time in the words; 'It would be well if those who are spending, would realise that it is necessary to go softly and behind closed doors and to realise that they are being watched by thousands of eyes, awakened to criticism by the grim education of war'.[1] After 1918, there was an expectation that things would improve. The reconstituted Labour Party was a strong democratic force; women over thirty were given the vote and the Fisher Education Act laid down compulsory schooling until fourteen. J. M. Keynes wrote *The Economic Consequences of the Peace*, and Trade Union men and women pressed for improvements in work and social conditions.[2] The Coalition Government made conciliatory noises and talked of 'homes fit for heroes'.

As W. G. Runciman pointed out, nothing was done. The Government intended a return to a pre-war state of high profits and cheap labour and the removal of war-time statutory controls. There were strikes but as hardship increased, they subsided in the deepening gloom. The workers lost heart and the whole country relapsed into a depression that was to last for the next fourteen years, and later described by Beveridge as 'a needless scandal'. Runciman made an interesting point that it is when there is an expectation of improvement and reform that industrial unrest occurs. However, it is when people are afraid of losing what little they have in the way of jobs that hopelessness and inertia set in.

It was in this atmosphere of poverty and deprivation that Marion Phillips in the February 1923 issue of *The Labour Woman* wrote her 'Open Letter to Lady Elizabeth Bowes-Lyon' on the occasion of her marriage to the Duke of York. It is a frank and fearless letter pointing out the contrast between the Royal prospects for a happy and comfortable life and those of thousands of deprived couples embarking on a similar path.

After declaring her good wishes for the future happiness of the Royal couple, she went on to speak of the anxieties of hundreds of thousands of young wives in the post-war era, plagued by unemployment and bad housing, and fearful that their children would know of the 'terrors of eviction, of overcrowding, of sickness and of hunger.'

Phillips stated that having learned from the press of the royal bride's beauty and goodness, she ventured to suggest ways in which her good fortune might be shared. There would be excessive spending on 'unprofitable luxuries,' and expensive gifts would be given in the forthcoming marriage to one who already had 'so much to make it beautiful and cultured and dignified.'

She continued, '....such expenditure can ill be borne by a country with one and a half million of its people unemployed, more than five million ill-housed and at least that number underpaid.'

Then, having mentioned that the Duke's income from the nation, of £10,000 would be increased to £25,000 upon his marriage, she added, that while the amount was not criticised or questioned, yet 'we know by experience that life on £10,000 a year is a hundred times beyond that to which many of our young couples can look forward to'. Phillips, therefore suggested that this was a moment when 'A royal gesture of a kind to suit our times would make reality of that stream of compliments which the Press has poured out upon you.' This 'gesture' would be, to celebrate the royal wedding in 'quiet dignity' shorn of luxurious spending, and that those who would be sending expensive gifts to show their affection for her, should instead send money to the bride to be spent on building homes for young married people who were without them. Further, in addition to these thousands of pounds spent on 'useless ostentation' Phillips suggested that the additional income promised to the Duke of York, should be foregone and used annually for the same purpose.

She concluded 'A princess who would thus make her happiness the cause for the happiness of other people, would indeed gain a place in the hearts of the people... We urge that you should consider these proposals, made with a genuine desire that your welfare should be increased by the joy of service to the community whose good wishes have been so freely given to you upon your betrothal.'[3]

Marion Phillips's emphasis in her letter was on *sharing* and bore no envy. It is interesting that the admirable Sue Ryder — Lady Ryder of Warsaw — in a totally non-political radio conversation on 4th July 1990, referring to the 'disastrous poverty' of those same inter-war years regretted that there was no sharing during that awful time. The waste in life, she said, was still here today. She talked of her own inability to go into shops [presumably expensive London shops], when children and people had no food to eat or ever would, or clothes or shelter. Hence her own declared habit of only wearing clothes from her own shops that are run to help to fund her homes in various countries for the sick, disabled and homeless.[4]

Meanwhile back in the early Twenties, the struggle for social justice through political means continued. Phillips was constantly travelling to various parts of the country, meeting her regional organisers, and attending conferences, committees and public meetings. Always looking for new means of increasing membership of the Labour Party, she decided that the Annual Women's Day should be replaced by an Annual Women's Week. She therefore announced in January 1925, in *The Labour Woman* that the Executive Committee of the Labour Party was inviting all Labour branches, Women's Sections, Women's Advisory Councils and Federations to make a special effort during the week 6th–14th June in order to double the membership of the Women's Sections in that year.

In the same issue, she referred to the National Conference of Labour Women to be held at Birmingham Town Hall on 28th–29th May, when she hoped that the number of delegates would exceed the high number — a thousand — of the previous year. 'Never before,' she remarked jubilantly, 'have the women in the Party been so great in number or enthusiasm.'

Phillips was also travelling further afield — to those International gatherings by which she sent such store. Immediately after the war, she had helped to form The International Federation of Working Women, becoming its first International Secretary. She sat too, as the representative of the Standing Joint Committee of Industrial Women's Organisations on a committee that ensured the presence of more women in the League of Nations. She herself of course, supported the work of the League as did other members of her family in

Australia, in particular her brother M. M. Phillips and her nephew A. A. Phillips.

During these years, she visited the Scandinavian countries, Holland, Belgium, Switzerland and Austria, addressing conferences and meetings on a variety of subjects. In the *Labour Magazine*, of July 1923, her article 'Internationalists in the Making' stressed the value of these contacts. She described in particular, the International Summer School to be held in August 1923 by the International Federation of Trade Unions. She also drew attention to other summer schools — two for young workers to be held respectively at Leipzig and Cologne and an adult summer school at Schonbrune Castle, Vienna.

She was particularly pleased that not only leaders at the congresses of the I.F.T.U. and the Labour and Socialist Congresses should have the opportunity to meet but that the rank and file people from various countries could also be involved through these arrangements. To her, this was essential. She wrote, 'Public opinion must be internationlised before international cooperation can be a reality. The intercourse of leaders becomes the right orientation of policy, but it can never be an accomplished reality until the intercourse has broadened down from the few to the many.'

She referred in her article too, to the fact that she herself would be present at the biennial Congress of the International Federation of Working Women at Vienna in August and announced that students would be allowed to attend their sessions and conferences. The various topics to be discussed there were listed, and she re-emphasised the benefits that resulted from regular international discussions of matters that were the concern of all.

As for her personal involvement in the Labour and Socialist Women's International Conferences, she found in them a splendid opportunity to secure specific reforms. Of these there were many. One of them — perhaps the closest to her heart — was the health of mothers and children. Her early interest in proper maternity provision; in the setting up of the Kensington Baby Clinic, and her publication of *The School Doctor and the Home* had already borne witness to her particular concern in this area. Throughout the Twenties too, and during her period in Parliament, childbirth and maternity care remained for her a constantly pressing concern.

Chapter 15: Maternity Care and Birth Control

In *The Labour Magazine* dated 7th May 1928, a long detailed article by Marion Phillips, bearing the title: 'Maternity: A Primary Problem of Socialist Policy' revealed that her continuing concern with this question was well-founded.

She led off with the sentence — 'The fundamental problem of Socialism, the acid test of all its policy, is the healthy birth of the next generation' and continued — 'The surest index of Poverty is the rise or fall of the death and sickness rates of babies and the next surest is that of young children'.

She then provided a table showing birth rate, death rate, infant mortality rate and total puerperal mortality applicable to four-year spans between 1891 and 1926. She inferred from them the now accepted fact that it is the first four weeks of a child's life that is most important. Maternal mortality, she insisted, had to be reduced, because the lives of mother and child are so clearly interlinked. There were too, high rates of maternal deaths in the U.S.A and Canada and also in Australia and New Zealand. The rates varied in Europe but everywhere there was need for research into the alarming incidence of deaths in childbirth. She listed many of the contributory causes: poverty, ignorance, poor health, unhygienic conditions, lack of medicines and proper nursing care before and after birth and lack of nourishment and warmth. Phillips, therefore, stressed the vital need for proper antenatal clinics as well as better training for doctors and nurses. Home Helps too were necessary. Much could be done in this country, she pointed out, by the full use of the Maternity and Child-care Act.

The subject had been prominently discussed previously many times, at the Annual National Conferences of Labour Women and the Labour Party, and she hoped that discussions about these matters at the International Women's Conferences would lead to exerting further pressure on Public Health Authorities in all countries and through the Health Section of the League of Nations, to attend in particular to the needs of backward areas.

Phillips always saw the housewife — overworked and overlooked, 'cabin'd, cribb'd' and 'confin'd' — often in more ways than one — as the most vulnerable member of society. It was especially necessary, she felt, that care and protection should be given to the pregnant housewife who went out to work. This view was shared by her colleagues in the Labour Women's Conferences and they, together with the Labour Party and Trade Union Movement, all supported protective legislation that would improve conditions of work in order to safeguard mothers and the new generation. The signatories of the Treaty of Versailles too, had endorsed the opinion of the Labour Party.

Under Part 13 of the Peace Treaty, the International Labour Office had been set up, in which, countries were represented by trade unions and employers and government delegates. The first I.L.O. Conference was held in Washington in 1919. The two women among the four members of the Labour delegation of Great Britain, were Margaret Bondfield and Mary Macarthur. Discussions were held on the following lines, according to the Treaty: 'Matters in connection with women's employment, included maternity and childbirth provision; night work relating to women, and women in unhealthy processes'. During th first discussions relating to maternity and childbirth, Mary Macarthur spoke. The following provisions were advocated: 'That women should not work for six weeks after confinement, and that they had the right to leave on a medical certificate, six weeks before confinement. Secondly, during that time, women were to receive monetary benefits sufficient for full and healthy maintenance of mother and child from public funds. Thirdly, that a mother was entitled to free attendance by a doctor or certified midwife.' The next convention was that of women engaged in night work, and the third concerned their employment in unhealthy processes.[1]

As a result of the deliberations at Washington, the conventions dealing with childbirth and night work were adopted.

But not all women were pleased with these provisions. In *The Labour Woman* of August 1924, Barbara Drake made a strong attack on them in her article, 'Middle-class Women and Industrial Legislation', with the sub-title, 'New Bills and Old Bogies'. Mrs. Drake had prepared this statement for the Standing Joint Committee of Industrial Women's Organisations and it related the history of attitudes towards protective legislation for women workers, and clearly stated the position of Labour women on the matter. She condemned the early feminists for opposing any legislation that applied solely to women and condemned with equal vigour, those feminists of her own time who were doggedly persistent in their opposition to the Washington Convention.

In the January 1925 issue of *The Labour Woman*; Marion Phillips in her editorial headed 'The Cry of the Backwoodswomen', asserted vigorously, 'There have been several attempts recently to breathe life into the dead controversy of special legislation for women workers'. After referring to Mrs. Drake's August statement, clarifying the position of the S.J.C. with regard to the subject, Phillips continued, '... Since that time, however, the ultra-feminists have gone on with their agitations and have endeavoured in vain to persuade the Executive Committee of the League of Nations Union to accept their line of opposition against the ratification for the Washington and other Labour Conventions concerning women's employment'.

She proceeded, 'In Great Britain, night work has been prohibited for women since 1901 but the British Government embodied the Night Work Convention in its 'Women, Young Persons and Children's Act 1920', thus confirming a law made many years ago'. Witheringly she observed, '... It is rather late in the day for the ultra-feminists to protest'.

But Phillips was not finished with the Opposition. Having declared that her forces were determined to secure the ratification of the Maternity Convention, she allowed herself a little fun at their expense. She related how "an opponent of the Maternity Convention has gone as far as to state that she would offer no objection to it provided that the word 'person' was substituted everywhere for the word 'woman'". Phillips went on, 'Could anything be more ridiculous? We have got to learn that the functions of maternity are independent of sex. Unless nature revises the processes of birth, we must accept maternity provisions and protection as applying to women and not to men'.

She declared her pleasure that the League of Nations Executive had confirmed that it accepted and worked for 'the application of the principles of these conventions adopted by the International Labour Conferences' but she still did not trust the tactics of the Opposition, and felt the need to indulge in a little special pleading. So after stating briskly that it was time that 'the theorists came down to earth' and insisting that a 'paper equality' was no good, she went on, 'it is useless to assume that men and women are the same in every way. To provide women with a real equality of opportunity, it is necessary to compensate them for their initial handicaps and we believe that their interests can be served by the improvement by law of their working conditions ... W do not believe in legislation as such but ... the bargaining power of women and children is less than that of men, and we want to give them therefore, the additional protection of the law ...' Typically, Phillips always chose to face facts rather than to indulge in symbols.

The campaign against protective legislation however, continued throughout the Twenties. Its supporters set up the 'Open Door' Movement with Dorothy Jewson, a member of the I.L.P. and a Member of Parliament in the mid-Twenties, as one of its leaders. It was the prohibition of night work for women that was most at issue, and in 1929 an 'Open Door International' was formed in Berlin, prior to setting up an office in Geneva with the purpose of seeking to influence the I.L.O. against protective legislation for women. Marion Phillips clearly regarded it as a confounded nuisance. In an article published in *The Labour Magazine*, under the title, 'Socialist Women meet in Switzerland' she described the proceedings of the annual meeting of the Women's Committee of the Labour and Socialist International held at Zurich in January 1930. To it came representatives of nine countries. 'The main business of the Conference' she wrote, 'was a report and resolution presented by Great Britain on the question of the Open Door Council and the Protection of Women Workers'. She explained that it was the formation of the Open Door International in the previous year, plus the fact that the Movement itself had started in Britain, that had prompted the necessity for the British Labour Party to make its own view clear 'before the world'.

The following resolution was then put forward by the British Labour Party:

This meeting of the Women's Advisory Committee of the Labour and Socialist International, declares that the policy of the Open Door Council is against the interests of industrial women workers and urges the Socialist parties in all countries, both nationally and internationally, to continue to support with all their force, the improvement of protective legislation for women, both as workers and mothers employed in industry. At the same time, we point out to women workers that they can only be adequately protected if in addition to laws, they are organised industrially, and that through their political organisations, it is important that they should exercise 'constant vigilance in order to assure themselves that any legislation proposed, which affects their industrial welfare is in accordance with their best interest, meets their needs and helps them in the struggle for better conditions and against exploitation'. The representatives of all the other countries present, apart from Sweden were unanimous in support of the resolution. Sweden's amendment 'softened the criticism of the Open Door organisation but declared that there was no moral justification for special protective legislation, save for women as mothers.

It transpired during the discussion, however, according to the article, that the Swedish delegate's criticism of protective legislation was based on the Convention banning night work. Replying to this, Gertrud Hanna of the Prussian Diet and Marion Phillips pointed out that while Sweden had seventy seven thousand in industry, Britain and Germany had seven million. Frau Hanna pointed out too, that the long summer hours of light in Scandinavia altered the circumstances. In addition, the view was expressed that if it was accepted that women 'as mothers' needed special protection then that protection surely 'could not begin and end with pregnancy and the period of nursing, but that a woman's potential motherhood must be taken into account even during her girlhood and her work must be subject to regulation with these facts in view, from the beginning.'

Miss Jewson who spoke on behalf of the I.L.P. Women's Committee, spoke in favour of the Open Door Council. Her amendment, recommending 'adequate protection for the mother before and after birth, and Protective Legislation for *all* industrial workers,' brought a terse comment from Marion Phillips. 'Once again', she complained, 'it was difficult to see how the former could be achieved if legislation was to be the same for men and women.'

All the other delegates present were in favour of the British resolution and Frau Hanna further reinforced the argument by saying that women in the trade unions were actually seeking *more* protection than their leaders were demanding.

On a personal note, Frau Hanna said that as an industrial worker herself, she had always been in favour of banning night work for women, and when the law had come into force in Germany, she herself had been among the displaced workers. Her conviction of the advantage of the legislation, however, had never wavered.

The resolution was carried, prompting Phillips to announce 'The position therefore as far as Socialist women in the International are concerned, is very clear and positive.'

Yet, the question of night work for women was to rumble on into 1931, when a proposal at the Prague International Committee of Labour and Socialist women in the January of that year urged, that as a result of various attempts to revise the International Convention on night work for women, that 'no opening should be given which would in any way weaken the position of women workers and that the prohibition of night work should remain in effective force.'[2]

Nevertheless, the I.L.P. delegates were still stubbornly pursuing their objective at the Vienna Congress in July 1931 as we shall see.

With her deep concern for the welfare of working-class mothers, what was Marion Phillips's attitude to birth control? She was of course, well aware of the misery caused by constant child-bearing and the struggle to rear large families in grinding poverty. She knew well enough that as many as ten or more children were often born and brought up in cramped insanitary cottages, resulting in a grievous toll on the mother's health. There had been generations untold of such mothers who 'rising before dawn, grew old before time'.

Independence and equality for women had been at the heart of the Labour movement from its early days. In 1913, a series of debates on the economic position of women under the title 'How Shall Women Live?' was held by the Central London branch of the Women's Labour League. Regular features appeared in *The Labour Woman* and in 1914 Phillips reviewed *Conflicting Ideals* by B. L. Hutchings, in which the question was posed, 'Woman, shall she be parasitic or self-dependent?' The endowment of motherhood was seen as some means of giving mothers a degree of independence. Pursuing the theme, Mrs. Sanderson-Furniss in her article, 'The Citizenship of Women' was to insist that the assumption that a woman '... is a drone in the hive — a non producer in the state' should be disposed of once and for all by the Labour-proposed endowment of motherhood. In her words, mothers should receive 'a direct financial consideration from the State for work and services in the home — as mothers, just as men demand the same consideration for work done or services rendered in the factory or the shop.'[3] This would give women equality and emancipation, and a degree of security unheard of in the past.

Even so, how much relief would this in itself, provide for mothers of large families overwhelmed with toil and fatigue and weakened by continual child-bearing? Family limitation was a subject of great sensitivity at the time, though an increasing number of women were beginning to feel that they themselves should be free to decide on the number of children they wished to bear. As early as April 1914 there were letters and discussions on family limitation in *The Labour Woman* and ten years later, it was still being discussed. It is incomprehensible today that the Maternity and Child Welfare Act of 1919, while providing treatment and advice for pregnant mothers, did not allow for advice on contraception.

In 1921 however, the first Marie Stopes Clinic was opened in Islington, while the Women's Co-operative Guild and Women's Sections of the Labour Party invited speakers on birth control to their meetings and as a result more clinics were opened in 1925.

Marion Phillips was always ready to publish articles on the subject in *The Labour Woman* and to supply information about meetings and speakers. She regarded the information supplied as a matter of education. She was equally ready to publish articles on venereal disease. In the March 1924 issue of *The Labour Woman* she published a letter from a number of women raising the question whether Labour women should urge the Ministry of Health to arrange that instruction and information be given at clinics run by the Public Health Authorities. This letter elicited an article by the Editor in the same issue headed: 'Birth Control: A Plea for Careful Consideration'.

She announced at the outset that the subject would be fully discussed at the Annual Conference of Labour Women in June, when the Report on the Year's Work would be presented. She then made the following observations. First, she stressed that the women of the Labour Party, while sharing the same political views, had differing religious convictions. Some women therefore, in the Party, because of moral considerations, were totally opposed to any form of birth control. She maintained that since this was a matter of private conviction and not political opinion, it merited very careful, sensitive treatment. She pointed out too, that the differences in this area among women of the Labour Party was a reflection of the differences among the public at large.

Secondly, Phillips emphasised that 'the practice and methods of birth control are still a matter of controversy and great uncertainty among doctors and scientists. Now, here we come to a very great difficulty. You cannot demand that a doctor or a health visitor or any public servant should give advice which he or she does not think is sound advice. You cannot ask your M.O.H. to give women teaching in birth control when he believes that the teaching itself is unsound or uncertain. Yet this is the case which a great many of the officers of the Health authorities and medical and scientific people have not yet reached any clear conclusions.'

She made a further telling point: that 'those who seek advice from people who can give or withhold it as they like, are in a different position, but when the State backs any particular methods on so vital a matter, it ought to be able to do so with reasonable confidence that it is doing the right thing.' Again she stressed the importance of scientific research and inquiry, adding that a great many women had become victims through this lack of medical knowledge of the subject. She argued that there should be 'a stringent and thorough-going enquiry by the Ministry of Health carried out by the best expert opinion it can secure, into the whole question of methods and effects of birth control on the physical and mental constitution of the Community. It is as important a question as research into the cause and cure of cancer and its urgency is as great. For there is no doubt at all that at the present time, there are few women who are not being forced to consider this question for themselves, often with the worst possible results upon the health of themselves or their children because of their ignorance or the bad advice they get.'

Lastly, she made it clear that there were two separate questions involved in the matter of birth control. One was the question of health. In some cases it was imperative that the number of children a woman might bear should be severely limited.

On the other hand, she said, there were economic reasons for limiting families. It is not surprising that Phillips — herself the youngest of seven children — should say, 'Now, a big family is not necessarily an evil in itself; it has certain very great mental and moral advantages over the one — or — two-child family. Big families are only a disadvantage where economic causes make it impossible to get them houseroom or food or a proper environment, or where the mother is worn out by the bearing of children. Let us realise therefore, that birth control is not an end in itself. The limitation of families is fast becoming an economic doctrine of Liberalism because the Liberals do not want to make any drastic changes in the distribution of wealth and not because small families are necessarily the ideal.'

Returning to the question of the health of the mother, she re-emphasised the need for immediate measures. The Ministry of Health should find means to offer these mothers sound advice based on scientific knowledge, and the necessary education for mothers — and fathers too — to deal with this personal matter.

She ended her article on the same lines as her earlier plea that 'the relations of husband and wife should not be treated as a political issue at all. Every sane woman must think about it, but it is not yet ripe for such a decision as would pledge a political party to any particular course of action other than full expert investigation of the medical side of the question.'

This balanced and closely argued article found an echo in the Report of the Standing Joint Committee prepared for the Annual Conference of Labour Women in June of the same year. The S.J.C. had appointed a sub-committee to look into the question of birth control and it was clear that its members were deeply concerned about the health hazards that could be connected with it. The account in *The Labour Woman* read:

> The Committee reported that in view of medical experts and others, they did not feel able to recommend that the Ministry of Health should require that information about birth control methods be given at clinics administered out of public funds, but that further expert inquiry was necessary and the Standing Joint Committee recommended that the Ministry of Health should be asked to make the question of birth control part of a special inquiry into the care of maternity and that this should be included in the resolution dealing with maternity to be placed before the Conference. This was reported to the Executive Committee of the Labour Party and endorsed.[4]

Meanwhile, the Women's Co-operative Guild had pressed resolutions at their congress of 1923 urging the Ministry of Health and local authorities to provide information about birth control in maternity and welfare clinics.

Resolutions were passed too in the annual National Conferences of Labour Women in 1924 and 1925. The 1924 resolution read that local health authorities should be allowed to provide birth control information to those who wished it. The resolution of 1925 was that doctors should be allowed to give birth control advice to married mothers. Both resolutions were rejected by the Labour Party Conferences in 1924 and 1925.

As for Marion Phillips herself, prepared as she was, to handle this issue carefully by publishing material on *The Labour Woman* she saw with deadly clarity that in making birth control a *Party* policy, there was great danger that it might alienate so many Labour supporters who held opposing views on the subject, that the future welfare of the very housewives she sought to help would be at risk. Arthur Henderson too, saw the shortsighted folly of incorporating it in the Party agenda.

Although the resolution was passed in 1926 by the Labour Party Conference in Margate, the verdict was reversed overwhelmingly by the Labour Party Conference at Blackpool in 1927 after hearing a powerful speech by Henderson.

It should be noted at this point, that Henderson had always been the women's champion in the battle against poverty, low wages, sweated labour, and 'dilution' in the munition factories during the war. He had stood like a rock, during the long suffrage campaign, and finally it was Henderson who won the day for the women. Mrs. Mary Agnes Hamilton tells us how Henderson stayed on, loyally in Lloyd George's Government, to see the war through. It was a time of great personal sadness for him as his eldest son had been killed on the Somme in 1916. When the new Representation of the People Bill came up for discussion, Curzon was against any extension of the franchise and above all he was against any admission of females. At this, Henderson thumped the table. He asked, 'Did he want the workers to get their rights by compromise or by revolution? As for the women, it would be an abominable breach of faith if they were not brought in and he for one would not stand for it.' Mrs. Hamilton went on, 'But for him and Cecil, who backed him stoutly, the women would almost certainly have been left out.[5]

There was therefore, enormous respect and affection for Henderson in the Labour Party and when he spoke about the resolution in a firm and balanced way at the 1927 Blackpool Conference the delegates listened to him. Mrs. Hamilton takes up the story:

> He stressed that they were not discussing the desirability or not of birth control, but whether it should be a part of Party policy. After saying that 'there are many of our numbers in the country who have deep religious convictions on this issue, I will frankly say they are not mine by any means; but that does not lead me the less to observe and recognise the convictions of the comrades who think differently from myself'.[6]

He went on to express his admiration for the determined policy of Labour Conferences from the beginning to avoid issues that would split the party on religious grounds. The Party Executive having listened carefully to the deputation from the Women's Conference, had in his opinion, acted correctly in refusing to support their resolution. To do so, he believed, would have had disastrous consequences in the constituencies and in Parliament. He asked the delegates to vote strongly in favour of the recommendation of the Executive and they did so over-whelmingly.

The women understood full well that Henderson's personal sympathy was with them. At the same time they realised the wisdom of his advice. The unity of the Party was paramount and it was vital to carry public opinion with them. This included Catholic and non-Catholic religious views.

Henderson knew his public. He was also more aware than most of the different strands of conviction in the intricate weave of the Labour Party. One of the stoutest and toughest of these strands was the Nonconformism from which the Party itself had sprung. Its members who attended the great Sunday night political meetings in the Welsh valleys, only did so — often in a great hurry — after attending chapel services. Egon Wertheimer's shrewd analysis of the difference between the Labour Party of Britain and the Continental Marxist Socialist Parties, bears witness to Labour's religious and cultural roots. It has been stated in various ways many times: 'Labour owes more to Methodism than to Marx' is one version.[7]

Wertheimer's *Portrait of the Labour Party*, published in 1929, emphasised that 'in all Continental Socialist Parties, there is a wide-spread tacit agreement on the necessity for a change in attitude towards contraception, interruption of pregnancy and revision of medieval legislation on homosexuality etc. Here, more than upon any other point, the difference between the Continental and British Socialist Parties becomes apparent, and the close connection of British Labour with British national culture and tradition revealed ...the wide-spread religious nonconformity of the working-class and close affinity with the Puritan tradition of the dissenting churches, militated effectively against the rise of any radical, proletarian culture'.

Reflecting that some differences lie deep, he further commented,

> ...the indignant disgust which the attitude of Continental women Socialists towards legalisation of abortion aroused, should have opened the eyes of many who believed these differences merely superficial or tactical. Those who participated in the International Women's Conference in Brussels will still remember the veiled but unmistakable condemnation uttered by Dr. Marion Phillips, speaking in the name of the Women's Organisations of the British Labour Party. The attitude prevalent among Continental women Socialists towards 'compulsory motherhood' she pointed out, 'would arouse the greatest opposition among the women of Great Britain, and the whole idea would only wound and outrage their tenderest sensibilities'.[8]

If Henderson knew his public so Marion Phillips knew 'her women'. She had the sensitivity and the compassion to understand the minds and the hearts of those who needed help, but practical as she always was, in order to help them, she realised that in the climate of the time, she and her colleagues would need to tread gently. Gertrude Tuckwell, Secretary of the Maternal Mortality Committee (which represented all the Societies connected with motherhood) had known Marion Phillips since 1911, and was to say of her, 'She never urged a line of action or pressed for an expression of feeling which would have aroused religious susceptibilities or Party feeling.' Labour housewives, while becoming progressively alert and well-informed, nevertheless, because of their upbringing remained in some matters, diffident and uncertain. A sustained programme of education about contraception, to remove shyness and embarrassment seemed to Phillips to be the way ahead.[9]

It is worth noting too, in connection with the determination of the Labour Party leaders of those days, not to make birth control a Party issue, that a free vote in Parliament, cutting across political allegiance, has always been the custom when deeply personal matters of this kind are debated.

As for the Brussels Conference itself, the subject of birth control was not even on the Agenda and Phillips with her British colleagues upon their arrival there, were surprised that it was being raised at all, since a decision had been taken at the Women's International Committee at Cologne in December 1927 that birth control would not be a subject of discussion at Brussels. The agreed Agenda dealt with two issues. The *first* was subdivided into three parts: (a), (b) and (c). 1(a) was headed 'For the Mother and Child'. This concerned the ratification of the Washington Convention, involving eleven measures in all. Draft Resolution of Delegates of the British Labour Party. 1(b) was headed 'For the Woman in Industry' and 1(c) was in respect of the care of the sick, crippled, invalid and aged — involving their financial provision, treatment and care. 'Adequate pensions, sufficient for honourable and independent retirement'.

The *second* issue concerned tendencies to mobilise women for military service.

However, a Declaration concerning 1(a) was made by delegates from the European countries stating support for abortion.

Phillips, as one of the six delegates from the Labour Party of Great Britain made a measured but totally uncompromising speech. While regretting being in disagreement with 'our Austrian comrades', she said that the British delegation could not accept their statement on behalf of the British Labour Party. She pointed out that the question of birth control in Britain had been discussed both at the National Conferences of Labour Women and at Labour Party Conferences for four years, and while the resolutions passed at the Women's Conferences had never been 'declarations in favour of birth control itself' they had been in favour of 'permitting clinics established by public authorities to give information on the subject' to those who sought it. She explained that the Labour Party had discussed the question three times but in 1927 had decided that it should not become a part of *Party* policy, but leaving individual members to make their own decisions on the subject. Since then the National Conference of Labour Women had accepted the decision.

Phillips further explained why the British Labour Party had arrived at such a decision. It was because there were people in the Party — no doubt a minority who were opposed to birth control, largely on religious grounds and it would be wrong to 'force out that minority' by a decision on birth control. She added pointedly, 'the Labour Party pays careful regard to minorities as may be judged from the fact that the Independent Labour Party, which is one of its affiliated organisations has been able here to express a view which is not that of the Party as a whole.' She was of course, referring to the I.L.P. delegate, Dorothy Jewson, a prime supporter of the Open Door Movement and opposed to special protective legislation for women in industry Phillips concluded this part of her speech by announcing that in view of the Labour Party decision, it would be impossible for its delegates at the Conference to vote on the question of birth control.

Moving on then to the question of abortion, she emphasised that this had never been discussed either by the Women's Conference or by the Labour Party Conference in Britain. She went on, 'so far as I can judge, the conditions in relation to this in Austria are very different from those in Great Britain, and I think that the conclusions to which we would come if we had discussed the matter, would not be those which the Austrian comrades have put before you.' Then came the short passage in her speech to which Egon Wertheimer referred. She said, 'The phrase 'compulsory motherhood' would, I think, especially arouse strong opposition and British women would, I believe resent its use in this connection. We regret that this question has been raised and I want to emphasise the fact that we do not wish the question of birth control to be excluded on the ground of timidity, since we have discussed the matter so fully in our own country, dealing with it, I believe, before any other Socialist Women's organisation had considered it. We are however, bound by the decisions that have been taken both by our Party and by the women of the Party.'[10]

Listening to Phillips and taking part herself in the discussion, was the Palestine delegate, Goldie Meirson, who would later be better knows as Mrs. Golda Meir.

In the year following the Brussels Conference, Marion Phillips contested Sunderland in the General Election and a smear campaign was directed against her by the opponents of birth control. There was, for instance, an anonymous note sent to the Liberal candidate (who honourably forwarded it to Phillips), outlining a strategy of Napoleonic ingenuity to discredit her. It involved mobilising an army of Roman Catholic canvassers, briefed to ask one earth-shattering question: 'Is Dr. Phillips a personal friend of Dr. Stopes?'

It is unlikely that Marion's rather off-hand reply, 'I have never even seen Dr. Stopes,' would be deemed by the enemy to be relevant in the slightest degree ...[11]

Chapter 16: Women and the Miners' Lock-out

'We are fighting not a fear of starvation but the actual presence of hunger.'

W hat was described by Ebby Edwards as the 'spirit and organising genius of Dr. Marion Phillips' was never more in evidence than in the magnificent seven-month rescue operation that she and her tireless committee of Labour women mounted, to save the hundreds of thousands of mothers and children — victims of the 1926 Miners' Lock-out in the coalfields of Britain. These had, according to Edwards, 'reached the limit of human endurance. Marion and her organisation of women workers saved them from final collapse ... Her district schemes to aid expectant mothers were an example of Marion's tact and foresight. Her efforts in the distribution of food and clothing cannot be forgotten. She placed thousands of miners' children in good homes until the struggle was ended. She gave help in every quarter ...'[1]

The main tribute to Phillips in *The Labour Woman* March 1932 describing her as a 'superb administrator,' maintained that the 'Women's Fund' had altogether collected and distributed £350,000 — in today's terms about six million pounds. It was indeed a heroic feat, executed by what has been described as an 'Industrial Red Cross' that averted a major disaster in the coalfields. This tribute also made the point that while 'most relief funds leave unpleasant memories behind, or surpluses that go no one knows where, every penny of the Women's Fund was ruthlessly accounted for. And was there ever a fund of such magnitude whose expenses amounted to so little?'[2]

In 1927, Marion Phillips published the story of how the Women's Committee for the Relief of Miners' Wives and Children, during the Miners' Strike of 1926, performed their gigantic task. She told the tale simply, with facts and figures. It was as follows:-

On Wednesday, 11th May 1926, A. J. Cook, the Secretary of the Miners' Federation, prompted it seems, by Barratt, the press photographer, asked Marion Phillips if she would form a Women's Committee to organise relief for the women and children of striking miners. A Central Committee was immediately set up, with Marion Phillips and Lilian Dawson as Joint Secretaries and Lady Margaret Slessor as Treasurer, and by 21st May the first appeals went out to the press from their headquarters at the Parliamentary Labour Club at Tufton Street. These premises were to be the centre of a round-the-clock marathon of urgent activity to combat distress for the next seven months. Within the next twenty-four hours, money began to arrive, as collecting sheets were printed and sent to various organisations across the country. Among these were Labour Party Women's Sections, Women's Co-operative Guilds, Adult Schools, various religious organisations, League of Nations' Union, Peace Societies, Women's International League, Branches of the W.E.A. Meanwhile, a demonstration at the Albert Hall on 30th May raised £1,000. Sibyl Thorndike, who was 'a warm-hearted friend throughout,' began to raise money and the Prince of Wales sent £10 to the Somerset Miners' Distress Fund.

Flag Days and 'Lamp' Days — (the miner's lamp soon became an emblem of their efforts) were organised and as early as the beginning of June, a scheme was developed for helping pregnant and nursing mothers, and a special further appeal went out for boots and shoes.

A special inquiry too, was initiated into the questions of school feeding and Poor Law Relief. This was necessary to counteract the claims of the Government and the Tory press that the needs were not urgent.

How urgent were they? They were real and intense, often harrowing. Chapter and verse of the actual suffering expressed in the coal-mining areas is provided in Marion Phillips's book by investigators on the spot, who reported back to her Committee. Some of these reports might well have applied to industrial Britain in the Victorian era. Indeed, it is inconceivable to us today, that such deprivation could have existed in the third decade of the Twentieth Century. At that time, alas, the Welfare State was still a long way off — a mirage in a desert of helplessness and despair. It was to take twenty years — nearly a quarter of a century — before a landslide Labour victory was to usher in a new order.

Phillips obtained her reports from reliable sources: from officers of Women's Sections and Advisory Committees, and from members of the London Committee and when she and Mrs. Bonhôte drafted a special Appeal to Lawyers, they were able to give detailed accounts of conditions in the coalfield. It starts:

> We know that there are many people who have not sent us a subscription for the miner's families because:
>
> i They think all children are wholly fed in the schools.
> ii The miners are getting good Union Pay.
> iii The expectant and nursing mothers are provided for in the welfare centres.
> iv The Poor Law Authorities supplement where there is need.
>
> But we think that if you knew the real position on these four points, you would help us to the best of your ability and we feel that it is only fair to you and to these sufferers to let you know the truth.

The four points are then clearly and factually dealt with in turn, revealing the real distress experienced in the coalfield. One section of her report soundly condemns the failure of the public authorities to provide succour to the needy. She quotes from a report from Pontypool, South Wales, made in August 1926:

> Five mothers having among them 33 children, pooled their resources and from Friday to Monday, when they would draw their Poor Law pittance, would have two small loaves and a ¼lb of margarine.

She mentions the attempt made in June 1926 to obtain information on Poor Law Relief in the coalfields and the use made of it by Susan Lawrence M.P., when the Labour Party raised the matter in the House. She quotes a few examples of the charity meted out by the authorities:

> The relief given to families of miners is, generally speaking, 12/- for women and 4/- for each child — the relief suggested by the Ministry of Health. In many cases, however, it is lower … Lydbrook, for example, in the Forest of Dean gives 10/- to the wife and 2/6 for each child. Lichfield gives 5/- for a woman, 2/6 for the first child with a maximum of 16/6 for a family.
>
> Boys of fourteen are almost always excluded from all relief, whether or not they have been employed at the pits; whether or not they had ever been at work. They therefore lived on their mothers' allowance.

She goes on to point out that for children of school age, meals were often given by the Local Education Authority, and while in a minority of cases, they were considered as an addition to Poor Law Relief, in a majority of cases, the cost was deducted from the Poor Relief. Milk and food were provided in a few places for children under five from Welfare Centres, but sometimes, again, this was deducted from the Poor Relief. In the majority of cases, Poor Relief was granted on loan!

One of the Committee's 'reporters' was Mrs. Adamson whose husband was M.P. for Cannock. Her references to the severe distress in that area is quoted. Lichfield and the South Staffordshire area similarly suffered great privation, examples of which are provided in the book. Mrs. E. F. Wise, who visited the area, says: 'Last week the relief was reduced by half. This week, that miserable amount was again halved. All relief is on loan.'

One of many examples of extreme distress, quoted by Mrs. Wise, is as follows:

> Last week, a man, wife, two children of school age and three girls over — one feeble-minded, another a cripple, tried to exist on 7/6. The woman was so weak she could scarcely stand and tears poured down her cheeks as she described how they had 'lived' for a week on tea and dry bread. This week they must drop the tea and some of the bread as they only get 3/9.

Other examples follow. Then, Mrs. Oliver, wife of the M.P. for Ilkeston, Derbyshire, went to the area to arrange immediate help to prevent starvation. She and a colleague 'saw the Co-operative Society and arranged for the distribution of food vouchers on the following day. They covered every part of the Lichfield Board [of Guardians] and distributed vouchers of 2/6 — 7/6 per family.'

A statement of indictment of the conditions in the Lichfield area was then sent by the Committee to the Press. It included the following:

> Last week the Committee was able to step in to save these fifteen hundred families from being without food for several days. Our investigators found that

practically all these people were without food in the house. A nursing mother for example, had not had anything for three days.

Similarly the Committee had to step in at Bolton where Mrs. Massingham in an article to the *Daily Herald* had reported on the dire poverty in the area because of the action of the Bolton Board of Guardians. Early in May 1926, the Board of Guardians at Lichfield stopped all payments as they had already done at Cannock, Tamworth, Nuneaton, Atherstone and at the Forest of Dean. Other Boards followed suit. Emergency relief was provided by the Committee in these areas, week after week and help was similarly sent to areas where the scale was especially low or where there was some particular emergency.

The claim of the Poor Law authorities that people could always come into the workhouses if conditions were so bad, was put to the test in the Forest of Dean. One of the local men describes his experiences at Westbury workhouse, labelled by him as 'One Black Hole of Calcutta.' Families, he said, were given 'dry bread greased with margarine' and tea that was 'dishwater slush.' Women were locked in their sleeping quarters and as there were not enough beds, many with their children lay on straw bags on the floor 'weeping and wailing.' Most of them made their way back to their villages the best way they could.

Another investigator — Mrs. Ayrton Gould, visiting Leicestershire, sent reports of appalling deprivation: of women fainting from hunger and children suffering from malnutrition. She wrote, 'No Poor Law Relief is given to families where there is not more than one child, and the highest relief for any family is 12/6 in one area and 9/- in the other.' She went on to describe individual instances of suffering:

> In one house there are fourteen including the parents to be fed. Bread bill is 11/8, leaving ten pence for all necessities beyond bread for fourteen people.
>
> No relief at all in another home because there is only one child. Mother, desperately ill is expecting baby in three months, if she lives. Constant fainting fits that last two to three hours at a time.
>
> Another women so ill, could hardly stagger across room to open door. Had two little boys, one had died of diphtheria a fortnight before, and the other, desperately ill with it. No relief, because one child living. Food equals potatoes from allotment.
>
> In one village, two heart-broken mothers. One had baby boy, born on Sunday, died on Monday. The other had a baby boy prematurely a fortnight before and died when I [Mrs. Ayrton Gould] was visiting her. The district nurse who was there, said she could suggest no reason for its condition but the mother's weakness through lack of food.

So the appalling chronicle of despair continues ...

Marion Phillips ends this section of the history by quoting from the *Labour Party Manifesto* which stated,

... it is clear that about one third of the Boards of Guardians in the coalfields suspended all out-door relief, thus fully confirming the findings of the Women's Relief Committee.

It was to deal as promptly as possible with the distress caused by the ruthlessness of the Guardians, that the Committee bent its energies during these months. The appeal that went out in May 1926 was aimed primarily therefore at helping mothers and babies. It read:

> In the wretched little houses clustered around the silent pit-head, children are being born in homes which have been stripped of every saleable luxury. The mothers have been ill-nourished and living in continuous anxiety and face childbirth without any of the care and comfort which they need.

About twelve hundred babies were born during the Lock-out and in order to deal urgently with the distress that was all around, the Committee called upon the Labour Women's Advisory Councils, composed of representatives of the Women's Sections of the Labour Party. These were well-organised local committees whose officers were known to the Central Committee. They were well-placed to investigate individual cases, to report on them and to take charge of the distribution of supplies to the needy. Thus the 'Mothers and Babies' scheme was set up. Detailed instructions were given to the local committees and these are described in the book. Priority was to be given to food and warmth for the mother and child. Forms requiring information and receipts were necessary and rules were meticulously followed, but the aim of providing food and clothing without delay, with the absence of red tape, was wholly successful. As Marion Phillips said, 'The enthusiasm and skill of the Advisory Councils astonished even those who thought they could forecast the result.'

Work in the London office proceeded round the clock as each post brought 'mountains of parcels' for distribution. 'The Committee' says Phillips, 'is very proud to recall that their original circular went out on Saturday 12th June, they received their first reply by return and the first cheque was posted on June 15th.' She quoted too, from pathetic requests as the scheme advanced. One letter read:

> One woman came here to seek a nightdress and a chemise to be laid up in. She had been in labour all night and had to be walked up to my house before eight o'clock in the morning. It took us all our time to get her home again. She had absolutely nothing for herself and child.

Another letter read:

> I went to visit a mother who had only just been confined a few hours. The child had been born in the same room in which they all had to live and eat. Six other children and no one to look after the woman, midwife had gone, only the husband.

Marion Phillips comments,

In the course of their work, these women came across confinement cases where there was no food, or only a loaf of bread in the house, houses where mothers were obliged to feed tiny babies on rice-water and meal-water, and in one small town we heard in the course of a fortnight five miners' wives had still-born babies.

Many of the secretaries worked twelve hours a day for weeks on end and wore out their strength and their shoe leather in trying to do what they best could to relieve the distress.

She goes onto pay tribute to the splendid generosity of food firms, praising in particular the response from Messrs Crosse and Blackwell, Messrs Wonder (Ovaltine), Marmite, Messrs Nestlé and Messrs King. A special mention is given to Messrs Neaves who sent eighty-one cases of infant food, and Rowntree who forwarded supplies direct to any district for which an emergency appeal went out. Two firms only, apparently, responded to the urgent appeal for soap: Messrs James Lindsay and Sons Ltd, Nottingham sent a free contribution of a ton of soap and Palmolive and the Co-operative Wholesale Society also helped.

By the end of January, £120,958 had been distributed for expectant and nursing mothers, sick women and children. The balance sheet is published. Further list are supplied of the numbers helped in the various counties. 'We had,' she said, 'established forty eight centres.' Altogether, five thousand women were involved in investigating cases and distributing and caring — almost all working women themselves who 'understood without explanation the conditions of those they visited. There was none of the usual sting of charity in the distribution; it was the generous help of equals to those in temporary trouble.'

The other serious problem with which the Committee had to grapple was the need for boots! In a chapter called 'The Clothes and Broken Boots', Marion quotes from a 'Report from Coalfields 1926'. 'We had one hundred and twenty five absent from school because they had no boots to wear.'[3]

Second-hand clothes and bedding and in particular, baby clothes were already being sent in response to urgent requests. Sometimes, Co-op stores and other shops made gifts of money or material to be made up into clothes. Knitting wool was also bought at wholesale prices. Sir Henry Simson sent money too for infants' clothes. Among the Committees' papers were reports of women who had actually cut up their underclothing for their children and had none for themselves. Five thousand packages were sent out by the London Committee, alone.

Yet, however great was this need for clothing and blankets, Marion Phillips goes on to say that the 'problem of boots dwarfed all the other needs.'

Many appeals were made to deal with this problem, particularly to various Co-op, Boot and Shoe Societies for gifts or supplies at low rates, and similar appeals to the Manufacturers' Association in the trade, met with similar success. Thirty four thousand pairs were distributed by the Women's Committee, together with grants, and in addition, in September a boot-repairing scheme was started through local committees which worked in two ways. Either leather and other mending materials were supplied, where miners in groups worked in centres specially set up for the purpose, or a grant was made after rates had been agreed with local cobblers to do the work. Soon, three hundred centres were established and forty thousand boots were repaired. The Society of Friends had already been operating such centres in the South Wales coalfield and grants were sent to them to continue their excellent work. Children had often to be carried to schools because they had no boots, and teachers in particular in these areas, were more than generous in helping to provide this basic need. Phillips mentions that in one centre a man on a motor-bike took the children's shoes in the morning and left them with carpet slippers, returning at night with the repairs done. 'We were frequently sent the boots the children were wearing to show the needs, and never, save on rubbish heaps would it be possible to match them,' Phillips adds.

In the chapter headed 'How we collected £313,000' she pays tribute to the generosity of the British public towards the families of the miners. 'The Press, in particular, the *Daily Herald*, the *Manchester Guardian* and the *Daily News*,' she says, 'gave a consistent prominence to the continuing appeal for help. They gave particular prominence to appeals signed by a cross-section of eminent people.' Among the long lists there appear the following names: Sir Henry Simson, Lord Haldane, Viscount Chelmsford, Sir Horace Plunkett, The Master of Balliol, Lord Dawson of Penn, The Marchioness of Milford Haven, Lady Emily Lutyens, Arnold Bennett, G. K. Chesterton, J. L. Garvin, Augustus John and Ellen Terry.

A great number of meetings and speaking tours were also arranged after covering two or three towns a day. A splendid women's meeting was held at Kingsway Hall in June, with Margaret Bondfield in the chair and with Sibyl Thorndike as one of the speakers and five miners' wives who addressed the audience.

Altogether a million leaflets were distributed, sixty-five thousand collecting sheets and twenty-five thousand collecting cards were issued, together with nine thousand special boot collecting cards bearing the picture of the boots of a miner's child, actually taken from her feet. Every collecting card had to be entered and registered at the office, with people working in relays. In addition to these, there were the local collecting sheets, issued by the Women's Sections.

A huge selling organisation then came into being. Miniature and real miners' lamps of varying quality were sold. Two hundred and forty miners' Lamp Days were held, in addition to the two in London that brought in over £14,500. Cards, pencils, calendars, Christmas cards were sold. Appeals for jewellery and watches produced a splendid result. These provided prizes for raffles and prize-draws. Sketches, pictures, hand-made rugs arrived to be sold. Great efforts were made by the Labour Party and Trade Union branches in towns and villages across the country. Woolwich took pride of place, contributing £6,361 to the coffers.

Much of the work at the office (or 'The Shop') at the Parliamentary Labour Club was done by post, but there was also a vast amount of over-the-counter business transacted there. Trade Union branches and individuals arrived there with their contributions. Phillips writes, 'One day's 'visiting list' would give interesting reading. Every class of community represented, came with cheques, pence, gold, silver etc. with little anecdotes. On Saturday afternoons, there were always family parties, bringing parcels of clothes, children's collecting cards, father's workshop sheet, and mother's collecting box.'

Religious organisations too, responded generously and Phillips acknowledges their help separately. Many individuals too, in religious organisations gave freely: bishops, deans, Free Church ministers, rabbis, Salvation Army officers, and missioners.

An interesting aspect of the huge task of collecting funds was handled by 'The Entertainments Section' of the Committee. It was responsible for approaching cinema and music hall proprietors for help. The Moss Empires — Glasgow, Birmingham and Liverpool sent their contributions regularly. Collection boxes were allowed in these cinemas, and appeals would often appear on the screens. Deep gratitude is expressed in the book to these proprietors and to members of the musical and theatrical profession who helped so generously. All local Relief Committees across the country were also asked to organise concerts, and often much light-hearted entertainment eased the strain of those dark days. Often too, Marion Phillips recalls, 'the Central Committee was asked to assist. It was not always easy, at a few hours' notice to send a baritone to Bromley, or a high-class entertainer to a town in the South West or to provide a place near the Scottish border with a programme, when our nearest troupe of artists who had offered assistance was at Doncaster. But we did our best.'

She mentions 'outstandingly successful' entertainment in London — at Battersea and Mile End and Tottenham, but she remarks that the West End of London, in regard to its music halls and cinemas 'proved itself more callous and indifferent, probably, than any other part of England.'

Almost all the Local Relief Committees were helped by choirs, quartets, glee parties who performed outside railway stations, at factory gates and public meetings. There were about sixty-five singing parties and bands. Welsh choirs were irrepressible — always rearing to go. Often they would arrive in London without having made any prior arrangement! One of them 'The Welsh Troubadours', worked from the Central Labour College throughout the period, while a Pontypool choir worked with the Clapham Labour Party. Three Welsh choirs went overseas, two to Germany and one to Russia. Other overseas help arrived from many countries in the form of generous donations to the miners' families.

A final and rather touching aspect of the work of the Committee was the arrangement of holidays and long-stay accommodation in comfortable homes for children from the coalfields — 'The Child Pilgrims', as Phillips called them.

It is a warm, compassionate story. Altogether, two and a half thousand children who were most in need, were fostered. Obviously it was a most demanding operation. First, the quality of the hospitality had to be closely vetted, and references were required from the 'hostesses' who came forward as a result of press appeals. Then, the selection of children needed thorough and sensitive handling. Preference was given to motherless or delicate children, or members of large families who were already receiving the maximum of Poor Law relief, so that the income would be unaffected. First-hand information about the children and their families was supplied by local representatives and miners' wives who came up to London for discussions with the Committee.

Railway companies gave specially low rates for parties of children, and railway staff showed them great kindness on their journeys.

Of course, there were all kinds of difficulties in spite of careful planning. Sometimes children or destinations had to be changed, and though every effort would be made to see that the children were properly clad and shod, often they would arrive in London without 'parcels', and clothes and boots would have to be hurriedly found for them before they could proceed to their new homes.

Some became homesick and returned to their families. Others stayed until the end of the Lock-out. A number were permanently adopted while many foster-parents became 'permanent aunts and uncles' to the miners' children and

enduring relationships were forged. The children improved in health after settling happily in their temporary homes. The 'hostesses' came from every class of society. Many refunded the children's fares to the Committee and often clothed them entirely. When the time came for the children to return home, extra coaches to carry gifts and supplies from their foster-parents had to be attached to the trains!

The tale told in this little book by Marion Phillips is about suffering and degradation in large tracts of industrial Britain in 1926. But it is also about the warmth and generosity of the British people and their immediate and instinctive response to need. Whatever the rights and wrongs of the dispute itself, the Innocent could not be allowed to suffer. The tale too, is about the will and determination of Marion Phillips and her helpers and their feat of organisation in mobilising and delivering help swiftly to the victims.

The great goodwill and generosity of the British people is always in evidence, most notably perhaps, in its response to Disaster Emergency Appeals and the BBC Annual Appeal on behalf of Children in Need. Interestingly enough, in relation to the latter, the BBC's Children's Appeal started in 1927 — the year following the Miners' Lock-out. It started within the framework of the 'Children's Hour' programme and the appeals were made at Christmas time. Later it was aimed at people of all ages. In 1951 the title was changed to 'Children in Need of Help' and from 1955 the appeal was presented on television as well as on radio. In 1980 it became an extended appeal and the response has grown each year since then, resulting in ever-increasing millions of pounds.[4]

In conclusion, perhaps we might reflect that while in 1926 the generous people of the Home Counties opened their doors and their hearts to the pitiful little children from the coalfields, thirteen years later, evacuees, threatened by Hitler's bombs, were streaming westwards, many of them to be welcomed into the homes of Welsh miners.

'Cast thy bread upon the waters ...'

Chapter 17: Member of Parliament

In the closing months of 1926, following her spectacular campaign to save the women and children in the coalfields, Phillips was nominated prospective parliamentary candidate for Sunderland by the Durham County Labour Women's Advisory Council. The political consciousness of the Women's Sections had grown to such an extent, that they themselves now sought to elect their own woman candidate to Parliament. The Durham women were particularly well-organised and forward-looking, as Margaret Gibb, in her article 'Diamond Jubilee — a Memory' recalled. She described the first magnificent women's rally in June 1923, that set the pattern for the famous annual galas that were to follow. There was great excitement, with huge crowds; seven bands; a procession carrying seventy white and green Women's Section banners; mounted police on duty and 'The City closed for about one and a half hours for everyone's convenience.' Many of the women organisers of the Gala were wives of miners who annually attended their own 'Durham Miners' Big Meeting'.

Mrs. Gibb captures some of the excitement as she refers in her article to the speaker at that first rally: 'First and foremost our splendid Chief Woman Officer, Dr. Marion Phillips ... she was an inspiration to all she contacted'. The other speakers were Jack (later Lord) Lawson and Sidney Webb. Perhaps there was rather too much enthusiasm, for, according to Mrs. Gibb when an M.P. called Bob Richardson was called to propose a vote of thanks, the heady atmosphere enhanced by the emotional singing so affected him that he excitedly 'declared loudly and long we'd sweep away the old order, and to stress the point flung out his arm and swept water jugs and glasses off the table, scattering their last remains all over the platform...'

It was the same women who organised this rally — the Durham County Labour Women's Advisory Council — who arranged to pay £70 a year into Sunderland's funds to sustain a Labour organisation. That was quite a feat in a community of miners in the nineteen twenties. Unemployment was very high and miners' wives were extremely hard-pressed: every penny counted. Yet there was this determination to strive to support a women candidate in an area in which most of the seats were held by miners. Maureen Callcott referring to the woman of their choice described her as 'probably the most important and most talented in the Party.' She continued 'Dr. Marion Phillips was appointed Chief Woman Officer in the Labour Party after a career already distinguished in academic and public affairs especially relating to working women and their war-time problems.'[1]

Phillips however, would have been well aware that the Sunderland Seat was fraught with appalling difficulties. Callcott concisely listed them: '...Though a predominantly working-class constituency, Sunderland contained a significant and growing middle-class, and Labour Party organisation developed slowly there and was beset with problems. Compared for example with Gateshead, there was no great surge forward after 1918 and Labour was bottom of the poll in 1918 and 1923. The local party was short of funds, failed to retain suitable premises or sustain the publication of a news sheet and by the late 1920s was functioning 'unconstitutionally'. Sunderland was a two-member constituency and between 1922 and 1929, the Borough was held by two Conservatives — both businessmen.'[2]

A bleak prospect then? For any hopeful Labour politician it would surely have presented a landscape of stygian gloom, totally unrelieved. The question then arises, how on earth did Phillips — an expert in psephology and the machinery of elections — come to accept the nomination? Were she so minded, she surely could have been nominated for another seat with less stress and worry and nearer to London. The continual travelling that her duties as Chief Woman Officer entailed, would in itself have justified the seeking of a more conveniently located constituency. It may be that the explanation for her acceptance lay in her loyalty to the Durham women. In view of their unstinting sacrifice, she had to respond. She therefore took up the challenge — with her eyes wide open.

Even so, Maureen Callcott informs us, from the beginning the situation in Sunderland dismayed and upset her. The other Labour candidate, Alfred Smith, as a nominee of the General and Municipal Workers' Union was assisted by union funds but there was no such financial backing for Phillips. Money worries were constant, with demands being made on her personally for contributions in addition to the £50 annual sum that she made available towards her agent's salary. These she could ill afford. Early in 1929 there were signs of tension, and no doubt she should have withdrawn from the scene there and then, for the sake of her health and peace of mind. But that was not her way, in spite of the ominous words in a letter to her agent Harry Leedale in February 1929, and quoted by Callcott:

> I begin to feel very bitter about the Sunderland Labour Party... it seems to me that the Sunderland Labour Party whose executive themselves approached me and asked me to accept nomination, are without any kind of friendly feeling and they continually treat their candidates as people whom they are obliging and not taking part in a common fight.[3]

This is the first time that the word 'bitter' appears in her writings as far as one can ascertain. 'Indignant' or 'disappointed' would be more in keeping with her cheerful personality.

Her agent however, clearly felt as she did and in his reply to her in March he deplored that he had not been paid any of his expenses. In fact, he left later in the year and the constituency Labour Party remained in total disarray.

How long Phillips remained 'bitter' is questionable. She certainly had very cause to be bitter, yet in April, and soon after her personal experience in Sunderland, we find her — nothing if not resilient — speaking with the utmost fairness about the allocation of Parliamentary seats, at the National Conference of Labour Women at Buxton.

Under the title 'Labour Women open the Election Campaign', an article published in *The Labour Magazine* began:

> In dealing with a report on the year's work, Dr. Marion Phillips pointed out how a great mistake was being made by those who said that women candidates got the worst seats. In a careful analysis of the position for the twenty eight women candidates who will fight for Labour, she showed that if the victories they might *reasonably* expect were achieved, fourteen of these would become M.P.s and if the men were equally successful Labour would have three hundred and forty seats in the next Parliament, thus giving them a clear victory overall. In view of the figures which she gave, the section which had a resolution expressing regret that women had specially difficult constituencies asked leave to withdraw and were accorded it.[4]

The General Election of 1929 took place a month later. Alfred Smith who was a joint candidate with Marion Phillips was a Catholic and it was deemed that the Catholic vote was about thirteen thousand. As far as Phillips was concerned, this was the first election in which women over twenty-one were eligible to vote. This was the election of the 'Flapper Vote'. In preparation for the campaign, Phillips had written a letter to all women in the constituency the previous year, emphasising the appalling effect of post-war unemployment on women and insisting that unemployed women should have unemployment benefit. Those women who were in work, she maintained, were in sore need of protection against bad conditions relating to wages and hours. Decent housing, of course, was a necessity for all women.

The joint Manifesto of the two Labour candidates attacked the record of the Conservative Government, high-lighting in particular, the daunting unemployment figures which stood in Sunderland at twenty five per cent of the working population. The neglected state of the mining industry was blamed on the Lloyd George Government especially for having failed to act on the recommendations of the Sankey Commission. Unemployment, low wages, high food prices, poor housing, with their attendant social ills all contributed to the low standard of life in the area. Both opposition parties, claimed the Manifesto, were responsible for the prevailing desolation.

In the ensuing election, in spite of difficulties, both seats were won by the Labour candidates. Phillips topped the poll with 31,794 votes, gaining 19.5% of the total. Smith ran a very close second with 31,085 votes — 19% of the poll. The two Conservative candidates followed thus: Raine received 29,180 votes and Thompson 28,937, each claiming over 17% of the total poll. Both Liberal candidates obtained over 21,000 each, amounting respectively to 13% of the poll.

So, in her forty-eighth year, Marion Phillips went to Westminster. It was abundantly clear, though, from the voting figures that Labour's only hope to retain the seat at any future date would be in a three-cornered contest without tactical voting among the opposition parties, and in conditions favourable to Labour. It was in any case, a dangerously marginal constituency and any hope of holding it at all entailed unremitting toil.

In addition the problems within the local Labour Party organisation persisted after the election. Although the constituency Party had been dissolved and reconstituted, all kinds of hostilities remained to plague Phillips. She, needless to say laboured tirelessly to serve the electorate and to combine her parliamentary duties with those of Chief Woman Officer. She visited Sunderland at least one weekend in every month, setting off from London on Friday morning and returning on the overnight train on Sunday. These visits would be packed with consultations, constituency meetings and gatherings of all kinds. With her unerring eye for detail, no defect escaped her notice, even suggesting in one letter a practical tip: that the committee-room floor should be covered with linoleum to make the cleaner's task easier![5]

To add to her workload, in January 1931, her colleague, Alfred Smith died suddenly and the Labour candidate who stood for his seat seemed to have incurred the animosity of all and sundry. He, himself was exceedingly unpleasant to Phillips, who in spite of that, worked 'like two men' on his behalf in the by election campaign, together with the women from other Durham constituencies who came into Sunderland to help. The seat, however, was lost to one of the former Conservative M.P.s — Luke Thompson. This meant that Phillips had the additional task of dealing with issues affecting her late colleague's seat for the remainder of the Parliament.

She shouldered the extra burden characteristically, and there is little doubt that the folk she served in Sunderland did appreciate her efforts on their behalf and that their continued affection for her went far to compensate for the wrangling within the local party organisation. Indeed, D. N. Pritt who was to stand with her later as candidate for the other Sunderland seat, remarked that she was 'idolised' there. She certainly was so regarded by the rank and file Labour women.[6] Nellie Suddick for example, the Advisory Council Member for Sunderland, calling her 'The Friend and Servant of All', emphasised two aspects of her personality: The 'incomparable' politician on the platform, and the 'motherly' Dr. Phillips who visited the homes of the poorer classes, sympathising with them and advising them.[7] Another local Party worker also mentioned her 'love of children' and her 'especial care of the poor'. But perhaps the most moving recollection of Marion Phillips is that of Mrs. Sarah Forster of Ryhope, Sunderland who was kind enough to write to me. I quote from her letter dated 3rd May 1991.

...I was six years old when she came to Ryhope. It was in July 1926 when the strike was on. She came to the Miners' Hall... My mother was a member of the [Women's] Section and I can remember her going to the hall to meet Dr. Marion Phillips. During her visit, she heard that my mother had become a grandmother. My brother's wife had a baby girl.

We were all poverty stricken at that time, no money and no hope. We lived in the colliery houses near the Miners' Hall and I'm not sure if she came across to see the new baby or not, but I do know that a gown, shawl and a bonnet was given to my mother... through this my sister-in-law christened the baby Marion Phillips Barnes. She will be sixty five years old in July and lives in Sunderland and knows why her mother gave her this name... At such a time ... she was an angel of mercy for the gift she brought.

Mrs. Forster continued

When the women decided they wanted a banner, it was decided that the painted photo of Marion Phillips would be shown and was always paraded with pride. It was displayed at the International Women's Socialist Rally in London.

The banner is now housed at the local Community Centre.[8]

Phillips had always thrived on hard work and her phenomenal energy and organisational powers had always enabled her to meet every challenge. In 1929 the challenge was greater than ever. How Members of Parliament without private incomes in those days, managed to survive, especially those with remote, demanding, marginal constituencies, is hard to imagine. They were certainly paid a small salary but no contribution was ever made towards their expenses. Secretarial help, telephone and stamp charges, away-from-home accommodation and other costs — all had to be met by the Member and incredible as it may seem, this arrangement persisted until comparatively recent times.

When Phillips arrived for the opening session of the new Labour Administration on 25th June 1929, she was one of fourteen women members, nine of whom were Labour. Among them was her old friend, Dr. Ethel Bentham — representing East Islington. Health care, and in particular, the needs of women and children were to be Dr. Bentham's special interests in the House. Her maiden speech was devoted to the causes of industrial accidents and the prevalence of the eye disease — nystagmus among miners.

Phillips made her maiden speech in the debate on the King's Speech, on 9th July.[9] It was a lively and vigorous condemnation of the previous Government's policies that had resulted in deterioration and poverty in the already distressed Sunderland area. In particular, she criticised the policy of 'safeguarding' as valueless. 'If you 'safeguard' food,' she said, 'the poverty of Sunderland will be greater than ever,' adding drily — 'It will not be a case of the last straw breaking the camel's back, because there will not be a straw left; all will have been eaten.

*The banner of the Ryhope Labour Party which is now housed
at the local Community Centre.
Photograph courtesy of Peter Hedley.*

With heavier taxation of food, people could not support even the low standard of life which is theirs today.'

The policy of 'safe-guarding' iron and steel, she maintained would have a similarly disastrous effect upon the shipyards. Higher prices of steel plates would ruin the industry, and managers and owners needed to build ships at lower, and not higher costs.

Speaking then, as an Australian in the United Kingdom, she was critical of the policy of Imperial Preference: 'It is not true to think that Imperial Preference is regarded as a great gesture of brotherliness from this country.' She related how as a schoolgirl, she remembered the dismay in her family when Joseph Chamberlain's policy of Imperial Preference was announced. Not all Australians then or now regarded such a policy as patriotic. 'No Australian is so foolish as to think that any other reasons than those of internal concern here, have led to that policy being adopted by anybody. After all,' she teased, 'Australians come from the same stock as people from this country and unless a little extra sunlight and a little extra heat have had a bad effect on the brain, their brain-power is probably very similar to that of the people of this country and they can see through the situation as well as can others ... The Australians, like anybody else can tell the difference between the sort of synthetic patriotic syrup of Imperial Preference and the real honey of genuine co-operation. They taste very different and one has a much better effect on health than the other.'

Her tone sharpened as she pointed out that there was no Imperial Preference given to manufactured goods from the Dominions nor to iron from India produced under sweated conditions.

Phillips concluded her first speech in the House by emphasising that Australians were anxious to see prosperity and a high standard of life in the Mother country. That in itself would be of advantage to Australia. She begged for co-operation with all-world resources and the development of the Dominions, re-iterating firmly that the policy of maintenance of Imperial Preference put forward by the amendment would not help the distressed areas of the United Kingdom, particularly those dependent on the coal trade, mining, and ship-building industries.[9]

The Rt. Hon. Runciman, rising to follow Phillips, congratulated her. 'Not only for the command which she obviously has over her subject, but for the Antipodean air which she has imported to our Debates.'

Two days later, Phillips was again voicing her concern for the distressed areas in a question to Sir Charles Trevelyan, President of the Board of Education. She asked for a report to the House on the work of the Lord Mayor's Fund for Distressed Miners including a number of important considerations which she specified. The Minister replied that the report dealing with these matters would soon be published. At this, Viscountess Astor intervened to suggest that the report might also include a list of subscribers 'seeing that some of us in our constituency have been accused by the Hon. Lady opposite of having done nothing for the Welsh miners.'[10]

Lady Astor's fleeting visit to the South Wales valleys during the 1926 Lock-out and her subsequent comments had certainly caused irritation among the Labour Women's Committee who had toiled day and night for months to relieve suffering in the coalfield. In any case, Phillips and Lady Astor were to clash on other occasions. Pamela Brookes in her *Women at Westminster* noted that although Phillips 'was popular in the Labour Party, she could be tough and cynical.'[11] Tough she certainly was in her exchanges with the equally tough Member for the Sutton Division of Plymouth.

She was persistent too, as well as tough. As early as 18th July she was again pressing for information on the Lord Mayor's Fund for Miners. She learned that the money was being kept back until autumn instead of relieving existing distress.[12] Her concern for the plight of mining families was ever present. Indeed, only three days earlier she had given the House a graphic example of the acute poverty in the coalfields in a long question to the Minister of Health. It asked 'whether his attention had been called to a summons for non-attendance at school, which was heard on 5th July at Blackwood (South Wales) Police Court; whether seeing that the reason why the child in question was not attending school was that it had no boots; that the mother stated that another child had only half-boots, and two at home had no shoes at all, and that further, having given evidence she fell fainting to the ground and was stated to be suffering from extreme hunger, will he state in what union this woman resided and whether he will make enquiries of the appropriate Board of Guardians on the matter'.[13] Phillips elicited a promise of inquiries with communication to follow, but a week later she was repeating her question.[14]

Poverty of course, was always a constant source of distress to her, but one particular aspect of it — the pathos and indignity of children without boots always seemed to touch a raw nerve. It was therefore, natural that later in the Parliament, the second reading of the Private Bill — The Children (Provision of Footwear) Bill, moved by Colonel Watts Morgan, should be seconded by Phillips. Its purpose was to enable education authorities to provide footwear and stockings for children in need. It proposed too that ninety per cent of the cost would be borne by central funding, leaving only the burden of ten per cent to fall on local authorities.[15]

In this connection, tribute should be paid to teachers in deprived areas during those harrowing inter-war years who used to make regular contributions out of their meagre salaries into a 'boot fund' to enable children to attend school.

Marion Phillips's compassion for children was again evident in her speech seconding the motion of the second reading of R. Sorensen's 'Children and Young Persons Bill'.[16] In November 1929 she began with a reference to her own 'protected and prolonged childhood', so different from that of children in working class families and she urged those who were as fortunate as she, to assist in getting the Bill on the Statute Book. The Bill was, she said, 'an effort to give all the children of the community reasonable protection against overburdened adolescence.'

She praised the Bill for placing all employed children and young persons under national regulation thus obtaining a satisfactory, consistent system of rules and regulations instead of the prevailing chaos. At the moment, she complained, there were no proper and regular inspections. Under the Bill, registers of all employed young people would have to be kept and the law would accordingly be enforced. As for hours of work, night work for lads under eighteen would be abolished as well as the two-shift plan.

Medical inspections would be made essential for every child entering employment with a certificate of fitness provided. If a child was found to be unfit, he could not be employed until treatment had restored him to health, and a new certificate of fitness issued.

Similarly close medical inspections would be essential for those engaged in work damaging to health, with the same rigorous procedures. The Bill also made more careful regulations for children in unhealthy trades.

Anticipating later legislation, the Bill also contained proposals that the term 'young person' should not apply to one between fourteen and eighteen, but under a new definition those under sixteen would be termed 'children' and those between sixteen and eighteen would be termed 'young persons'. Given the new definition, special regulations relating to hours, governing those in the younger group would give them protection against long hours of employment. She enlarged on this matter, comparing the arrangements existing in other major industrial countries for their junior employees.

She ended her speech by urging the support of all members of the House for the humane reforms embodied in the Bill.

A matter of a different sort, in connection with young people, reflecting her concern as a magistrate, was tabled by her with reference to the Children Act 1908 Amendment. In the same month as Sorensen's Bill, she asked the Home Secretary what action he proposed to take to put into operation the recommendation of three Departmental Committees on Sexual Offences against Young Persons, on the treatment of Young Offenders, and on Metropolitan Police Courts and Juvenile Courts respectively.[17]

Although she had barely entered the House, November 1929 seems to have been for her a time of great activity in the Chamber. There were questions concerning Sunderland Borough Council's loan application, its unemployment relief schemes, rent overcharging in the constituency, and other problems to which she would return time and time again.[18]

She spoke too in the Debate on the Bill to provide annual holidays with pay to workers. She questioned the suggestion that it was a new principle, reminding the House that Lloyd George's Reconstruction Committee — of which she was a member — had discussed the principle of providing a holiday with pay to everyone engaged in munition work. Although there was much support for the proposal, no unanimity had been achieved on that occasion.

She suggested that the present Bill's general provision for an annual holiday with payment was 'part of the normal industrial condition.' She drew attention too, to workers and their wives who badly needing a little respite, would nevertheless dread the prospect of a holiday without pay, because of the debt it would involve.[19]

Before the year was out an attempt was made by Phillips in the House to right a long-standing wrong, in the debate on the Unemployment Insurance (No. 2) Bill. She sought to introduce a new clause — 'A very small amendment' as she called it — to secure justice for industrial workers who went into agricultural work, and industrial workers who went into domestic service. The anomaly may seem bizarre to us today, but there it was. She explained: 'They go into non-insurable trade in order that they shall work rather than live on benefit, but if they become unemployed again, they lose everything they have paid into the fund; and though they may have been on benefit at the time of taking up the non-insurable work, they will not be able to return to it.'

Her proposal was that they should be able to do that up to a maximum period of two years. She was supported by Ellen Wilkinson who hoped that the Minister would accept the clause.

The Parliamentary Secretary, Ministry of Labour agreed that there was a 'serious difficulty' but promised, after making certain adjustments to the clause, he would bring it up on the Report Stage, so that 'the Hon. Member for Sunderland will then have the satisfaction of having ended a difficult position which has continued for a long time.[20]

In the event, the 'difficult position' of this group of workers was to remain unaltered for many years to come.

Throughout 1930, Marion Phillips managed to combine her duties as Chief Woman Officer of the Labour Party and other work, with a sustained surge of activity in the House, bombarding Ministers with questions on a wide range of subjects and speaking in important debates. In March she was pressing the President of the Board of Education for information about the number of comprehensive schemes operating in England and Wales to supply milk to schoolchildren, and from that month onwards she was waging a prolonged campaign for the establishment of nursery schools particularly in deprived areas like Sunderland.[21]

Another question on the same day concerned the complaint of a number of people whose disablement benefit had been reduced under the National Health Insurance Act of 1928.[22]

Yet another question, though of a totally different nature, was tabled on that 27th March. Because of her own hatred of drudgery, Phillips was always anxious to introduce all modern electrical equipment into training for housewifery. With this in mind she asked the President of the Board of Education 'whether he will consider the advisability of requiring as a condition of grant, the installation of electric cooking lighting and cleaning apparatus in all domestic science teaching centres,' so that the tuition could be carried out 'on the most scientific lines.' In spite of the Minister's answer that these arrangements were a matter for the local authorities, she still persisted valiantly that the 'very best methods of housekeeping,' would be helped by such apparatus, until the Speaker's intervention rescued the Minister.[23]

Tied up with good housekeeping was good housing — another of Phillips's great concerns. In April her question to the Minister of Health took her to the purlieus of Tunbridge Wells — of all places, to a slum area known as Albion Square. It consisted, she said, of fifteen houses, sharing two outside taps as the sole water supply and a group of water closets in the centre of the square — a few yards from the front entrance of the houses.[24]

Two days earlier, she had spoken in the Debate on Housing (N° 2) Bill, dealing with the slum problem of the area which she represented, and pointing out that overcrowding in the towns of Tyneside and Wearside was thirty per cent. She said that the degree of poverty and unemployment made it 'a matter of the gravest difficulty to move the population from tenement flats into decent homes. Even when adequate accommodation was found people could not afford to pay the rent. There was, she maintained, 'a desperate need for five thousand houses, and of the existing ones, three thousand were desperately in need of repairs.'

She stated that the Bill proposing a programme of slum clearance and rebuilding would be welcomed in such areas. She asked the Ministry of Health to make suggestions to help local authority schemes and made a telling point that has echoed down the years — that building costs in this country were far too high, and that expert advice to produce cheaper building was sorely needed.[25]

In April too, Phillips was pursuing the need of training schemes for women and asking the Minister of Labour for specific details for such schemes carried out by the Central Committee on Women's Training and Employment and the financial provisions of work in this direction in the year 1930–31.[26]

She was still tenaciously pursuing this question of women's employment in her speech in the debate on the address — the Economic Situation — on 4th November. She deplored the lack of openings. The textile industry was in a poor state with an increasing number of women losing their jobs. She blamed the lack of consumer power for the high unemployment rate. There was 'rampant poverty' because there was no buying power and she hoped there would be no lowering of unemployment benefit.

The remainder of her speech on the address was devoted to the dire prospects of the ship-building industry in her constituency. She made a plea that it was vital to retain the existing body of skilled workers in the area. To this end, she suggested the provision of a large credit facility to produce ships that would not immediately be of great trade value in order to keep the work force together. She was glad of the existence of unemployment benefit in preference to making these men dependent on Poor Law dispensations.

She declared too that she was in favour of the Government's policy on Import Boards dealing briefly with the fall in world prices as it affected 'the suffering people of this and other countries.'[27]

A fortnight later, Phillips, speaking in the debate on the Agricultural Land Utilisation (Money) Bill, made a strong plea for allotments and small holdings.

Like Lansbury, she saw the value of allotments as therapy, and as a substitute for gardens for those deprived of them. But most important of all she saw them as a source of fresh food: vegetables and fruit so often denied to the poor. Women too could keep poultry. She suggested that unemployed skilled miners and shipbuilders would soon learn the techniques of growing food and she referred to the intensive cultivation in Palestine. She thought it far better that men should remain to till the land in their own country than to emigrate to till new pastures overseas.

As for the concern expressed that it would be money extravagantly spent if people settled down on an allotment with the dole, she observed crisply: 'Hon. Gentlemen opposite have a good deal of knowledge of people who have settled down with an allotment and the dole. The great difference ... is that [their] allotments were very large indeed and that they themselves did not ever have to work on them.'

She developed her theme with vigour before ending with a further appeal, for support for the Bill that was 'bringing hope to thousands of people.' It was, she said a constructive effort to make use of our own land and she referred to the success of small holdings in countries like Denmark. They could be run equally well here, she maintained.[28]

The last debate in 1930 in which Marion Phillips spoke was the Nationality of Women Bill, moved by Ethel Bentham and strongly supported by four Labour Women Members and Miss Eleanor Rathbone. The occasion would be a farewell to Dr. Bentham because she died suddenly two months later.

In the debate, Phillips spoke indignantly about the treatment of British women married to aliens. She maintained, that after the 1914–18 War, the legislation introduced with regard to aliens had made the position of a British woman married to an alien intolerable because of the burdens imposed on her. 'I know of no greater indignity,' she said, 'than a law which compels a British woman who has married an alien to change her passport and her manner of proceeding from this country to another, to lose in her own country the elementary right of being a voter and to have to register at a police office in her own country as an alien.' She claimed that because of the existing legislation, 'we have definitely worsened the position of British women; the position of a British woman who became an alien on marriage was not, from a practical point of view, as bad as it is today.'

After giving an example of the experience of one of her friends, she pleaded with the lawyers, to seek to remedy any flaws which they might detect in the Bill and to support it.

She hoped too, that the Dominions and the United Kingdom would co-operate in this matter to settle any difficulty that might have arisen, and accept this legislation.

She remarked too, that at recent international discussions between Socialist women all agreed that a woman upon marriage should choose her nationality, and pleaded that this country should not lag behind Scandinavian countries on a matter of this kind.[29]

At the end of her speech Marion Phillips turned her attention to Lady Astor. She complained that Lady Astor often criticised her Labour colleagues 'with extreme severity' but noted that 'she either criticises them when they are absent or after making her criticism she retires while they take part in the debate.

The Speaker called Phillips to order, as the noble Lady was absent. There were further exchanges between Phillips and the Speaker before Marion repeated her charge of Lady Astor's fondness for attacking Labour women, adding 'She has several times attacked me personally when I was not present and when I did not know she was going to attack me. On this occasion she is absent during the period when replies are being made. That is all I desire to say on that point.'

A clash between these two women was not totally unexpected, though there were certain similarities in their character. Both were brought up in former British Colonies: Nancy Astor in America and Marion Phillips in Australia. There was therefore in both of them a predictable lack of inhibition and more than a streak of irreverence towards the traditional morés and institutions of the country which became their home and to which each was totally devoted. Both too, were forthright and fearless and unlikely to be at any disadvantage in a male-dominated House of Commons, Phillips because of her formidable intellectual powers, and Astor because of her quick defiant repartee. Both spoke with directness and clarity without waffle or fudge. Both held strong opinions, gave as good as they got, and no doubt disliked each other heartily. Their tactics in the House in waging hostilities, however, differed. Nancy's favourite weapon was a sly one-line remark, while Marion would make a frontal charge — all too often to find that her opponent had silently slipped away — as she had done during this debate ...

Continuing to champion women's rights, Phillips in her speech in the India debate on January 26th 1931, congratulated the Indian women delegates for their splendid work at the Round Table Conference.

She was heartened, she said, by the rapid advance of the Women's Movement in India from a recent state of non-existence. Saving the lives of women and children there, would not only be a particular challenge to them but also the 'greatest test of Indian Government in the future.' She was confident that these dauntless women would fight hard to remedy the wretched plight of India's poor.

However, the negative attitudes displayed by certain Members of the House, including Winston Churchill, during the debate, dismayed her. She felt that the Round Table Conference had restored Indian confidence in the Government's declaration of Dominion status, welcoming too the release of Gandhi and other leaders, and the continuation of discussions. In her opinion, the House should now build upon the progress already made and 'use our imagination as well as our brains, and our hearts as well, to develop into a real and successful constitution that small and feeble plant already set in the ground.'

'There are,' she proceeded, 'good constitutions, bad constitutions and work-able constitutions, and the workable constitution lies between the good and the bad.' She strongly urged the need to find a workable constitution for India but it would only be found with the 'trustful co-operation of the Indians them-selves.' No constitution imposed on India would be a workable one.

In conclusion, she again warned of the dangers inherent in an atmosphere of discouragement and delay created by some Members of the House, and urged the Government to move forward rapidly with the Indians to develop the 'germ of the constitution, which they have settled at this great Conference.'[30]

Marion Phillips had by now served for eighteen months as a Member of Parliament and in view of her performance at Westminster during this period, Pamela Brookes's comment, that she was 'not often heard in the House,' may seem a little puzzling.[31]

Chapter 18: Electoral Reform

Since the early years of the century, support for proportional representation or for the alternative vote had found favour among Members of the Labour Party at all levels. Many of its leaders, notably W. C. Anderson and Philip Snowden championed proportional representation while Arthur Henderson voiced his staunch support for the alternative vote. Ramsay MacDonald, on the other hand, was resolute for the retention of the prevailing electoral system with its 'knock-out' contests.

The need for change was raised repeatedly in Labour Party Conferences between 1909 and 1926 with varying degrees of success. In the Party Conferences of 1909 and 1910, Henderson, submitting resolutions on Electoral Reform had included among them an item which read, 'The prevention of the Election of Members by a minority of votes'.[1] Such a priority should surely be at the very heart of any democratic voting system.

In the 1911 Party Conference a motion in favour of proportional representation was overwhelmingly defeated. In that debate, MacDonald made a powerful speech in favour of the status quo, arguing that proportional representation would result in coalition governments and compromised policy based on bargaining between the parties.

Nevertheless, the argument continued. At a special session of the 1914 Party Conference in Glasgow, many Party leaders spoke in support of one of the alternative systems of reform, but both proportional representation and the alternative vote were turned down by a two to one majority. Four years later, proportional representation was agreed to in the Party Conference, then defeated in the 1919 Party Conference on a card vote. It was agreed to again in 1926, but neither of the resolutions carried in support of proportional representation was effective because there had been no card vote, and the necessary two-thirds majority required by the Party Constitution was not secured.

The 1917 and 1918 Parliaments were similarly involved in discussions of proportional representation and the alternative vote in advance of the Representation of the People Act. The Speaker's Conference of 1917, prior to the introduction of the Bill, had proposed the adoption of proportional representation in the large cities. Unfortunately for the reformers and unfortunately for the Prime Minister himself as time would tell, Lloyd George was less than enthusiastic about proportional representation. The House of Commons rejected it but adopted proposals for the use of the alternative vote.

When the Bill reached the House of Lords, proportional representation was reintroduced and the alternative vote eliminated. Discussions followed to attempt to settle the differences between the two Houses. A compromise was reached which included the appointment of a commission to report on the application of proportional representation in a given number of constituencies. In the proceedings, Arthur Henderson on behalf of the Parliamentary Labour Party, stood for the alternative vote. But no commission was set up and in 1927, the clause of the Act relative to this matter was repealed.

The failure of Lloyd George to support proportional representation in 1917 resulted in the dwindling fortunes of his own party in the Twenties. Then came a new opportunity to change the electoral system. When Labour gained power in 1929, Lloyd George declared his support for a 'prompt, bold, energetic policy'. He was in favour of State intervention — of a National Development Loan — as later advocated by the Macmillan Committee and it was the failure to implement this policy that contributed in such large measure to the economic disaster of 1931. In 1929 however, and indeed in 1930, in spite of the paralysis that was gripping the Labour leaders, Lloyd George and the Parliamentary Liberal Party continued to support the Labour Administration. The Prime Minister in return, conscious of the concern of the Liberals to make the electoral system more representative, proposed the setting up of a Speaker's Conference on Electoral Reform.

Consequently in November 1929, under the Chairmanship of Viscount Ullswater — a former Speaker, the Conference was set up. Seven members were selected by the Chairman of each of the Labour and Conservative panels of submitted names and four from the Liberal panel. One peer from each of the Parties was added to the list. Among the best known names were: Lord Hugh Cecil, Sir Samuel Hoare, Sir Herbert Samuel, Sir Archibald Sinclair, Lord Arnold and W. M. Adamson. The two women members were Miss Megan Lloyd George, representing the Liberals, and Dr. Marion Phillips, representing Labour.[2]

At the outset however, the National Executive Committee of the Labour Party, decided that the Labour representatives were not to put forward proposals on proportional representation or the alternative vote, although those matters were bound to arise.

According to the letter dated 17th July 1930, written by Lord Ullswater to the Prime Minister at the conclusion of the Conference, the first meeting was held on 4th December 1929, "when it was decided that the first matter to consider was the suggestion of the Liberal section that some system should be adopted with a view to 'Securing that the composition of the House of Commons shall properly reflect the views expressed by the electorate'". The letter went on to state that during ten sittings the merits of proportional representation and those of the alternative vote, as well as those of the present system, were examined and debated in great detail. The letter explained too, that information had been presented by H.M. British Ambassadors and High Commissioners to the Conference about electoral systems in various parts of the world.

In addition, Mr. J. H. Humphreys, the Secretary of the Proportional Representation Society presented memoranda and gave evidence, while Mr. W. Clough, a former M.P. submitted memoranda of the alternative vote. Lord Craigmyle too, submitted a statement in support of the alternative vote, should the system of proportional representation not be adopted.

Because of the difficulty of obtaining general agreement as to the system of election that might be recommended to supplant the existing one — if a change was deemed necessary, it was decided to take a provisional vote on the proposals put forward by the Liberal section, which were moved in four resolutions.

The first resolution stated that any change in the present system of Parliamentary elections should include proportional representation with the single transferable vote. This resolution was opposed by the Labour section but received the total vote of the Liberals and the conditional support of the Conservatives.

The second resolution — that certain divisions should remain as single-member constituencies, was carried by eleven votes to eight, the Labour section constituting the minority.

The third resolution — that the method of the alternative vote should be adopted in the said single-member constituencies was negatived by twelve votes to five. The Liberal section accounted for the minority vote and one member of the Labour section abstained from voting.

The final resolution — that special provision should be made in proportional representation constituencies to permit by-elections being held in divisions of a constituency — was carried by eight votes to nil, with nine members abstaining from voting.

The Liberal section explained that in the event of proportional representation not being finally accepted, they would be prepared to consider the adoption of the alternative vote generally as being preferable to the present system.

The Conservative section indicated that they were not prepared to agree to the alternative vote in any circumstances.

The Labour section explained that none of them was willing to support the alternative vote *per se* but that some of them were prepared to accept it on condition that other reforms were adopted at the same time'.

These reforms — nine in number — were mostly concerned with election expenditure and expenses plus the question of plural voting, and were, in the view of the Chairman, matters outside the scope of the inquiry.

The Chairman ultimately concluded: 'The main purpose of the Conference — viz some general agreement as to the amendment of our electoral laws — had failed, as no agreement had been reached, or was likely to have been reached ... I have, therefore to inform you with regret, that our proceedings have been discontinued.'[3]

So ended the Ullswater Conference on Electoral Reform, on 17th July 1930. Yet the matter was not allowed to rest there. After negotiations between the Labour and Liberal Parties, the Labour Government introduced an Electoral Reform Bill which contained a clause in favour of the alternative vote and on February 3rd 1931, The Representation of the People (Nº2) Bill came before the House. Phillips made a forceful speech beginning with an attack on plural voting which she described as being unfair and undemocratic. Concentrating first on the Business Premises Qualification, she lamented that as 'one of the unfortunate residents of the City of London,' her vote was rendered useless since it was swamped by the business votes of those who worked in the City and lived elsewhere. She appealed to the Government to remedy the situation by giving an equality of vote to the City residents.

Second, as a university voter, she stated she would approve of the loss of that vote when the Bill became law as she had never thought that graduates had any right to an extra vote. She went on, 'If I may say so, a great deal of sentimental bosh is talked about the University electorate and the quality of the votes which these electors give.' She complained that 'apart from a handful of dons, those accorded this franchise were spread all over the country and all over the world without any corporate interest in political questions nor the corporate interest which people in the same constituency have.' However she argued provocatively, that if it was deemed that 'special values shall be given to different types of voters' then at a time when the problem of unemployment was of paramount importance, perhaps giving a second vote to the unemployed might be an effective way of putting pressure on Parliament rather than bestowing it on graduates. As for the cloistered academic she remarked drily, 'The life of dreamy contemplation is not the life that makes a man or woman capable of judging the world practically.' She briefly dismissed the notion that university representation provided more independence of judgement as being 'a very poor compliment to the members of this House.' The university representatives, she continued, were elected by a handful of voters so scattered that they could never take cohesive action.

She maintained therefore that both the business and university constituencies should be abolished in the name of equality for every voter.

Referring next to her membership of the Ullswater Conference, she explained that 'our difficulty was that the three parties had three different points of view. The Liberal representatives had as their primary object a change in the method of voting. The Labour representatives had as their primary object equality in the value of votes by sweeping away the privileges that wealth gives in our electoral system. The object of the Conservative representatives was no change at all in the method of election.'

She elaborated further on how the Liberals had proposed proportional representation in all the industrial areas but were in favour of the alternative vote in large County Divisions. 'We were unable to find out how many Divisions the Alternative Vote would affect' she said, adding that Labour agreed to consider the alternative vote if it was coupled with the question of the privileges of wealth. The Liberal representatives were ready to consider this, but the Conservative representatives were not of that mind. Labour, she said, was anxious to reduce election expenses, while the Conservatives felt it was fair for them to spend more to pay for the help that was available voluntarily to Labour.

She stressed that the object of this Bill was to equalise voting power. While the object of previous Bills had been to extend the franchise to sections of the populace previously excluded, '... what we are now trying to do is to give equal weight to every vote cast in an election.'

Phillips then moved onto the discussion of proportional representation and the alternative vote, finding much merit in the latter system. She was content to go on fighting under the first-past-the-post system to obtain a majority 'that was a clear majority backed by a majority of the electors,' nevertheless, aware of the 'extreme danger to the poorest in this community of a system that makes it possible for a Conservative government to be returned by a minority of the electors' thus repeating the appalling experiences of the years between 1924 and 1929, Phillips stated that she was content to try the method of the alternative vote in order that such a danger might be averted.

As for proportional representation however, she believed that it would not only encourage 'minority parties but a succession of compromise governments built up on agreements between a number of small groups.' It was too early, she said, to pass judgement on Ireland, but she had little faith in the system practised in Germany. Furthermore, she warned, once proportional representation was adopted it would not be easy to get rid of it. She referred to a number of countries who were dissatisfied with their proportional representation system but could not change it because of the preponderance of small parties who were anxious to prolong their existence.

Returning to the question of the alternative vote, she pointed out that in Australia it had certainly helped to increase majorities. She explained further: 'The Party that is on the upgrade tends to gain by the alternative vote but this is also certain — that the Party that comes into power after an election under the alternative vote, has got a majority behind it. I would rather, perhaps, that we had the present system of having occasional compromises within the House than we should have to compromise outside. But it is clear that under the alternative vote, whatever the government of the country is, that the government is there because the majority of the electors have sent it there.'

She ended her speech by warning that if a minority government after the next election was to be prevented, the electoral system should be changed without delay. 'A good electoral machinery is enormously important to a civilised democracy' she said, reflecting on her recent experiences in Poland where many excesses took place because of the 'extremely defective' machinery of elections. In conclusion she re-emphasised that 'Every additional perfecting of the electoral machinery helps a democratic state to function satisfactorily and peacefully, and even if this Bill is not a great and world-shaking measure, it is one which will secure equality of voting powers, will restrain the privilege of wealth in electoral matters and will ensure that the next Parliament will have a majority behind its government.'[4]

Alas, the measure failed to reach the Statute Book. Plural voting was abolished during the Attlee administration and measures taken to regulate expenditure during elections, and there are clear signs that sixty years after the Ullswater Conference, proportional representation may well be adopted early in the new century.

Chapter 19: Gathering Clouds

A month before the debate on Electoral Reform, Phillips was in Poland, observing the conduct of the Polish elections and upon her return recorded her impressions in the press. *The Daily News* of Perth, Western Australia, under the heading 'Revelations of Polish Elections' and sub-titled 'A Campaign of Tyranny and Brutality' quoted Phillips's description of 'astonishing atrocities' which she blamed on the Pilsudski regime. She described the arrest of an old Socialist, Dr. Lieberman, at Brest Litovsk in the early hours of the morning, and his imprisonment on 'a trumped up charge'. After the election, he was, she said, set free — 'a broken man with fifteen grievous wounds'. She related too, how a woman was imprisoned for six months in Poland for saying that Jozef Pilsudski, the Prime Minister of Poland, was insane. As for the election itself, it was she maintained, 'dishonestly and tyrannously' conducted, with highly irregular procedures which she carefully listed.

The article too, appeared in *The Morning Herald*, Sydney, and in *The Sun*, Melbourne, which also published a reprint of a cartoon of Pilsudski.[1]

She had denounced the abuses in Poland, to the press in London, immediately after her return, before leaving to address a series of meetings at a Bristol by-election.

Phillips was to raise the matter of the Polish elections again the following month in Prague at a meeting of the International Committee of Socialist Women. The meeting, having spent three days preparing the programme for the International Conference of Socialist Women to be held at Vienna in July, went on to discuss in some detail the situation in Poland and a resolution by Phillips was unanimously adopted. It read as follows: 'The International Committee of Socialist Women expresses its abhorrence of the illegal and brutal actions of the Polish Government against its political opponents throughout the Republic. It declares that the imprisonment and barbarous treatment of the prisoners at Brest Litovsk and the persecution of minorities have roused a sentiment of horror and disgust throughout the world. It sees in the activities of the Polish Government a further development of Fascism in Europe and pledges itself to help in every effective way to bring success to the struggle so courageously waged by the Polish Socialist comrades and those co-operating with them to establish the rule of law and democratic freedom in the Republic of Poland'.

Present at the meeting was Mrs. Kluszynska, a member who had been re-elected to the Polish senate and who had managed to leave the country, though another delegate had been arrested. Mrs. Kluszynska spoke of the imprisonment and brutal treatment of deputies and talked of their determination to continue to oppose Fascism in their country. She appeared in the photograph taken of the delegates in Prague, reproduced in *The Labour Woman* as an attractive as well as an extremely courageous woman. Phillips referred to her 'utter intrepidity'. What fate awaited her before the end of the decade is a matter of bleak surmise. The other women in the photograph, including the German delegates were all aware of the storm clouds that were already darkening the skies over Europe. The brave young Toni Sender — a member of the Reichstag — was to speak at the Vienna Conference on 'The Political Reaction and its effects on the emancipation of Europe'. As an articulate and determined Socialist it is unlikely that she would have been spared. Phillips expressed her concern thus:

> The reason for putting forward this subject is easily understood. A great wave of political reaction is sweeping over Europe. There are dictatorships in Italy and Poland and the last German elections were a victory for the Right Parties and the German Fascists. In Hungary and Spain there are autocratic Governments and everywhere there is a tendency to turn towards old reactionary politics.

That in itself, she added, made women vulnerable. It was, therefore especially important that the improvements in their position should be maintained.

The second resolution carried at the Prague meeting was concerned with the nationality of married women and ran as follows, and bore echoes of the debate in the House in November 1930: 'This Conference of Socialist women regrets that the representatives of the nations assembled at the Hague in 1930 have not yet agreed to the simple principle that a woman on marriage with an alien, should have the right to choose whether she will take the nationality of her husband and that she should not, except with her consent, lose her previous nationality and become an alien.'

The third Prague pesolution was in connection with night work for women. There had been some proposals to revise this international convention and fearful that such proposals could lead to serious exploitations of women workers through changes in 'hours, rest periods and general provisions,' the Conference urged that 'no opening should be given which would in any way weaken the protection of women workers and that the prohibition of night work should remain in effective force.'[2]

Meanwhile troubles for the Labour Government at home were gathering in intensity. At the beginning of 1931, Susan Lawrence in her New Year's Message in *The Labour Woman* wrote prophetically: '... though we believe in the ultimate victory, we have a period of struggle and confused fighting in front of us', and she called further for courage '... to live in a sense of our responsibilities'. Ominous words.

It was true that the minority Labour Government, in spite of growing difficulties, had tried to pursue a Socialist policy. The Widows and Old Age

Pensions Act had been improved, and Arthur Greenwood at the Ministry of Health had brought forth a Bill to deal with slum clearance, maintaining too, housing subsidies. There had in addition, been an effort to raise the school-leaving age to fifteen, but this because of opposition, had to be withdrawn. There were also, other small reforms, but eclipsing all else, the spectre of unemployment loomed large, until by the end of 1930, those afflicted by it had increased to 20% of the population. Against a background of world depression, the Government seemed incapable of finding a solution.

Phillips, like Susan Lawrence, deeply worried about the situation, tried to produce some words of cheer in her Editorial letter in *The Labour Woman* in April. She emphasised gains such as Henderson's peace-making missions to Paris and Rome and praised the helpfulness of Labour Ministers in trying to solve the problems of constituents, but she could not hide her anxiety. She referred to the month of March, in something of an understatement, as 'a month of varied experience sad and happy, troubled and hopeful'.

More forthright were her comments in her May letter in which she admitted openly '... we are beginning to look back on the first year and a half of this Parliament as a terrible period of trial and testing'. She talked of the limitation of the Government's position and of the 'hard tough work' that lay ahead and of the need to 'save our people who are falling victims to poverty'. She did not pursue the plight of the Government beyond that point but turned instead to a matter she had raised in the Commons, mainly the treatment meted out by some Public Assistance Committees to old age pensioners receiving medical treatment in Public Assistance Institutions. She proceeded to inform the pensioners of their rights and promised full discussions in the June issue of the magazine.[3] Her speech in the Supply Committee debate in April was a scathing attack on bureaucratic incompetence and inhumanity in the treatment of these old people.

She complained first of all of the difficulty of eliciting information on the actual administration of Public Assistance Committees. She had however, ascertained that it varied from area to area. How, she pursued, were the old age pensions administered in relation to public assistance authorities? She believed that the Ministry did not always have 'adequate or accurate information from those authorities as to what they themselves are doing. The old age pensioner has a right to his pension. He is not disqualified from receiving his pension if he enters a public institution under the Poor Law for medical or surgical treatment'. However, she maintained, there were pensioners in Sunderland who were in receipt of pensions, but upon entering these institutions, were required to sign a form giving the right to draw their pensions to the local relieving officer. 'In theory' she said, 'the old-age pensioner is quite free to sign his pension over to the relieving officer or not, but in fact it is the custom to place the form before him and to say 'Sign there', and if he protests at all to say, 'Oh, that is the usual thing'. I have one form here signed by an old man with his mark, and one can well imagine that an old man so ignorant that he cannot write his own name, is not going to read and understand a complicated form.'

In this way, she continued, the pension was signed over, the old man got nothing while he was temporarily in an institution, and on his return home found an accumulation of rent arrears that he would never be able to pay, or that the landlord had sold his possessions to claim the rent. She added that it was only in 'rare instances' that the Public Assistance Committee would pay the rent when pensioners were in our institution temporarily.

Phillips then drew a picture of 'these poor old men'. Their plight was such she said that '... they have not a penny to buy tobacco. They have not a penny to make flat racing a little more interesting or to put on the Cup-tie; they are just stuck there in an institution without anything in their pockets at all — they cannot even buy a newspaper'.

Her fury increased as she approached the most bizarre aspect of the whole matter. No money for the old men even to buy a newspaper! But, she insisted, someone was getting pocket money all the same, out of this arrangement. She explained: 'The Public Assistance Committee does not get the whole of their 10/- pension; the relieving officer who draws the pension gets a ten percent commission on the money which he recovers from the Public Assistance Committee. Ten percent of 10/- is 1/- a week so that the relieving officer gets 4/- a month on each old-age pensioner. It comes in with the general commission for the recovery of money due to the Public Assistance Committee; he gets 4/- pocket money and the old age pensioner gets nothing'. Phillips stressed that that money was not used to reduce administrative costs, because there was no reduction in the salary of the relieving officer. He was just getting 'an additional bit of commission as pocket money'.

Was the ghost of Dickens in the House still taking short-hand notes for Hansard? If so, did he feel that the parsimony of his Scrooge had a kind of shining directness in comparison with the convoluted cruelty of such insensitive bureaucracy?

Phillips doubtless would have agreed, for she ended her speech with a plea to make the most careful inquiry into 'this scandalous thing'. She felt that everyone in the House would wish for better treatment for the old than that described. The 'best authorities' she said, already returned a small weekly sum to them, and she pleaded that that should be made the rule in every area.[4]

Two other matters concerned her in the same debate. One was the inadequacy of housing programmes. She produced facts and figures relating to the unsatisfactory situation in her constituency. Five weeks previously she had been pressing the Minister on the same issue.[5]

The other matter was the need for a national maternity scheme. She claimed that local authorities alone could not deal completely with the problem and urged that urgent action was necessary to deal with it.

Again in July, Phillips was making detailed inquiries about the response of local authorities to the Ministry of Health Circular (of 30th December 1930) aimed at providing better maternity services. The Minister's reply indicated that a large number of authorities had now replied though the list was yet incomplete.[6] Phillips however, was still pursuing the matter in the autumn. On 17th September in a question to Neville Chamberlain, the new Minister of Health in the National Government, 'whether the Circular 1222 (11th September 1931) urging local authorities to make further economies in their work, is to be taken by them as superseding the Circular of December 1930, urging them to extend their work for the saving of maternal and infant life'?[7]

Chamberlain's unsatisfactory reply brought a sharp supplementary question from Phillips. She asked the Minister bluntly whether he proposed to carry out his predecessor's intention to obtain more information from local authorities or as it seemed more likely, that they would 'drop the matter altogether'? Chamberlain answered that he did not know.

Still undeterred, on the same day she went on to press the Minister of Health about another aspect of the same matter. She wanted to know if, in view of the proposed reduction in unemployment benefit, he would advise local authorities to extend the provision already in existence, of supplying milk to the needy,[8] and still undaunted, on two separate occasions in September, she was again hammering away at the need for a national maternity service, obtaining alas, little reassurance.[9]

Throughout that summer, unemployment and all its statutory complications claimed a great deal of the attention of Parliament. In July, Phillips spoke on the position of married women in the debate on the second reading of the Unemployment Insurance (N° 3) Bill. It was a measure to deal with anomaly and transfer in the provision of unemployment benefit. In her speech, she said that as Secretary of the Standing Joint Committee, she had been involved in compiling and giving evidence before the Royal Commission on the question of unemployment insurance concerning women. The Committee, she explained, represented about a million working women in the Labour, Co-operative and Trade Union movements.

In times of industrial difficulty, she commented ironically, the code of chivalry — of women and children first — was all too often applied. As money became scarcer, women especially married women, became the target for economies. She spelled out the difficulty with regard to married women in employment, first making the point that while the majority of women did not continue to work after marriage, apart from those in the textile and pottery areas, they only went out to work, when there was poverty in the home. Because of the prevailing level of unemployment among both sexes, it was inevitable that more married women were, at that time drawing benefit. Many people she said, had jumped to the conclusion that most of these women were drawing benefit unfairly.

Her organisation, she said, had made detailed inquiries into the situation and found that there were 'individual cases where there was undoubtedly a wrong position, a position never intended by the Insurance Acts, in which women who were not in the true sense available for employment and therefore had not a right to benefit, were drawing benefit'. She thought that those cases were fewer in number than yet realised, and that there were genuine misconceptions on the part of some of these women. She added however, that there were others who were undoubtedly 'taking advantage of the present situation and the regulations laid down by Parliament to stay on the fund when in fact they do not desire wage-earning employment'. To some extent umpires' decisions, she believed, might be to blame for that because of the ambiguity of the term 'available for work'. In any case, she was quite firm that if such cases existed they should not continue, insisting staunchly that 'the working class who are infinitely more honest in their outlook than many people who have been for a very long time members of political organisations within this House, have a straightforward and honest sense of what is right and wrong'.

She repeated that there had been great exaggeration of the situation and that her own committee had indicated to the Commission that they were opposed to 'any proposal to sweep married women out of unemployment insurance'. She emphasised that the evidence her committee had given made it clear that they would not object to regulations which made it certain that no one should draw benefit who was not genuinely available for work, provided that they 'penalised no one who was genuinely entitled to benefit, whether married or single.' She believed that the proposals in the Bill would enable such a principle to be carried out. Elaborating on the proposals, she emphasised again that the regulations needed 'the most careful consideration and the most careful safeguards.' Seasonal workers too, she added were in need of 'suitable regulations' to safeguard them against abuse.

In conclusion, Phillips referred again to the moral stance of working people in this matter. Her constituents, she said felt acutely the injustice of a situation in which 'men and women should draw unemployment benefit as a subsidy.' While, quite naturally they would be glad of an increase in benefit and other improvements, they would also welcome the Bill which if properly worked out, would remove from the working class as a whole, the charge that they wanted 'everything for nothing'. That she insisted, was the moral outlook of the workers. Desirable as it was to see more money going into their homes, the taking of money for one purpose to which there was no entitlement, made unemployment benefit or any form of state assistance demoralising in itself and akin to the hated Poor Law system. The Bill was an attempt to prevent anomalies without damaging those workers who were fully entitled to benefit.[10]

Outside the chamber of the House, much of Marion Phillips's time was taken up with committee work. On 24th October 1930 an inter-departmental committee was appointed by the Ministry of Health under the Chairmanship of Lord Marley 'to enquire into and report upon the present working of the Rent Restriction Acts (excluding the provisions relating to agricultural cottages) and whether any modifications or amendments should be made to them'. The Rents Restrictions Acts Committee as it was called, had been appointed because landlords had been complaining about the effect of rent restrictions and were seeking decontrol, while tenants were fearful of the results of such an action. Landlords and tenants sought justice and security.

The committee consisted of fourteen members apart from the Chairman and included seven M.P.s of differing political views. Phillips was the only woman member. The report was submitted on 11th July 1931 and submitted to Parliament in the same month.[11]

The inquiry entailed looking at the historical background of previous Acts, taking oral and written evidence, and examining statistical aspects regarding housing and rents. Altogether, complicated matters under eighteen headings were considered in detail before conclusions were drawn. It was a long, arduous process. The committee first met on the 14th November 1930 and then on forty other occasions. They heard oral evidence during thirty sittings and examined thirty-two witnesses. They received written memoranda, evidence and representations from fifty organisations and individuals.

Among its recommendations were: that working-class homes should be controlled and that control should apply to the house and not to the tenant; that gradual control should be attached to the next grade and that there should be complete decontrol for the most expensive houses.

Phillips herself, was also in favour of Rent Courts or Conciliation Committees to mediate between landlord and tenant, possibly on the lines of the Rent Assessment Committees of the present day.

Among the conclusions of the long detailed report too, there appeared a paragraph: 'We do not share the same philosophy but (with the exception of one of our colleagues) we are unanimous in recommending these proposals as a reasonable settlement under present conditions of the difficult and complex social problems which we were appointed to consider'. The colleague who did not sign the Main Report was D. M. Graham who submitted his Minority Report.[14]

The Chairman too, in his letter accompanying the report to the Minister confirmed that the committee members had worked with 'complete harmony and goodwill' and had agreed, 'regardless of Party to support the passage of a Bill embodying the recommendations of the Committee'. These he stressed had not been arrived at as 'a series of compromises' but were based entirely on the evidence of witnesses and on the relevant statistics.

In conclusion, the letter stated that 'while some landlords derive benefits from our recommendations, the number of tenants who directly benefit from abolition of decontrol by possession runs into several millions, and ninety percent of those left out of the category are not made worse off, but merely remain under control as at present'. So ended the labours of the Marley Committee.[12]

Another departmental committee on which Marion Phillips served was that set up by the President of the Board of Trade in 1930, under the chairmanship or Lord Gorell to consider art and industry and to look at the possibility of a standing exhibition of articles of good design in daily use. There were thirteen meetings of this committee between 1930 and 1931.[13]

Her interest in art and well crafted objects led her to experiment on her own. While pursuing a gruelling work schedule she still found time to design what she called a convenient House of Commons uniform for women members. It was, in her words a well-cut overall of thick crepe de chine lined with bright silk which buttoned over her dress and apparently much admired in the House.[16] It would have been interesting to hear Arthur Phillips's comments on her creation, since his general view of his aunt's sartorial preferences was anything but complimentary.

Chapter 20: The Cinderellas

During the first week of June 1931 the Annual National Conference of Labour Women was held at the Tower Ballroom, Blackpool. It was heralded by Phillips in *The Labour Woman* as 'Blackpool's Great Conference'. Although she conceded that there had been many other conferences at Blackpool, yet 'we women may be forgiven if we think this is the best of them all ... for the National Conference of Labour Women is our own show and we are proud of it. It has more inspiration to the hour and shorter speeches and more speakers than any other, and what is more still, it consists of the people who hold the future of our country in their hands. Yes they do. It is the women in the homes who count more than anyone else ... The mother is the centre of life for the child. The responsibility of the mother is a heavy one and at our Conferences we try to see our way into the future.'[1]

The delegates to the Women's Conference represented the Woman's Sections, Divisional Labour Parties, Local Labour Parties, Co-operative Organisations, Socialist Societies, Trade Unions and the N.U.R. and A.S.L.E.F. Organisations. They totalled 754 delegates including those who represented 1,824 Women's Sections and it was reported that the fully-paid up membership was just under 250,000. Throughout the country there were at that time 61 Labour Women Advisory Councils, 24 Central Committees co-ordinating the work of Ward Sections in Boroughs, and 70 Federations co-ordinating the work of Sections in County Divisions. Nevertheless, the delegate and membership figures showed a slight drop, partly due it was thought to the 'extreme poverty' of the times.[2] Further proof that penury was freezing 'the genial current of the soul' was supplied in the Private Business Conference held for delegates of the Women's Sections and Labour Parties, when Phillips reported on the small number of replies received during the year on the question of a fund for assisting the candidates of working women for Parliament. It was agreed not to press further with the matter at that time.[3]

How could it have been otherwise? These women were only too aware of the struggle in the homes of the poor to make ends meet, especially when the need to buy a new pair of boots for a growing lad blotted out all other considerations.

A large number of resolutions was adopted by the Conference. One congratulated the Government on 'the success with which it has pursued a policy of international peace and disarmament' and a general policy of arms reduction, though an amendment in favour of unilateral disarmament was lost by three hundred and fifty five to three hundred and three votes.

An emergency resolution was adopted on unemployment, as were resolutions on maternal mortality, social services, trade union membership, venereal disease and India.

Another resolution called for more Labour women to serve as magistrates and as members of Government Commissions of Inquiry. The Conference urged too that there should be a national scheme of adequate super-annuation for all classes of workers and that persons should receive pensions under this scheme at sixty years of age.

However, the two most important matters for discussion at this Conference were 'The Domestic Workers' Charter' and the report on 'Hospitals and the Patient'.

The latter had been prepared by the S.J.C. and the Public Health Advisory Committee of the Labour Party, and presided over by Dr. Somerville Hastings, M.P.. Phillips was among the members of this committee. The report concentrated on patients' care in hospital — from the point of view of the patients and not from the point of view of doctors or nurses or general management. It was well-received and fully discussed.

On then to 'The Domestic Workers' Charter' which in this Conference reached an important if not its final goal. The Charter was presented and there was general agreement to its terms. Delegates speaking on various aspects of the Charter, welcomed the long-overdue reforms embodied in it. However, Phillips warned that its acceptance by the Conference was only the first hurdle and that an enormous task lay ahead to turn its provisions into reality. The following month she would be seeking an international charter for the 'Cinderellas' on the same lines, in Vienna.

Marion Phillips's long campaign to secure a better deal for domestic servants had been waged throughout the Twenties and culminated in 1931 in this production of a 'Domestic Workers' Charter'. It attracted more interest (and vituperation) at home and abroad than any other reform which she had sought.

Margaret Bondfield in her article 'Women as Domestic Workers' in the publication, *Women and the Labour Party*, while conceding that there were indeed, some households in which servants were treated in a civilised and kindly fashion, nevertheless insisted that the general lot of those employed in domestic service between the declining years of the last century and the outbreak of the First World War was wholly deplorable.[4]

Frank Dawes in his book *Not in Front of the Servants* described their standing in society during that period.

...Servants remained near the bottom of the social ladder. Only the unemployed, the criminals, down-and-outs and prostitutes were lower. [5]

He reminded us too how important it was for domestics not to 'get above themselves'.[6] Dawes also referred to a text for the benefit of servants, printed in

The Servants' Magazine, in 1867 which read: 'Never change your place unless the Lord clearly shows it will be for your soul's good'. Dawes commented drily, 'But some servants were apt to give notice without consulting the Almighty first.'[7]

Bondfield too, listed among the servants' grievances, their lack of freedom, their long hours and low wages.

Their isolation, ever under the watchful eye of their employers, made it difficult to organise themselves into unions, even if they had had the courage to do so. Yet during the First World War a few servants had actually dared to approach a union in Birmingham and through its good offices, had secured comfortable quarters in their employers' homes, paid holidays and a minimum wage. In Scotland too, Miss Jessie Stephen started a union by venturing to call at houses to interview servants when their employers were out.

During the war, however, rather than seek better jobs 'in service', servants had gone in droves to seek freedom in munition factories, preferring the dangers therein and the hazardous journeys on dark nights to and from work, to the incarceration from which they had escaped.

With the cessation of hostilities, they were in consequence reluctant to return to their previous employment, thus precipitating the crisis known as 'The Servant Problem'. So acute was the shortage of domestic workers after the war, that the Government found it necessary to institute an inquiry. Sir Auckland Geddes, the Minister of Reconstruction, therefore appointed a committee of which Phillips was a member, to look at the effect of women employed in war work on the domestic service situation. It reported to the Minister in 1919 and consequently 'The Report on the Domestic Service Problem, Ministry of Reconstruction' was presented to Parliament.[8]

It was clear from its findings that all members of the committee were agreed on the need for reforms, but there was disagreement about some of the recommendations that would appear to us today to be eminently sensible. These were: the setting up of local joint committees of employers' and workers' representatives to negotiate matters like free time and holidays, the number of working hours and the setting-up of training centres in which the domestic arts could be taught. Trade unions too it was felt, should be encouraged, and reasonable conditions of work should be discussed to everyone's advantage.

Yet there was dissatisfaction among some of the members of the committee. The Marchioness of Londonderry for example, was adamant that she would not sign the section on organisation and conditions because she felt that many of the recommendations 'would interfere unduly in the individual character of relations between employers and workers, and widen still further the breach that already existed.' Lady Birchenough agreed. She was convinced that 'servants in 'better service' would greatly resent interference by outside regulations and Trade Union methods 'so inappropriate to their circumstances and to themselves''.

On the other hand, Marion Phillips refused to sign for a different reason. There was no precise recommendation with regard to wages and hours of work. Her memorandum read:

> I believe that the reason why it is difficult to get servants today is not lack of training but because servants are dissatisfied with wages and hours of work. They are also dissatisfied with many matters which may roughly be classified as questions of social status, but hours and wages are fundamental.

Phillips argued too, that in addition to the use of labour-saving devices, the whole question of domestic service should be looked at anew. It should be municipalized and be made available on the basis of need and not of wealth.[8] The women workers should be regarded in the same light as modern Home Helps — paid in the case of ill-health and family crises by the community.

She urged too, (as she did in *The Working Woman's House*) the use of national kitchens and municipal laundries to ease the burden on housewives and domestic workers alike.

Further, the servants themselves felt that their uniforms bore the stigma of their lower social status, and that the custom of being addressed by their Christian names, was also unacceptable. Neither did the word 'servant' appeal to those who bore the appellation. Marion Phillips herself hated it. Like them, she preferred the term 'domestic worker'.

In the event, all the proposals came to nothing, and though the writing was on the wall — warning that the pre-war army of resentful cooks and 'skivvies', tweenies and nursemaids was gone for good, the nettle was not grasped and the subsequent inquiries and other efforts throughout the Twenties were to prove abortive. They all failed to deal with the situation in a positive, constructive way. A large file of correspondence relating to the problems of domestic service between 1923 and 1930 in the Phillips Archive at the Labour Party Library bears witness to her efforts in this direction during those years.[9]

The Central Committee on Women's Training and Employment set up during the war, was re-appointed in 1920 to deal with post-war unemployment problems. It also ran courses in nursing, cookery, housecraft, and 'home-making' — the two latter courses being combined into a 'home-training' course. All in all, by 1924 about 25,000 women had attended them. Many women's organisations urged additional courses like short-hand, typing and midwifery to improve the chances of employment. Leading Labour women pressed for an education for girls on general subjects to broaden their lives, as suggested by Rebecca West in her essay in *Women and the Labour Party*. But still there remained the insoluble problem: a clear demand for domestic servants on the one hand, and on the other, a pool of young women who were unwilling to supply the demand.

In 1922, however, the Central Committee funds ran out so that it became totally dependent upon the Ministry of Labour. The result was that the girls were increasingly coerced into domestic service because of the withholding of the unemployment insurance benefit. In 1920, the Coalition Government had extended State Unemployment Benefit so that it covered twelve million out of nineteen million at work. But, as Sheila Lewenhak explains, '... among the groups still excluded were home-makers, cleaners and domestic servants. This was their predicament: anyone who went into domestic service no longer had any insurance claim because of having been in previous insurable employment. But if those who had been in previous insurable employment, on becoming unemployed, refused to take up domestic work they were then classed as 'not genuinely seeking work' and therefore lost their claim to a 'dole' payment. The coerced women therefore fell into a trap.'[10]

In 1922, the unemployment situation among women was so serious, that a deputation from the T.U.C. Women's Group went to see Macnamara at the Ministry of Labour, urging work or training and the inclusion of all women under the Unemployment Insurance Act because so many women were in the excluded group, but no assurance was given.

The following year, 1923 — the Ministry of Labour did indeed recommend that private domestic service should be brought under the Insurance Scheme and secondly because of the difficulty found by domestic servants over fifty years of age in finding work, a pension fund should be set up to which employers would be required to contribute.

Neither recommendation was implemented.[11]

Again in 1923 another Government inquiry was set up under the chairmanship of Mrs. Ethel Wood to investigate the shortage of women domestic workers. Among the large group of witnesses was Countess Bathurst for the employers and Councillor Jessie Stephen representing the domestic servants and the Hotel Workers' Union. It reported to the Ministry of Labour (*Report on the Supply of Female Domestic Servants*, Ministry of Labour, 1923).

Throughout the report, it was the reluctance of girls to enter domestic service because of its inferior status — so regarded by other workers — that was the only matter to emerge in addition to the need for labour-saving devices. No proposals of any importance were made and no further action was taken.

Nevertheless such were the crushing pressures of poverty and unemployment that throughout the Twenties, and increasing number of young women were forced into domestic service, until by the 1931 census, there were 1,325,300 of them, including unemployed domestic servants.[12]

In 1928 the Labour Party and Women's Sections published a pamphlet about domestic servants in private residences in London and found that they accounted for a quarter of the female electorate aged twenty-one and over in Kensington and a third of all women voters in Westminster and Chelsea.

In 1930, at the Annual Conference of Labour Women in Birmingham, it was agreed that a questionnaire on domestic employment should be drawn up by the Standing Joint Committee of Industrial Women's Organisations and circulated as widely as possible. Fifteen thousand copies were placed on sale and sent to Women's Sections, advisory committees, trade unions, Co-operative guilds and other concerned organisations. Marion Phillips, secretary of the S.J.C. had found the questionnaire method extremely effective in the past as a means of gleaning factual information, first in the preparation of *The School Doctor and the Home*, and in the compiling of *The Working Woman's House*.

The intention now was that from the knowledge obtained from the replies to this questionnaire it would be possible to submit a 'Domestic Workers' Charter' to the Annual Conference of Labour Women the following year at Blackpool. The *Manchester Guardian* was later to comment that the 'Domestic Servants' Charter' was for Phillips 'another leading ambition. ... In this cause she laboured with all her push and drive' adding that 'getting things done ... was always her strong point.'[13]

So, the questionnaire was drawn up in the form of a pamphlet entitled 'What's wrong with Domestic Service?' and published by the Labour Party. It contained a list of questions with spaces provided for replies. The first question was 'What do you think the chief reasons are for the unpopularity of domestic service?'

A small press conference was held to launch it and this was followed, in Phillips's words, 'By very informative reports and correspondence in several newspapers. Some of this was serious and valuable for the information it gave. Much of it was violent and hysterical in tone, treating us as fools and meddlers and occasionally as something even worse.'[14]

The *Daily Herald* commented,

> The Tory papers have gone off at the deep end about it without taking much care to know what the Pamphlet says. It merely asks everybody concerned to send information and to that end, gives a questionnaire to which it would be glad to have answers from mistresses and maids alike, with a view to finding out if there were any widely expressed desire for a Trade Union.

The newspaper then proceeded to reproduce the list of fourteen simple questions relating to training hours, wages, accommodation, employment agencies, uniform, holidays, recreation, organisation into a union, joint councils etc, and then added that Phillips in some quarters 'has been accused of a desire to impose an army of inspectors to see that rules of hours of work are kept, if and when trade union rules are imposed'.

The columnist herself made a more realistic comment:- 'Blink the question as you may, domestic service in spite of efforts to 'raise its status', is not an occupation which is rushed 'by application for jobs — over abundant as domestic jobs are'.'[15]

Meanwhile, a Buenos Aires journal, under the heading 'Trade Union of Mary Anns' with a sub-title 'Sitting-rooms and Higher Wages' and yet a smaller sub-title, 'Housewives Smitten with Dismay', pin pointed the 'demands for an eight-hours day, sitting-rooms, higher wages and the dole' in a so-called manifesto issued by Phillips. It stated too, that 'a large volume of protest from housewives and servants is being published'.[16]

However, the *Daily Standard*, Brisbane was much more supportive. It praised her for doing 'great work for the working girl, despite the enormous amount of hostile criticism which poured in upon her as soon as it became known that she intended to investigate the conditions of the domestic worker'. It went on '...Think of the disadvantages! A social outcast in the home of her employer, consigned to the doubtful privacy of the worst room in the house, with the kitchen as her own reception room; long hours (she is liable to be called at any hour of the day or night as long as she is on the premises; low pay, and most terrible of all, for the majority who live in, never away from her employer. It is an occupation to which there is no future. Is it any wonder that the worst factory is heaven by comparison?'[17]

Others took a different attitude. Months later, Marion Phillips published the following paragraph under the 'Items of Importance' column in the August 1931 edition of *The Labour Woman*,

> A reader of *Pearson's Weekly* has been greatly, amused at Dr. Marion Phillips's scheme for Domestic service. What appears to *entirely* escape Dr. Marion Phillips is that if this reform, as she calls it, was put into practice, nobody would require these new servants, so the number of unemployed would greatly increase. That the suggestions of a handful of men and women who busy themselves unasked in the private affairs of an English household would *not* be tolerated, so if this reform is to take place the servants must look elsewhere for their food and wages. This is only one more blunder of the Labour Party, and these blunders are the laugh of the whole countryside.

Phillips's comment: 'We thought our readers *also*, would be amused at the anonymous letter sent here!'

Meanwhile, the replies from organisations, and Women's Sections were arriving. They could be regarded as representing the views of some twenty thousand people. Phillips was still rather disappointed that there were only one hundred and nineteen replies from domestic servants directly and fifty two from employers. Nevertheless, she felt that from the received information it was possible to 'put forward a Domestic Workers' Charter which will be a sound basis for future effort'.

She said that answer of the majority to the question 'What do you think the chief reasons are for the unpopularity of domestic service?' was long hours followed by lack of freedom and dislike of the status and loneliness of the domestic servant. Other reasons followed.

It was also felt that training was necessary after leaving school — at centres as well as training on the job; that special departments of the Employment Exchanges should be responsible for recruitment and be the agency for the taking of references; that the number of working hours should be agreed allowing reasonable elasticity; that sensible holiday times should be negotiated; that bedroom accommodation should be arranged but not in the basement. As for uniform, special clothing would be desirable but without 'any badge of servility' such as a rather pointless cap. Recreation and the preference of daily rather than resident help was also discussed. The 'Charter' itself listed fourteen proposals. With regard to wages, the overwhelming opinion was in favour of a scale. As to the issue of the insurance of domestic servants, the Charter stated, 'The results of our inquiries are definitely in favour of bringing these workers, whether daily or residential into Unemployment Insurance. We are, however, bound to point out that we have fifty five replies against it and that the press correspondence showed a strong feeling against insurance. But it was still more against Trade Unionism'. That, she said was understandable as mistresses would be in opposition just as they were in regard to health insurance. She added that those women 'already in insurable trades are unanimous in favour of the extension of the Act to domestic workers.'

As for trade unionism, Phillips was of the opinion that lack of organisation made the fulfilment of any Charter an impossibility. She urged the unions catering for large bodies of general workers to make every effort to bring in domestic workers.

Finally she stated that the proposals made in the pamphlet for Joint Councils were agreed. She praised the work of the Whitley Councils, seeing the co-operation of employers and employed as the way ahead.[18]

The task of implementing the terms of the Charter would be 'tremendous ... and one which we shall need all our energies to carry through to success', Phillips warned in the June edition of *The Labour Woman*. She referred again the following month to the work ahead, stressing that at Blackpool, the Domestic Workers' Charter had 'only laid the foundations on which we must now build'.[19]

That same month — July 1931, Phillips was again pleading for 'The Cinderellas of the industrial world, the Women Domestic Servants' — this time at the Fourth International Conference of Labour and Socialist Women in Vienna. In her report, she paid tribute to Austria for being the most progressive country in improving their situation and recorded the resolution adopted by the Conference to provide, a 'Domestic Workers' International Charter' on the same lines as the Charter adopted by the British Labour Women at the Blackpool Conference.[20]

Phillips never allowed the grass to grow under her feet and before attending the Vienna Conference she was present at a meeting of the S.J.C. on the 6th July. The minutes of that meeting referred to the work to be undertaken to put the Domestic Workers' Charter into operation, and the decision to invite the Minister of Labour — Miss Margaret Bondfield — to the September meeting to discuss these matters.[21]

Miss Bondfield accepted the invitation and at the September meeting, she gave a report on the progress made with regard to the extension of Unemployment Insurance and the setting up of Employment Exchanges for domestic workers.[22]

In the General Election of October 1931 which swept the Labour Government out of office, Miss Bondfield and all the other Labour women Members of Parliament lost their seats. In the S.J.C. meeting in early December, Phillips reported that she had received an invitation from the Trades Union General Congress Council to attend a small conference of representatives of the two unions concerned with the organisation of domestic servants on 10th December 'in an advisory capacity'.[23] The S.J.C. meeting was the last in the year for the Committee. Sadly, it was for Marion Phillips, the last in her life.

Pressure persisted upon the unions during the Thirties to persuade domestic servants to join them. Unfortunately the unions would not co-operate because of the difficulties involved. It was not until 1938 that a 'National Domestic Workers' Union' was launched and at the same time the T.U.C. when producing a nurses' charter, also produced a domestic servants charter, proposing hours of work and conditions on a par with those proposed for factory and officer workers.[24]

But it was too late in the day. Where had they been during the misery of the Twenties? In the event, war and the provisions of the Welfare State after 1945 rendered the belated gesture of the unions superfluous. By that time, the 'skivvy' had been replaced by the 'treasure', and the little maid-of-all-work known by the absurdly pompous name of 'cook-general' in countless suburban villas had disappeared. Instead there was the daily help who arrived by car. Today there are au pair girls who have their own pleasant quarters, home helps, 'dailies', and professional cleaners who provide their own equipment — just as Marion Phillips had anticipated so many years ago. How she would have beamed with delight at the present arrangements.

The *Daily Herald* said of her: 'She was the foremost friend and champion of the domestic servants of this country'. As for the domestic workers' charter which she drew up, the comment continued, 'Dr. Phillips would have preferred to call it 'The Household Workers' Charter' for she was not fond of the word 'servant' and was never tired of pointing out that few tasks call for more skill and character'.[25]

The likelihood is however, that more than anything else, it was the trampling upon the human dignity of generations of women servants that prompted Marion to battle so hard on their behalf. After all, it was respect for the personality of the individual that was the cornerstone of her political faith.

Chapter 21: Vienna

The Fourth International Conference of Labour and Socialist Women since the war, meeting at Vienna, was an impressive gathering of a hundred and thirty full delegates representing twenty-four countries, and forty-one fraternal delegates. Among them were sixty-six women Members of Parliament, and many delegates had come from non-European countries like the United States and Palestine. The Women's Congress preceded the Congress of the Labour and Socialist International which met the following week.

'In accordance with the Constitution a special Commission of that Congress considered the Resolutions adopted by the Women's Conference and reported them at a plenary session which unanimously accepted them'. So explained Marion Phillips in her lively account of the Vienna proceedings in *The Labour Woman*. It fell to Phillips, as one of the British Labour delegates, to prepare the report and deliver the speech encapsulating the deliberations of the Women's Conference to the Congress. She was clearly pleased to inform them that 'We hope soon to have two million organised Socialist Women throughout the world'.[1]

A photograph of a large group of delegates appears above the article in *The Labour Woman*. Marion, holding flowers presented to her by her colleagues from many lands, sits in the place of honour — in the centre of the front row. It is not a particularly clear photograph but it is evident that she is looking worn, unlike her usual ebullient self, and certainly much older than her forty-nine years.

She explained in her speech to the Congress that what was new and distinctive in the work of the Women's Conference was their attempt to 'formulate a body of doctrine with regard to women's problems, seen through the eyes of women themselves. For the first time in history, it is the representatives of the ordinary women in the home, it is the representatives of the wives of working men, the representatives of industrial wage-earning women — it is these representatives who are formulating policy which will meet their needs in the Socialism of the future as well as mitigate the rigours of the present.'

The first resolution concerned women's suffrage in those countries that unlike Britain, had not granted full adult suffrage.

She called attention to the women's 'indignation at the scandalous backwardness' of such civilised, democratic countries as France, Belgium and Switzerland 'whose women are completely or partly without political rights' and she appealed to the Congress to work to rectify the wrong, insisting 'that no country is fully civilised that has not given free and equal political status to the women of that country.'[2]

The Women's Conference had previously pledged itself to 'unreserved solidarity' with the women of those countries who were fighting for better political and economic equality in those countries and called upon men in the Labour and Socialist International to strive hard on their behalf for 'this modest share of Democracy'.

As for the organisation of women within the L.S.I. much needed to be done in many countries. The Conference resolved to continue 'International Women's Day'. Films, wireless, the socialist press and particularly the socialist women's press should be used more extensively. House to house sales should be encouraged, to promote propaganda, and women's organisations should collaborate with sports organisations, friends of the children, youth organisations and friends of nature. As for those women who were politically indifferent, social activities should be arranged to stimulate their interest.[3]

In her speech to Congress, Phillips urged the men to take the women seriously. 'I speak here,' she said, 'as a rather old organiser. I have been a national organiser of women in the Labour Movement for twenty-one years and I should like to make a personal appeal — especially to the husbands of these women — never let her feel she is at a loss; never let her feel that she is anything but an equal comrade in the Party which men and women both love.'[4] In these words, she was reinforcing an earlier plea in her address that women's education should be equal to that of men.

Another Conference resolution concerning the nationality of married women was in four parts. It stated that efforts had to be made to obtain for a woman:

> A right of option upon marriage: to retain her own nationality or adopt that of her husband's. In order that a change of nationality during the course of married life on the part of the man shall not automatically apply to the wife, should this be contrary to her desire and interests, the woman shall also have the rights of option in this eventuality. Should she desire to change her nationality at the same time, however, she shall not be compelled to commence a separate process of nationalisation.

> The right of a woman to repatriation (the right to the acquisition of her former nationality) in consequence of the dissolution of the marriage by legal separation or by the death of the husband, which right exists in many Countries, should be made general by international agreement.

> In order that women ignorant of the law shall also be in a position to benefit from the laws, women must everywhere be informed of the legal position on marriage as well as in the event of a change of nationality on the part of the husband, and their declaration demanded.[5]

On motherhood questions, the resolution was that 'The International Women's Committee be asked to conduct investigations as soon as possible in all countries as to legislation and practical conditions in all fields of population policy; the results to be submitted to the next meeting of the International Women's Committee'. It is clear that in the countries affected by the slump, the need for population control was rapidly becoming a matter of the most pressing concern.[6]

The second section of the report bore the heading 'Political Reaction and its effect on the Emancipation of Women'.

Fascism was the great threat, not only to the general social and political achievements that had come in the wake of international socialism but also to the political emancipation and independence of women. The relevant resolution therefore read:

> Rejecting the Fascist tendency which is driving humanity towards new slaughter, Social-Democracy calls upon the women, as creators and protectors of new life, to take their place in the ranks of the workers in their fight against Fascism and war-mongering.[7]

The third set of resolutions came under the heading 'Women in the Economic System'. The first section centred upon 'Women's Right to Work'. It contained a stern warning of attempts to create a rift between men and women in employment. It stated that the fight against unemployment was being used unscrupulously by employers to divert the attention of workers away from the real causes of unemployment and ways of dealing with it, towards the employment of women, with the intention of creating antipathy towards them. The warning continued: 'The International Women's Conference vigorously opposes the campaign against the employed women whether single or married'. All attempts to create dissension among workers were repudiated and there was a re-affirmation of the demand for 'the equal right of women to work'. While accepting that the circumstances of the individual should be considered when dismissals were being made, 'so that the economically weaker in particular should retain the job' it was pointed out 'that the economically stronger is not necessarily the single woman, nor even the married woman'.[8]

Under the title 'Modern Industry and the Employment of Women' it was reported that there were more women than men and this fact in addition to hardship produced a constantly growing 'reservoir of female labour'. Women were to be found in a large diversity of occupations — in industry and trade, in offices, in manual work, and in 'responsible jobs'.

Women however, had become victims of the economic crisis and of rationalisation. 'Of the millions of unemployed, one third are women'. Women bore an unfair burden.

> Women receive lower wages for equal work. They suffer the same distress through unemployment but their right to equal support is disputed; though qualifications be equal, they do not enjoy equal possibilities of promotion; under equal compulsion to work, their right to employment itself is questioned ... Only Socialism which liberates all working people can shatter the fetters of women workers ... Therefore, the International Socialist Women's Conference proclaims itself enthusiastically in favour of the aims of Socialism.

In the meantime, the report continued, it was imperative to alleviate the plight of working women and to this end, the Women's Conference were making eight minimum demands. These related to the admission of women at all levels of occupation so far as their 'special physiological constitution permits; to the reduction of working hours and to the principle of equal pay for equal work; to the removal of any injustice borne by women in regard to unemployment benefit; to the extension of the protection of motherhood and children's welfare, and the care of widows and orphans; to the extension of the protection of workers and the collaboration of women in all tasks connected with social administration; to the erection of houses well equipped with labour-saving devices and provision for the care of children, and finally to the setting up of an inquiry into the effects of industrial employment on women, with the co-operation of representatives of working women'.

The Conference called upon working women to co-operate with men in political and trade union organisations, to strive to implement these 'immediate demands'.[9]

It is lamentable that this urgent call in 1931 to implement these demands had to be made again, in 1991 — 60 years later — by the Equal Opportunities Commission. Today, as in 1931, there is an unusually high proportion of women in the workforce — higher than in most of the countries of Western Europe. Today as in 1931, the earnings gap between the sexes still exists, and indeed is wider than in other European countries. We are informed that in 1990, women in full employment earned only seventy seven percent of the hourly wage of their male counterparts. In addition, just as in 1931, today, in spite of equal qualifications, women's chances of promotion are far fewer than those of men. Men are appointed to most of the senior posts. Training for women also lags behind that given to men. As for working mothers, the lack of satisfactory arrangements for paid maternity leave and child-care provision in Britain, sixty years after the demand for the greater protection of motherhood and children's welfare rang out loud and clear in Vienna, is truly deplorable.

'Women' concludes the E.O.C. 'are still under-utilised and under-valued in Britain'.[10]

Women in agriculture, performing very different work, also claimed the attention of the Conference and were the subject of another resolution. This read, 'The Women's Conference notes with indignation, that as regards legislative protection and social insurance, agricultural work is still at a disadvantage, and it demands protective measures for women land workers, analogous to those which exist or are being demanded for industrial workers'.

The Conference further demanded that the backwardness with regard to social welfare and vocational training that marked agricultural work, should be 'remedied by adequate measures as speedily as possible'. Additionally, the Conference expressed its sympathy with the women landworkers and urged them to join trade unions and to unite with other socialist women to seek an improvement in the standard of their lives and that of their families.[11]

The threadbare poverty of rural workers alas, was to continue in Britain until the 1945 Labour Government, when Tom Williams's Agriculture Act, together with the social welfare provisions of that government, transformed their lives.

The final resolution of the Conference was concerned with domestic workers — the 'Cinderellas'. Though there were millions of these skilled women workers throughout the world, constituting a large proportion of wage-earners, yet as the Conference pointed out 'in most countries their employment is unregulated either by law or trade union agreement', and because of this, wages and conditions varied from place to place so they were, therefore, in a worse position than any other women workers. Accordingly, in order to make 'the 'servant' of today, the free domestic worker of tomorrow', the Conference of Socialist Women was demanding the following for all domestic workers: full suffrage rights; protective legislation and social insurance; inclusion in unemployment insurance; regulation of working hours and holidays; vocational training; the establishment of free public employment exchanges and abolition of private employment agencies; hostels for unemployed domestic workers.

The Conference delegates pledged themselves to co-operate with trade unions in their respective countries to ensure that these demands were met, also urging the domestic workers in all the countries in which they were enfranchised, to use their political power to improve their conditions and to fight for their rights by organising themselves in trade unions. The resolutions were akin to those embodied in the Domestic Workers Charter which had been received so enthusiastically at the National Conference of Labour Women at Blackpool the previous month.[12]

In her speech to the Congress, Phillips described this resolution as one 'which when we carry it out, will mean that the domestic servant will be in an honourable position, an independent position as a worker, and I hope some day ... we will have the richest constituencies in our different countries represented, not by reactionaries but represented by domestic servants who form very often, the bulk of the population within them. We want to get in our rich London areas, the housemaids, cooks, parlour maids and domestic workers of all kinds to express through their own representatives in Parliament, their advocacy of Socialist policy.'[13]

All the resolutions at the Conference were passed unanimously with two exceptions, the Independent Labour Party of Great Britain through their representative Miss Dorothy Jewson, voted against the resolution on the motherhood question. They voted too against the resolution on women in industry. The I.L.P. all along had been totally opposed to any legislation reflecting a bias towards women, believing it invalidated the concept of equality with men. With this in mind Miss Jewson and her colleagues had established the 'Open Door' Movement to try to counter the protective legislation already adopted by the Washington Convention. In the circumstances of today, they would doubtless reject the proposals for flexible hours and childcare facilities, ignoring Marion Phillips's dictum that 'a paper equality' was no good.

Finally, what about the housewives so long championed by Marion Phillips? Their turn would come at the next Congress. In the meantime, their position, like the motherhood question, would be thoroughly explored by the International Committee who would submit detailed reports to that Congress.

Nevertheless, it was to the 'Woman in the home' that Phillips chose to pay the greatest homage at the end of her speech to the Congress of the Labour and Socialist International. Inviting them to adopt the report on the Women's Conference, she reminded them of 'the enormous strength that the women of the different countries are giving to the Socialist Movement.' She described that strength as being more powerful than force. 'It is,' she said, 'The deep, profound instinct of protective love. It has mitigated the horrors of individualism and capitalism.' She expressed her belief that it was those deep instincts in women that prompted them to serve humanity all the more. She ended with an impassioned appeal to the men: '… the woman in the home, the keeper of the hearth, the protector and comforter of the young life of the community — she is the greatest force that Socialism can bring to our movement. We ask you to give us in the fullest possible measure all the help you can.'[14]

Marion Phillips described the Vienna Conference as a great conference — the best they had ever had. For all her colleagues it would also be a sadly memorable one.

Chapter 22: Crisis

Meanwhile, the economic situation at home was critical. The collapse of the German economy and the general depression in other major industrial countries had placed Britain in jeopardy. In addition, the financing of speculative enterprises in Britain and abroad, and lack of investment in basic industries, aggravated the situation. Nevertheless, in the hands of a competent Prime Minister and Chancellor, able to supply in good time remedies recommended by bodies like the Macmillan Committee and the Economic Advisory Committee, the worst effects of the looming crisis might have been avoided.

Instead, neither the vague, visionless Prime Minister nor the rigid doctrinaire Chancellor had the will or the weaponry with which to deal with the realities of the situation. Snowden clung to the two icons of his economic faith: the Gold Standard and Free Trade with the fanaticism of the closed mind. He also closed his ears to any other course suggested to him. According to Commander J. M. Kenworthy, one such way out of the morass was certainly put to him. In the *Manchester Guardian*, 25th January 1932, Commander Kenworthy wrote that Dr. Marion Phillips had acted as Secretary of a Special Committee set up by the Parliamentary Labour Party during the Labour Administration to examine questions relating to currency and exchange. 'The work was invaluable' he wrote, adding, 'Before the financial crisis, she warned the Government of what was coming. If she had been listened to, many of the present troubles would have been avoided. The Committee drew up very valuable reports but although these were sent to the Cabinet no attention was paid to them'. He concluded, 'she was one of the most far-sighted prophets in the Labour Party and a great economist'.[1]

Unfortunately it has not been possible to trace the documents to which Commander Kenworthy referred. It is believed that these papers, together with many other valuable documents, were probably destroyed during the war-time bombing raids on London when the House of Commons suffered a direct hit.

However, she made her views on the economic situation perfectly clear in her writings and in her Budget speeches. In both, she emphasised the lack of policy and inertia of the Prime Minister and his Chancellor. Robert Skidelsky too, in his book *Politicians and the Slump*, speaks of this 'policy of negation', the 'want of courage and the intellectual paralysis that gripped the Labour Government'.[2] He clearly indicates the options open to them in 1929 and early 1930 when they had the confidence of their people. There was support too from Lloyd George and

Liberal backing for a National Development Loan. Skidelsky refers also to the evidence given before the Macmillan Committee, 'when employers argued repeatedly ... for Government subsidised investment'.[3]

The City and the Treasury and consequently Snowden, opposed any suggestion of a State Interventionist policy. The Labour Chancellor was a total disaster. Skidelsky puts it better: 'With him at the Exchequer, no Government stood much of a chance in the circumstances of 1929'.[4]

With Snowden's constant rejection of every course presented to him, by 1931 the Government was finished. Skidelsky concludes: '... there was nothing to do but govern without conviction, a system it did not believe in but saw no real prospect of changing. It struggled to defend the working class as long as it knew how and when it could defend them no longer, it resigned'.[5]

Even as late as 1931, had Snowden been capable of adopting new policies, there is a view that the effect of the world crisis on the economy of this country could have been greatly alleviated. It is suggested that such policies would have involved suspending the Gold Standard, so producing more competitive export prices and replacing free trade with arrangements more advantageous to us. He might also have stopped the export of capital from the United Kingdom. He did none of these things.

Instead, although faced with rapidly rising unemployment and huge increases in unemployment benefit as a consequence, he still, rigidly and obsessively, saw as his main priorities the twin tasks of balancing the budget and the annual repayment into the Sinking Fund to pay the National Debt. This was at a time of grave financial difficulty when both activities might well have been suspended.

To balance the Budget, the Chancellor decided that there would be large cuts in unemployment benefit. The poorest human beings in the realm, the victims of greed and incompetence, were to be further squeezed. The May Committee set up by Snowden, damaged the credibility of Britain at home and abroad and succeeded in creating a large scale crisis. Snowden with Sir Montague Norman at the Bank of England, secured loans that soon disappeared, and eventually on 21st September 1931, there was the abandonment of Snowden's cherished Gold Standard.

In the meantime, in August, the Labour administration came to an end when half the Cabinet refused to agree to the cuts in Unemployment Benefit. Marion Phillips was present at the Joint Meeting of the National Executive of the Labour Party and the General Council of the T.U.C. held at Transport House at 3pm on Thursday, 20th August. Within days, Ramsay MacDonald became the Prime Minister of a 'National' Government composed of Conservatives and Liberals and they carried through the Budget which the Labour Party could not swallow. Phillips wrote personally to MacDonald to express her disgust that he should have given 'his blessing' to a reduction in unemployment benefit, saying,

> It means so definitely less food and less clothing, the loss of such meagre comforts as they may have had, that I cannot bear to hear the words 'equality of sacrifice' without a furious anger boiling up in me.[6]

In the weeks that followed, Marion Phillips carried on with the task of explaining to Labour women, exactly what had happened to destroy their Government. Later, she was to refer to MacDonald with icy contempt: '... he finds himself now the pictorial head of a Tory Army. He has become the moral dupe of his own vanity and the political victim of his own ignorance.'[7] Immediately after the rift however, she was more tempered in her comments on the erstwhile Leader in order to avoid a stampede of the confused rank and file out of the Party. In the September issue of *The Labour Woman* she did say clearly though, 'I cannot yet understand why the Prime Minister, if unable to apply Labour principles to the situation should remain as a 'National' Prime Minister, to administer a reactionary policy of retrenchment at the expense of the poorest'. She went on, 'Why is it that we revolt so instinctively against these economies that hit the unemployed? I think it is because we realise that to talk of 'equality of sacrifice' in the same breath as we speak of a ten percent cut on benefit and a 'tightening-up' in administration is sheer hypocrisy. The unemployed have been bearing the brunt of the sacrifices throughout these lean years since the return to the Gold Standard. Inequality of sacrifice, year in year out has been their lot. Further sacrifice must be measured in what they have left rather than what they lose. Cut down a bare living and you go below the fodder base. There is no equality when from one family you take the children's chance of fresh milk and from another no more than a possible luxury'.[8]

1931 was only five years away from the misery of the 1926 Miners Lock-out. In fact, since the end of the First World War, vast numbers of our people lived in obscene poverty. During the thirties, the unemployment figures reached three million and it is a sobering thought that it was the preparation for another war, in the munition factories of 1938 that restored their self-respect! It was only then that they were enabled to feed and clothe their families adequately and to provide the simple comforts that make a home.

Meanwhile, Phillips continued to work energetically as a member of Parliament and as Chief Woman Organiser of the Labour Party. Regular meetings of the Standing Joint Committee of Industrial Women's Organisations, as always claimed much of her time. The meeting held on 17th September for example, discussed matters as various as secondary school fees; the health of the unmarried mother and her child; the Children's Bill; the nationality of married women; maternal mortality; the National Conference of Labour Women; the Domestic Workers' Charter; the International Labour and Socialist Women's Conference and 'The Economy Proposals' as they affected women. In connection with the last item, the committee agreed to endorse the manifesto issued by the Labour Party and General Council of the T.U.C. and the attitude taken by the Co-operative Party.[9]

In the House, business went on as usual, pending the announcement of a General Election. That September, most of the questions asked by Phillips, related to the distress caused by the Slump: the cuts in benefit as they affected various sections of the community; the details of transitional benefit and means test; the difficulties experienced by allotment holders, and the burden placed on temporary women staff in the Civil Service with increased work, coupled with wage reductions. She voiced her concern too about the exploitation of consumers as a result of the depreciation of the pound.

There were questions too, to the Chancellor of the Exchequer and to the Financial Secretary about loans.[10]

On 10th September she spoke in the debate on Budgetary issues (Ways and Means — Financial Statement). 'We are discussing' she said, 'whether this Budget will save the flight from the pound and … will not only balance, but help the country to get back to a better industrial and financial condition.' She warned that unless there was such an improvement on both fronts as a result of the government's financial policy, the Budget would be 'entirely useless and we shall within a few months … be faced again with exactly the same crisis that faced us a few weeks ago. We shall, however, be faced with it under much more serious conditions than we were then, for we shall have already borrowed and paid for a loan of eighty million pounds for the previous credit and will therefore be in a worse position to meet a new crisis.' She stated that the issue was whether the method now being taken could save sterling at its present value. She went on to emphasise that Britain was a creditor nation: that countries owed us money and could not pay because of the present value of the pound. The Budget, Phillips insisted, was the wrong way of dealing with the matter. She did not want to talk of 'a bankers' ramp' but there was little doubt that the economic solution proposed by the leading banks for regaining financial health was to bring wages down to the level of prices. This theme, she stated, ran through the banking literature of the world, She referred in particular to a recent speech by Dr. Sprague, the American economic adviser to the Bank of England, adding that there appeared repeatedly in the banking press of the world, 'the criticism that the economic blizzard is the result of falling prices for primary products, that the only way to deal with that situation is to reduce the cost of production, that the best way to reduce it is to reduce the level of wages, and that the great barrier to reducing that level is the system in Great Britain of unemployment insurance and the present level of insurance benefit.'

The Budget, she maintained, carried out absolutely the principles advocated by the leading economic advisers to the banking world.

As for unemployment benefit, since the sum was 'comparatively small,' she did not think that such a sum of itself would have been a part of the conditions on which our country's position was to be assisted. However, she maintained that there was 'something more' to it, which was 'the breaking down of unemployment insurance as a system and the breaking down of the level of benefit which gave the unemployed person a possibility of living …'

She went on, 'I am asked whether those principles are right. They are going the wrong way about it. You cannot get back to prosperity by ruining the consumer power of the people of this country.

What is more, you do not by that means touch the real problem — the problem about which the financiers are getting anxious — as to whether the countries that owe us money are going to be able to pay.'

She went on to explain what had happened as a result of the very high value of the pound.

She pointed out that the countries who owed us money had to pay in goods as that was all they possessed. Because the value of sterling was high, these countries were bound to pay goods in higher quantities. She mentioned that Sir Oswald Moseley had referred to Britain as 'being in pawn'. On the contrary, retorted Phillips, 'It is really the other way round. Our trouble is, that we are the pawnbrokers with a very large business, that we have an enormous quantity of goods in the shop and that the people who put them there cannot even pay the interest that is owing in the normal and ordinary way of trade.'

British trade, she emphasised, was in difficulties not because of the amount spent on unemployment insurance but because the assets of the country were beginning to look doubtful and she regretted that the Budget did nothing to reassure the world on the matter.

Meanwhile, she said, Members of the House were trying to 'Make our blood run cold ... with pictures of the horror that would come upon us if there were a flight from the pound.'

At this point, another member — Mr. G. Gibson — intervened to ask: 'Does the Hon. Lady deny it?' Phillips who was said to be autocratic on occasion, was certainly autocratic now. 'If,' she said loftily, 'the Hon. Member will listen to me, he will see whether I do so or not. I am perfectly ready to stand by everything I am going to say.' She maintained that many wild statements had been made about the value of the pound. She quoted the Prime Minister's words that if action had not been taken by the Government at a certain exact moment, the pound would only be worth ten shillings by the following morning. She poured scorn on such a statement which was not backed she said, by 'a real foundation of fact,' and adding for good measure that the value of the pound was not based on imagination. She insisted that not even the panic-stricken 'sentimental romanticists' of whom there were many in the financial world 'could have driven the pound down to ten shillings in a night,' because of the valuable assets of this country at home and abroad, although the assets abroad were more doubtful than they used to be. She continued, 'the financiers, the bankers, the people who deal in the money market, know that very much better than members of this House. We keep finance as a sort of closed mystery.' She recommended the report of the Macmillan Committee set up by the Labour Government to members of the House. That report, she said, was 'an analysis of the money market and finance ... [and] will enable people to see at last what has been held to be a mystery, is something which any intelligent person who will devote some time to it, will understand.'

The report too, she continued, exposed the fallacy of comparing the situation here with that of Germany. When the mark fell in Germany, it was during a period of great disturbance and anxiety — in circumstances totally different from those at the present time in Britain.

'Of course,' she added, 'everyone would prefer to avoid any period of panic or difficulty, would like to see the pound maintain itself at a very high value, but we have to look facts in the face and to consider whether we can maintain the pound at its present price, a price above its real value.'

At this point, Phillips regaled the House by quoting some of the price rises projected by a Member, on bread, meat, sugar and tea and possibly all in one night! 'He had,' she said sarcastically, 'worked it out with an exactitude which, I am sure, would enable him to make a wonderful future by manipulating foreign exchanges.' He had too, at a later date, forecast even higher rises — a prophecy described by Phillips as 'the kind of vague, mysterious talk to which people are so much addicted when dealing with financial matters.' The worst thing about such talk to her was 'the kind of inexactitude with which they try to frighten the people of this country ... until poor women with pensions write and say that they are glad to give their sacrifices to this great and wealthy country. We ought not to stoop to such exploitation of the sentiments of the people.'

Warming to her subject, she referred to another member who had told the House that unless it agreed to action being taken — she was not sure what action he had in mind — the country would be in the same situation as Germany. 'He took a note for ten thousand marks, or a million marks out of his pocket and showed it to us. He said that would be our lot and that those who did not agree with him were lunatics.'

Phillips was clearly appalled that the level of discussion should sink to such depths. That there should be a comparison of the financial situation in Britain with that in Germany, showed, she said 'ignorance to the last degree.' Ignorance of the facts often breeds fear bordering on hysteria, and this resulted in some of the wilder utterances of the time. Later on, during the election campaign, as the panic grew, even the Chancellor himself in vituperative outbursts, was to make wholly absurd statements. Their stampeding effect on our apprehensive and bewildered public was predictable.

Phillips's final indictment of the Government's policy to maintain the pound was the burden it placed on the families of the unemployed through the reductions in unemployment benefit. 'We are told that we must not borrow any more for unemployment ... Is it very much worse to borrow to maintain the consuming power of your people, to distribute wealth among them so as to keep the home market occupied, than to have to pay six percent which we are paying on a loan, in order to bolster up the pound?'

She ended with a plea to face the facts: 'Would it not be better to face boldly the situation in the financial markets of the world — to realise that the old days have passed and that a new policy must be developed in order to meet the new conditions of our times?'[11]

Before many days had passed, Britain had indeed come off the Gold Standard and in the continuing debate on the financial situation on 23rd September, [the Finance (N° 2) Bill 1931] Phillips reminded the House that the Chancellor had been warned in the first discussion that the main object of the Budget — preventing a flight from the pound — could not be achieved and 'within a very short time we were proved right.' She added, 'It is not the Government that has taken us off the Gold Standard; the facts of the case have made it impossible for us to remain on it.' She believed that 'properly handled' it was a good thing but feared that the Chancellor would try as soon as possible to put the country back on the Gold Standard, thus depriving Britain and the world of the benefit of what had happened.

However, she said, there was another matter at stake. This was the question of internal finance. They had been informed that it was necessary for the Government to produce a scheme of economics and heavy taxation in order to save the pound, and further, in order to obtain the loan, it was necessary for the Government to decrease unemployment benefits. Not merely was this strategy an attack on the unemployed but on all wage earners and salaried workers, and was, she insisted part of a pattern seen in other countries. She referred specifically to the situation in the U.S.A. making a powerful attack on the bankers in America and Britain.

Quoting first, details of the policy of American bankers and its results, as outlined by Mr. McGrady, legislative representative of the American Federation of Labour, Phillips elucidated further: '... the incomes of the wage-earners were cut twelve percent while stock-holders' dividends increased twenty eight percent. That is a situation so remarkably like the situation in this country that we may very well see in what is happening here, an equally strong attempt by the financial interests to carry out that policy of depressing wages, of which the most effective method is to reduce unemployment benefit.' She believed that it was a desire to see that policy carried out by a Government that 'was not hampered by Labour supporters' that led to the downfall of the Labour Government. In support of this theory, she quoted the words of David Lawrence, the editor of *The United States Daily* — the 'pet organ' as she called it of the U.S. President. She read Mr. Lawrence's Statement to the House. 'There is no doubt that British bankers themselves are in accord with suggestions of foreign bankers, and it would not be surprising if the true British situation were exaggerated to bring about the fall of the Labour Ministry.'

She went on to say that the fall of the Labour Ministry had been truly accomplished as a result of which, the working-class woman would be heavily penalised when she sought to buy her household necessities.

Turning then to examine the state of the economy and the plight of the twenty-eight thousand unemployed people in her own constituency of Sunderland, she stated that the direct loss in purchasing power there was assessed at one hundred and eighty-one thousand pounds. The wages of teachers, policemen, and others in the same category would be cut and they would be further pilloried by a rise in income tax. She sympathised too with shop-keepers who would pay 'at least double the tax they paid last year and they will be paying it for a year of better trade than they are now going to experience.'

She said that while the whole would gain from a lower pound there was the need to prevent profiteering. She repeated that wages were down, unemployment benefit was down, transitional benefit was reduced, and there was an increase in income tax for the smaller middle-class people. She observed that the only ones to receive the care of the Government were 'the classes who receive interest and live by bondholding and similar methods.'

She described as 'abominable and callous' the tactics of the Government of taking credit for not reducing children's allowance of two shillings, while at the same time adjusting the family allowance downwards to two shillings and ninepence. Obviously, said Phillips in such circumstances milk would have to be sacrificed. She herself, she added, had tried to elicit reassurance from the Minister of Health about the provision of milk for needy mothers and babies but that no such reassurance had been forthcoming.

In conclusion she criticised the Chancellor for being so bereft of any schemes to improve the prosperity of the country or indeed to balance his own Budget. 'We have never seen a Budget so hopeless in itself and never, I am sure, has this House listened to speeches from a Chancellor which have been so devoid of any intention, any expectation of doing anything during the coming winter except to press the standard of life down still further, depressing the purchasing power of the people and doing more and more to damage the home market.'

After deploring once again all that was being taken from the little people, she remarked on the 'small and dismal economy at the expense even of the allotment holders — that failure to continue one of the most useful pieces of work for the unemployed workers — that the Labour Government carried out.' Phillips had always set great store by the wholly commendable system of allotments, and now she commented sadly, '… thus the people who helped by growing their own food were penalised, and all for the saving of a few thousand pounds.'

She reiterated that there was nothing in the Budget 'to help us but a good deal that is going to hurt us,' and she hoped that the House 'by a strong vote' would declare its strong opposition to the methods used to deal with the difficulties that confronted the country.[12]

On the same day as the continuing debate on the financial situation — 23rd September, a sub-committee of the S.J.C. agreed upon a statement headed 'Women and the Political Situation' for the Executive Committee of the Labour Party, in preparation for a General Election. It was a concisely drafted statement by Phillips in five sections. Briefly they read as follows: The purpose of Section One was to allay fear and panic among women about the effect of the departure from the Gold Standard.

Section Two dealt with the Government's proposals that would reduce Women's Purchasing Power. These were: Cuts in unemployment insurance and the increase in income tax on small incomes, and cuts in wages. The use of simple examples was recommended and a warning about profiteers. Section Three dealt with the treatment of the unemployed 'in regard to cuts and destitution tests for Transitional Benefits' and should be looked at from the point of view of the family. This subject was dealt with in some detail. Economising on allotments, for instance was bad because of the moral effect of idleness. Section Four showed how the attack on social services was particularly bad for women. It would affect among other things the supply of milk, Local Authority provision for mothers and babies, the creation of a national maternity service, education services and nursery schools. Section Five expressed opposition to tariffs since they caused a heavy burden on household budgets.

In conclusion, the statement suggested that in the event of an immediate election, four special pamphlets be issued, in addition to Speakers' Notes, in a special series. There were too, other suggestions.

But Phillips never left anything to chance. If the election should be delayed, the issue of a special pamphlet similar to that prepared for the General Election of 1929 was suggested. That, she said, 'would give (a) A short statement on the break-up of the government. (b) A criticism on the lines above given of the present Government's policy. (c) Its programme, if returned with a majority.'

In this way, there would be available for the active workers 'something comprehensive' for them to use and it would act as a discussion document in 'special conferences of Women's Advisory Councils, Central Committees and Federations, as well as Women's Sections throughout the country.'[13]

The Labour Women were therefore geared for every contingency. It was just as well, for events moved rapidly. Parliament was dissolved on 7th October and the Government, calling for a 'Doctor's Mandate' declared that the General Election would be held on 27th October. A 'Doctor's Mandate'! Was there ever such a cynical misnomer? The Labour Party were venomously attacked by their former Prime Minister and Chancellor in a climate of hysteria and panic and were even accused of taking people's Post Office Savings Deposits. 'The Savings of the Poor', they laughably described them.

In the October issue of *The Labour Woman* of that year, Phillips was at her most vigorous as she awaited the General Election. 'Be ready, stand steady' she warned. Her 'Letter' was unusually long and she used it to spell out patiently what exactly had happened in the economic life of the country since the War. She said that she well understood that 'it is difficult for a woman who has to spend her time cooking, shopping, cleaning and mending — and thinking about making Friday's money last the week out, to know just what has happened,' but she did ask her to try to understand. She explained simply the international borrowings and the interest payments on debts, the value of the pound, and then, either through sheer frustration, or by design — in order to hold the attention of the reader, there was a sudden explosion: 'Just stop dusting the kitchen, or peeling the potatoes or whatever you are busy with, and try to follow this because your very existence depends on your voting right and to do so, you must know why.'

After this burst of urgency, she went on to explain carefully the value of the pound at home and abroad in terms of goods and prices. Unemployment, wages and the Banking interests, past and present policies were made clear. As to the future, well:

> We have now a great opportunity to get an international agreement on War Debts and Reparations and to place a truer value on the pound thus helping ourselves and other countries. We must use our currency wisely to stabilise prices and restore prosperity.
>
> We must control the money power of the world as we control health and education, war and peace. We must tear open the veils of the money temple. We must end the madness which keeps the world's millions poor in the midst of plenty.[14]

Chapter 23: The Last Campaign

On 7th October 1931 Parliament was dissolved and the General Election was held on 27th October two days before Phillips's fiftieth birthday. For Labour it could not have come at a worst time. Among its rank and file supporters in the country, there was shock and bewilderment, following their betrayal by the Party leaders. As for those who knew and understood the facts, there was no escape from downright bitterness and despair.

In Sunderland, Phillips's fellow candidate this time, was the barrister D. N. Pritt. He recalled that she asked him soon after the split, 'Where do you stand — with Ramsay Mac or with Uncle Arthur?'[1] Pritt added that it would have been difficult not to have supported Henderson especially in Sunderland where he saw for himself evidence of harrowing poverty. The desperation of the poor was such that 'one by one they killed their dogs because they had no scraps with which to feed them.'[2]

Pritt drew attention to Marion's personal qualities. 'She was idolised in Sunderland and I could see her real merits, one of which was a great capacity for organisation.'[3]

The latter resulted in a well-run election campaign in spite of overwhelming local obstacles. Pritt soon found, as others had done before him that indeed it was a difficult task to establish a good relationship with the local Constituency Party, and after contesting the seat in 1931, he left. In 1935 he fought and won the North Hammersmith seat.

In 1931, however, he and Phillips together fought the good fight. In their joint address, they explained how the world-wide depression had come about and condemned the National Government for its failure to deal with the situation, apart from imposing further hardships upon the poorest in the land.

They offered in detail Labour's plan for the future and ended: 'The National Government burks all the real issues. It can only agree in its desire to destroy the Labour Party, but while it asks for a 'free hand' and a 'blank cheque', it is so predominantly Tory that a victory for Mister MacDonald would in fact be a victory for tariffs and food taxes, reductions in social services, wages and unemployment benefits.'[4]

They returned to the 'morally intolerable' cuts in benefit in the closing stages of the campaign, fiercely attacking the international bankers who had insisted upon them.

Phillips's own 'Personal Message' to the electors of Sunderland, was an understatement of her efforts to minister to their needs. It was described by

Maureen Callcott as 'brief and modest' from an M.P. who, she emphasised, due to the ill-health of Alfred Smith had carried a heavy burden both at Westminster and in the constituency.[5]

She had indeed worked extremely hard, helping individuals with their problems, ranging from pensions, health insurance, maternity benefits to housing and agricultural wages and had constantly and forcefully brought Sunderland's difficulties in the areas of employment, education, shipping, ship-building and mining to the attention of the House. Naturally, she never missed an opportunity to speak on matters affecting the lives of women and children.[6] In return the working people of Sunderland in spite of the national panic, showed their appreciation of her gallant fight on their behalf by supporting her and Pritt, but the mathematics of the contest made victory impossible. The Election in Sunderland followed the pattern throughout the country of being a straight fight between the National Government candidates and those of the Labour Opposition. The Conservative candidates in Sunderland thus won both seats easily. Phillips could, however take comfort that her vote held firm. In 1929 she had taken 19.5% of the poll. In 1931 it was 18% — a drop of only 1.9%. Surely a remarkable feat in such disastrous circumstances. Pritt's vote too, maintained the 1929 percentage. He commented, 'We retained about 99% of the 1929 Labour vote in the Borough, but were overwhelmed because the Liberal candidates withdrew, leaving the Tories to collect every Tory vote, pretty nearly every Liberal vote and every panicked 'floating voter'.'[7]

In Durham County, Labour held only two seats out of the eighteen. Throughout the country only forty-six Labour candidates were elected compared with two hundred and eighty-eight in 1929. All the Front Bench leaders, with the exception of Lansbury, Attlee and Stafford Cripps were defeated. All the nine Labour women M.P.s lost their seats. The National Government had truly swept the country, almost annihilating Labour. Communities in which Labour thrived, were dazed and incredulous.

This was without doubt, the darkest hour in the Party's history. For Labour, however there would be another dawn. For Marion Phillips alas, her day was almost done. It was during the election campaign that Mrs. Deacon, her house-keeper, who was helping her in the fight, realised that she was ill.[8] Mrs. Gibb, too wrote in a letter, 'She was then a very sick woman — how she went through that Campaign, no one will fully understand'.

It must have been her indomitable spirit, because reading her Editor's letter in the November issue of *The Labour Woman*, we find her in cracking form, rallying the troops for the time 'when the next fight comes'. There were no lamentations or recriminations about the electoral devastation, only praise for the efforts of the 'heroes and heroines of the Labour Party' and in particular for the 'magnificent body of workers in Sunderland'. In fact, it was praise all round: for the audiences — for the quality of their questions and for their enthusiasm. Yet, being human, she did confess to being 'a little stunned still', but 'not yet shattered', as she pointed to the six and a half million voters who kept their heads and steadfastly refused to be engulfed in the panic created by their opponents.

They were beaten, she said by their betrayal by MacDonald and Snowden, enlarging on the shock and confusion that Snowden's bitter public attacks on Labour had produced. By describing the policy he himself helped the Labour Party to draw up, as 'bolshevism run mad', he undermined the trust among his former followers and frightened floating and first-time voters. She said that the 'finishing touch came when Runciman and Snowden terrified people into believing that Labour had endangered their savings though Snowden himself as Chancellor of the Exchequer had throughout been their guardian'.

Her contempt for MacDonald was withering. He had, she said, used the 'panic for all it was worth. It came well on top of the German mark nonsense which by that time in the campaign was wearing thin. His personal triumph is a strange one. It is the success of a beautiful voice, a fine presence, a careful use of romantic sentiment — of everything in short that can be used in the place of policy'.

After this curt dismissal of the former Labour leader, Phillips made a prophecy: 'Labour will rise stronger than ever and swing back to real power, but it may be a long time before the chance comes'. In the meantime, there would be a period of great economic and social problems at home, and of 'international distrust ... I cannot help fearing again the coming of war in this troubled world' she added sadly.

Then, returning to the present situation, she urged all Labour women to apply themselves to the task of reorganising and rebuilding. It was vital to try to win back the faint-hearted who had abandoned them. She advocated: 'Do not let us be bitter against them but set about the task of educating ourselves and them. For in knowledge alone can we find the barrier to panic, fear and puzzled despair. We must face our difficulties with courage, knowing that truth will in the end prevail'.[9]

This was Phillips at her best: calm, cheerful and courageous as she looked towards the future.

The relaxed tone of the November letter contrasted with that in the preceding issue. The October letter was a mini-lecture, delivered urgently, on the economic facts of life and written under great pressure. The November letter, post-bellum, was more of a fireside chat: good-natured, hopeful and positive. It suggested too, a feeling of great relief. Since the early summer, the growing tensions in the House culminating in crisis and betrayal, had produced anxious minds, heavy hearts and frayed nerves. It would account for the 'phillipsy' outburst in the October issue when she almost frantically had tried to make the housewife understand the impact of the forces arrayed against her, with the words: 'Just stop dusting the kitchen ... and try to follow this because your very existence depends on your voting right ...'[10]

Indeed, there can be little doubt that Labour M.P.s in 1931, fighting against the combined forces of the other parties, knew for certain that an overwhelming landslide defeat awaited them. In the circumstances of those tragic days, the landslide could have buried them all. It did not, and although the election result was devastating, the Party was not decimated. In the words of a popular song of the time, they could still pick themselves up ... 'and start all over again'.

Phillips seemed to voice this sense of relief in the November letter in *The Labour Woman*. It may too, have reflected a sense of personal deliverance. The election was over and done with and, although lost, she had battled bravely in two campaigns and during the two years between them, had toiled unremittingly in the service of Sunderland. Now that the seat was irrevocably lost, one wonders whether a gigantic burden had suddenly and mercifully been lifted from her shoulders.

We can only surmise. What we do know, however, is that with her usual gusto, immediately after the election she began to organise the campaign to secure one million new votes for the Labour Party. There is no evidence that she sought any rest after the election; nor is there a hint of any fear or anxiety.

'We must face our difficulties with courage,' she had said, and now, with faith and hope as well, she started on the task of reconstruction. By early December, she had held a considerable number of meetings in the North East. For her, speed was ever of the essence, and now she worked as if there was not a moment to lose. She visited West Hartlepool on 13th November and was cheered to find there 'a crowded hall' and great enthusiasm. Thirty new members had joined the Women's Section, she was able to inform the readers of the December issue of *The Labour Woman*. She announced cheerfully, that 'the Party ... is still solid and united' but she warned that if they were to win the next fight, 'there was a lot of educating to do and we are going to begin by educating ourselves'. She was full of plans and ready for action. There would be study circles and speakers' classes and one-day schools. For light relief, dramatic groups would be formed and from time to time, plays would be published in *The Labour Woman*. The December issue, in addition to the usual book page and short story, carried an announcement for those intent on merry making at Christmas, that patterns for fancy dress costumes, suitable for dances or carnivals could be obtained from Transport House.

But, even as she sought to lift the spirits during that festive season, Phillips was only too aware of the heavy hearts among the ranks of the unemployed, as minds daunted by despair grappled with the insoluble problems of existence. In an article in the same issue, headed 'How Shall We Pay The Rent?' She examined the appalling housing problem. The root cause of 'the rent difficulty' she insisted, was the need to build new houses. Wages were low and they and unemployment benefit were being cut at a time when an increasing number of houses were coming under decontrol, making the difficulties of finding accommodation worse than ever. Tenants too, were sub- letting rooms at high rents — a scandalous practice in her eyes. It was, of course another ugly aspect of penury. Because of the widespread misery caused by this lack of housing, Phillips even suggested that landlords might consider making a general amnesty, or a special reduction of rents because of insufficient funds.[11]

The plight of the poor that Christmas time was further discussed in her Editorial letter. She flatly blamed the Government for adding to it. She deplored that 'under the terror of the Bankers, we are setting out to ruin our trade and to threaten the peace of the world'. The pressure for food taxes alarmed her. The great need was to plan our own economic development and 'to co-operate with other countries so that the needs of each was met without harm to any'. She continued with a ringing appeal: 'Let us say, this Christmas: we are tired of the Money Terror. There is plenty of food, of raiment, of every material need. Let us stop this madness of misery amidst plenty, and pledge on Christmas Morning to use our own strength of body and mind to bring plenty within the reach of want'.[12]

The economic, social and moral philosophy of Marion Phillips was ever thus. The 'madness of misery amidst plenty'? What would she say today about the Mad Hatter's tea-party and the food mountains? What of the headless bureaucracy that actually pays farmers for NOT growing food, while the grim horsemen of famine and death ride relentlessly across desolate acres of the earth?

Back in the 1931 winter of despair, she saw that the first step on the way forward to creating a saner world, was to restore the faith of the British populace in the Labour Party, and she applied herself energetically to the task. She was already working on new projects, for instance, envisaging a new format for *The Labour Woman*, and possibly a change of name. In early and mid-December she attended two meetings of the Labour Party National Executive Committee and two meetings of the Standing Joint Committee. Among the matters discussed in the S.J.C. meeting on the 10th December were the Domestic Workers Charter; motherhood questions; unemployment insurance as it affected married women and the hours and conditions of work of shop assistants.[13] A great batch of correspondence relating to the S.J.C. claimed her attention, as well as more meetings although Christmas was drawing near ...

Margaret Gibb takes up the story: 'I saw her last in late December 1931 when we had a staff conference in Transport House. After the meeting she asked me to join her in her room for a chat. I think the last words I remember were, 'We are all so tired. I have so many things to do. I don't know where to start'.[14]

Two days later, she was admitted to hospital. Her housekeeper, Mrs. Deacon said, 'After going round her flat on December 20th, saying goodbye to the home she could so seldom afford time to fully enjoy, she turned and walked bravely away to face the end.

'I little thought that when I saw her sitting in bed, writing her New Year's Message for *The Labour Woman* that the end was so near.'[15]

For even from her bed in the Empire Nursing Home in Victoria, she carried on with her work. In her January letter,[16] she mentioned the series of conferences just completed in December and saying how she had been looking forward to some 'quiet days at the office and at home' between Christmas and the New Year, planning study pamphlets and a 'host of other jobs before renewing the National Campaign with six National Conferences, each to be held on a Saturday between January 16th and February 20th'.

All this, she wrote, she had planned, when 'Bang, like a hammer down on my head comes one of the plagues of Job'. She had, she said, for twenty years been 'in the thick of the fight and now had to be out of it for this splendid effort'. It was, she said, a nightmare following the previous nightmare of the Labour defeat. The second nightmare was the operation that lay before her.

The 'splendid effort' to which she referred was the campaign to win another million Labour votes. The remainder of the message, therefore, was devoted to exhorting her women to greater effort to swell the Party membership. She hoped that the women would supply half the number. As for the campaign itself, she wrote, 'Well, I am out of it. I hope each of you will do an extra turn for me' and appealed to each Women's Section to send her a 'present' of twenty new members to help her convalescence. Then, after advising delegates about framing resolutions for the National Conference of Labour Women to be held in Brighton in the following June, she briefly returned to her own plight: 'I am writing this before Christmas, though you will get it after January 1st. How I shall welcome 1932! Indeed, I wish it were June already'. She herself loved June, 'England's month of sunshine' as she called it. It was too, the month of the Women's Annual Conference. She would, according to Annie Townley, one of the regional organisers, encourage a little liveliness at a meeting with, 'Cheer up, you are a DULL lot. Think of June and come to Brighton'.[17]

Alas, when the women would next meet at Brighton, it would be without 'The Chief'. Surgery revealed wide-spread cancer of the stomach. She died on 23rd January 1932.

Barbara Ayrton Gould, Chairman of the Standing Joint Committee of Industrial Women's Organisations, visited her friend constantly during those last weeks of her life. She remarked later, "Marion faced death with the same high courage with which she had faced life and her last message to Labour women was, 'Tell them to carry on and consolidate the Movement; the future of Socialism depends on the work of the next few years'". Another frequent visitor to her bedside was her old colleague for over twenty years — J. S. Middleton. He too, described her fearlessness as the end drew near.[18]

Margaret Gibb recollected — even after a span of fifty years — seeing the notice of the death of Marion Phillips on a newsagent's board in Leeds, and immediately hurrying down to London feeling 'lost and bewildered'.[19]

The same feeling of loss was evident in Arthur Henderson's comment to *The*

Daily Herald,: 'The keen sense of personal love I had for her is shared by every member of the National Labour Party Executive'. He went on to describe her as 'a woman of striking intellectual force, powerful personality and great industry'.[20]

Soon the press at home and overseas were recounting details of her life's work and paying tributes to her. One of the first newspapers to carry the notice of her obituary was the *Arbeiter Zeitung*.

The *Manchester Guardian* expressed the view that she was, by education, special training and experience, the best equipped of all the Party's leading women. It added that 'getting things done was always her strong point'. Another edition published on the same day mentioned 'her organising ability and genial and persuasive personality' but tended to regret that she had concentrated her work in the narrow field of working women's interests.[21]

Considering that Phillips had, in the words of Lucy Middleton, 'constructed the most formidable organisation of politically conscious women in Britain — probably the world',[22] it is not surprising that the latter part of the comment in *The Guardian* set up a storm of protest from women. It is however, fair to point out that her long-standing friend and colleague made a not dissimilar observation in her own warm tribute to her: 'Her great intellectual gifts and powerful personality might have brought her greater renown'.[23]

Phillips had certainly concentrated on that very segment of the population that needed the most help and encouragement to develop into well-informed human beings, equal in every way to their male counterparts. Education was the key to their new existence and she slogged with might and main to provide them with the knowledge essential for their advance. As social and political awareness grew in working-class wives, they followed her into the Labour Party. However, this special commitment of hers did not exclude other aspects of her interests and training. Indeed both *The Morning Post* and *The Manchester Guardian* Obituary Notices carried the reference by Commander J. M. Kenworthy, earlier quoted in this book, to the 'invaluable' work performed by a special committee of which she was secretary, set up by the Parliamentary Labour Party to examine currency and exchange questions. Commander Kenworthy, as we saw earlier, concluded his remarks thus: 'She was one of the most far-sighted prophets in the Labour Party and a great economist'.[24]

The *Daily Herald* was supportive of this view. It noted, 'In Parliamentary work, Dr. Phillips's chief interest according to her own statement, lay rather in the direction of monetary policy and international finance than in any of the less fundamental reforms'.[25] The *Herald*, then continued, 'her contributions to debate were not feminine in the ordinary sense of the word, for she had the clear brain of the organiser and something of the masculine outlook'.[26]

Marion Phillips herself without doubt, would have found that to be an extraordinary statement. Since women, unlike men, seem to have a specific talent for dealing with a whole raft of duties simultaneously — while for example, running a household — does not that in itself, give them a flying start as organisers?

As the British and foreign press paid tribute to Phillips, personal messages flowed in from abroad — from politicians and colleagues and delegates to the international gatherings that had been so close to her heart. From Germany, Austria, Belgium, Holland, Czechoslovakia, Finland, Hungary and France came words of profound sadness and appreciation. Perhaps it was Josef Buchler, Member of the Hungarian Parliament who best summed up the widespread sense of loss: 'She ... understood our difficulties ... I shall never forget her'.

Truly, she did have a thorough knowledge of these countries, visiting them as often as she could. A few months before her death, after briefly visiting the Hungarian capital, she had written of its sad and poverty-stricken state under the Horthy regime.[27] The previous January she had witnessed the abuses of the Pilsudski regime in Poland, as well as helping the victims in a practical way.

From Belgium, Alice Pels, Member of the Presidium of the Women's Committee of the Labour and Socialist International, wrote of Marion's intellectual and moral strength adding, 'I am afraid she will not be replaced so easily ... not internationally'.[28]

Her old colleague Adelheid Popp, Member of the Austrian Parliament, mourning 'so beloved a friend', made a special reference to the 'rapidity' with which Phillips would always grasp ideas expressed in foreign languages, which secured an even closer bond between them.[29]

Both the Secretary of the Finnish Women's Social Democratic Federation and Member of Parliament, and Mrs. Karpiskova, Member of the Second Chamber of the Czechoslovakia Parliament wrote of her tireless work for international understanding and for raising the standard of women's lives.[30]

From all over Europe, came the same message: the woman with 'the remarkable personality'[31] had become their leader. It was Marion Phillips who was invited to draft the minutes of their meetings and at that last Conference in Vienna in July 1931; it was she who was invited to present the Report in a speech to the Congress of the Socialist and Labour International a few days later in the same city. The women looked to her, admiring her intellectual capacity and warming to her humanity and understanding. They sensed her internationalism: her eagerness to improve the lot of women in a world at peace.

The funeral service took place at Whitefield's Tabernacle, London on 27th January before cremation at Golders Green. It was described with great feeling by Hannen Swaffer in the *Daily Herald* under the banner headline 'Women Honour Marion Phillips'. Swaffer led off: 'Never was a woman paid greater honour than when in Whitefield's Tabernacle yesterday, humble folk laid flowers around the coffin of Marion Phillips and a large gathering of women, well-known and humble, listened to words of burning eulogy. It was a service of rededication to a great ideal, 'Marion Phillips lived and died for the people' that was the keynote of all the speeches'.

Swaffer described how the Rev. A. D. Belden, after he had read *St. Paul's Hymn of Love*, said of Marion, 'She was Jewish by birth ... a member of the race which in the judgement of many of us, gave the Supreme Revelation of God to mankind and from which there emerged The Saviour of the World. Certainly, the spirit of Saviourhood dwelt richly in Marion Phillips because she gave of her strength and her talent prodigally to bring social redemption to the womanhood of the world.'

The crowded congregation heard too, prayers of thanksgiving for her life and quotations from *In Memoriam*. They sang *Jerusalem* and *England Arise* and afterwards Mrs. Ada Salter laid a laurel wreath on the coffin on behalf of the Women of the Labour Party.

Swaffer referred too, to Lansbury's tribute that told of her long fight for the working woman, of how she had forced child welfare upon the local authorities and how she struggled and endured. George spoke of William Morris and Hyndman and Keir Hardie and he classed Marion with them. 'She had a heart that made her hate preventable suffering and for the embodiment of the brotherhood of all ... I think we ought ... to be exultant that although she lived so short a time, she lived so great a life.'

Barbara Ayrton Gould eloquently referred to Marion's heroic task in raising money to save the families of miners during the 1926 Lock-out, 'knowing how women without food and without clothes were giving birth to children ... Behind all her talents was a passionate love for humanity ... She hated misery, injustice and poverty ... She built up the Women's Movement with her heart and soul and blood ... All through her life, she desired to give service to the world. Her one thought in dying was to give service ...'

Swaffer commented further, "Service' was the keynote of yesterday's memorial ceremony,' adding movingly, 'It was something never to be forgotten.'[32]

Later, as the extent of their loss was borne in upon the whole Labour Movement, more tributes appeared in print. To Walter Citrine, the General Secretary of the T.U.C. Phillips was 'a radiant personality, a massive intellect, a fighter without fear or venom, who hated cant and snobbery'.[33]

Mrs. Ayrton Gould who agreed to serve temporarily as Chief Woman Officer, commented further on her 'vitality and immense energies that swept away all difficulties', and she referred to Henderson's pronouncement that the 'Monument of her Life' was the Women's Movement itself. The importance of the Women's Organisation was described by him as one of the most remarkable phases of Labour's progress, re-iterating, 'to no one more than Marion Phillips is credit due'.[34]

At the same time, Henderson echoed the regret of many others, that she had gone 'in the heyday of her splendid powers', because the future seemed to promise richer opportunities.[35] The conviction that Phillips was destined for a shining future was shared by other Party Leaders. Ellen Wilkinson declared:

She would have made a magnificent minister ... When men say we have not yet produced a front rank statesman, remind them that Marion Phillips's death robbed us of a promising candidate for the highest honour.[36]

Margaret Bondfield too, the country's first Woman Cabinet Minister, wrote,

Always she gave the impression of having reserve powers, as yet unused.[37]

Alas, the 'reserve powers' tragically remained untapped as the night closed in upon her. Had she lived, with her administrative experience during the First World War and her deep knowledge of European politics, she would have made an extremely valuable contribution to the execution of the war against Hitler.

As to the pre-war period of the Thirties, the collective wisdom of her Parliamentary colleagues at the time of her death was that 'on the Opposition benches she would have easily been the outstanding figure ... As Secretary of the Labour Currency Group in the House of Commons, she showed a grasp of essentials, coupled with a lucidity of statement that showed how able a Minister the Labour Premier lost by not giving her the Front Bench rank that would undoubtedly have been hers in the next Labour Government.'[38]

There is no doubt that Marion Phillips would have brought a wealth of talent and expertise to any high office at any time. Margaret Gibb was firmly of the opinion — shared by many others — that 'she could have been our first Socialist Woman Prime Minister.'[39]

She certainly had the qualities of leadership: vision, capacity, courage and infinite common-sense. Her talent to inspire loyalty and devotion was such that a quarter of a million women in the early Twenties were ready to trust and follow her. One of them said when she died, 'Because her life touched theirs, a hundred thousand women will take up the task she has so well begun.'[40]

However, after the death of Marion Phillips, no other woman in the Labour Party found herself in such a position of power and influence. Phillips, given a free rein, had driven a coach and horses through every conceivable obstacle in order to 'get things done'. Although she had emphasised shortly before her death that the next few years would be crucial to the Party's recovery, the drive to educate women, to interest them in social and political affairs, to train them to sit on governing bodies and to acquire complete equality with men — all this, somehow lost its momentum. As one of her colleagues said: 'There can never be another Marion Phillips.'[41] She was right, and consequently there was no Second Crusade.

It is now nearly seventy years since the death of Marion Phillips. What would she think of the present position of women? She would certainly be dismayed at the continuing failure to appoint more women to top posts in the professions, and while there are at present more women Members of Parliament than ever before, she would, without doubt have regarded the quota method of selecting

Labour women candidates as unworthy and demeaning. Women, she would have insisted, are perfectly capable of standing on their own two feet and of proving their worth, with pride and dignity. In particular, she would have stressed, competent and politically involved mothers, who at some stage, wish to stand for Parliament are especially well-qualified to do so. Rebecca West, in her essay in the book *Women and the Labour Party*, took the same view, observing that bringing up a family is a far better preparation for Parliamentary duties than 'prosecuting scoundrels'.

However, Phillips — always a realist, would still be aware of the obstacles. While J. S. Middleton applauded her 'contribution to the growth of independent thought and to the political use of the influence she herself had created' in the campaign for equality of status for women; for the right to work for equal pay and conditions; for decent homes and schools; for the provision of maternity care and child welfare, and a host of other reforms, she herself, nevertheless, understood well enough, that women as childbearers would always be at a disadvantage, and that their special ability to tackle a whole range of tasks at the same time, was always likely to be exploited to the full. It is the working mother, who in addition to any post she may hold, still has to run the home with all its myriad responsibilities, unless she is able to afford domestic help on a fairly substantial scale. Always insisting that 'a paper equality' was not enough, Phillips would today be strongly urging a development in the system of maternity leave and wholesale provision of child-care facilities jointly funded by government and the employers for mothers who need or choose to go out to work. By the same token she would be strongly in favour of extending similar funding to those women who choose to remain at home to look after their children themselves, during their early years. Should this financial provision come from tax reforms and substantial personal allowances for the children, it would be in line with the Family Endowment Scheme advocated by Labour women earlier last century, namely that all working women should be treated alike. There is a long way to go and Phillips's concern for the overworked woman, expressed in her best-known lines is still valid today!

> The nation has not yet attempted to repay the debt it owes to the patient toil of tired women, a toil that could with thought and determination be replaced by lives in which happy hours of work alternated with the joys of fruitful leisure.

The visible public memorials to Marion Phillips were few: a block of flats bearing her name in Islington; an endowed bed at the Mary Macarthur Holiday Home for Women; a plaque presented to the Labour Party by the Standing Joint Committee of Industrial Women's Organisations. In addition, the Marion Phillips International Fund was set up to provide educational opportunities for women from developing countries. Annual contributions made by the Women's Sections towards the Fund, are administered by the National Labour Women's Advisory Committee.

Yet, perhaps her most fitting epitaph lies in her father's prophetic words uttered in 1888 when his youngest daughter was in her seventh year. A reference to his address to the Melbourne Jewish Literary Society is found elsewhere in this book and it may be recalled that, looking to the future, he pledged the co-operation of his own people with others to strive to achieve a worthwhile world:

We will assist in the making of wise and just laws, in the promotion of charity, in the amelioration of social conditions. We will aid you to elevate, to beautify, to refine existence.

It was left to Hannen Swaffer to write the postscript to her life. His moving words issue a challenge to the women of today:

One woman alone had done so much ... and there are so many women. If they copied Marion Phillips they could transform the world.

Notes

Chapter 1 The Family
1. Fox, Len   E. *Phillips Fox and his Family*, 1985, 97.
2. Chapman, M. *The Humanist Jew*, 1981, 91.
3. Fox, Len   E. *Phillips Fox and his Family*, 1985, 30.
4. ibid, 31.
5. ibid, 62.
6. ibid, 59.
7. Chapman, M. *The Humanist Jew*, 1981, 82.
8. Fox, Len E. *Phillips Fox and his Family*, 1985, 130.
9. ibid, 113.
10. ibid, 112.
11. Reid, M.O. *The Ladies came to stay*, 1960.
12. *The Labour Woman*, March 1932, 37.
13. Fox, Len E. *Phillips Fox and his Family*, 1985, 116.

Chapter 2 London: Attractions and Influences
1. Crocks, Will *Labour MP for Woolwich*, 1903–22.
2. Fox, Len E. *Phillips Fox and his Family*, 1985, 123.
3. Blatchford, R. *My Eighty Years* (Cassells. 1931), 184.
4. Williams, F. *Fifty Years March. The Rise of the Labour Party*, 1950, 74.
5. *The Book of the Labour Party, Vol 3*, 232 –7.

Chapter 3 The League, The Vote and the Unions
1. Collette, C. *For Labour and for Women*. The Women's Labour League 1906–1918 Man. Univ. Press 1987, 30–4.
2. Hollis, P. *Ladies Elect: Women in English Local Government 1865 - 1914*. Clarendon Press Oxford 1987, 412.
3. Annual Report Women's Labour League 1913–4, 62. & WLL Leaflet No. 6 Labour Women as Guardians of the Poor.
4. Hansard. Vol 251. Cols. 123–6. 14 -4 -1931.
5. Hamilton, M.A. *Mary Macarthur —A Biographical Sketch*, 1925, L Parsons.
6. ibid.
7. Bunbury, H.N. ed. *Lloyd George's Ambulance Wagon — Memoirs of A. J. Braithwaite*. Methuen. 1957, 235.
8. Hamilton, M. A. *Mary Macarthur — A Biographical Sketch*. L. Parsons.

Chapter 4 The Crusade Begins
1. Tribute. *Daily Herald*, Jan. 28 1932.
2. Hansard. Col. 1816. Children and Young Persons Bill 29 Nov 1929.
3. Collette, C. *For Labour and for Women. The Women's Labour League 1906–1918*, Man. Univ. Press. 1987. 132–4.
4. MacDonald Papers 1157–8.

5. Collette, C. *For Labour and for Women. The Womens Labour League 1906 –1918*, Man. Univ. Press. 1987. 133.

Chapter 5 Babies and Children
1. *The Labour Woman*. January 1924.
2. *The League Leaflet*. Jan. 1913
3. ibid. Dec. 1911.
4. ibid. Nov. 1911.
5. ibid. Jan. 1913. 1st Annual Report on the Baby Clinic.
6. Conference on "The Care of Babies and Young Children" March 1912. Later published as booklet: "The needs of Little Children" 1912.
7. Report of the Registrar General dealing with Births in England and Wales printed in Oct 13 issue of *The Labour Woman*.
8. *The Labour Woman* Oct 13 quotes Chief MO for Local Government Boards. 1913.
9. Fabian Tract No 10 'Life on a Pound a Week'.
10. *The League Leaflet*. Oct 1912. Refers 1910 Report of Sir G. Newman MO Board of Education supporting Open - Air Schools as advocated by MP.
11. *The School Doctor and the Home*. Booklet published in 1913.
12. Report of the Chief Medical Officer for Board of Education published 1909.
13. ibid. published 1910.

Chapter 6 1912
1. Hansard Col 1816–9. Seconding R Sorensen. Children and Young Person's Bill 29 Nov 1929.
2. *The League Leaflet*. Dec. 1912.
3. Fox, Len. *E. Phillips Fox and his Family*. 105.
4. Women's Labour League 8th Annual Report 1912–13.
5. Hollis, P. *Ladies Elect: Women in English Local Government 1865–1914*, 1987, Clarendon Press, p.413–4.
6. Women's Labour League, 6th Annual Report, 1913–14, p.59.
7. Hollis, P. *Ladies Elect: Women in English Local Government 1865–1914*, p.406.
8. ibid. p.430.
9. *Women's Labour League Leaflet*, Sept. 1912, Review of MacDonald's book on Syndicalism.

Chapter 7 Take Your Tickets, Ladies
1. *The League Leaflet*, Feb. 1912.
2. ibid. June 1912 (No. 18).
3. ibid. April 1912 (No. 16).
4. ibid.
5. ibid, May 1912, refers to *Life As We Have Known It*, edited by M. Llewelyn Davies, Hogarth Press, 1931.
6. *The League Leaflet*, July 1912 (No 19)
7. ibid.
8. ibid p.5.
9. ibid. Feb. 1912, p.20.
10. ibid. Aug. 1912, p.7.
11. ibid. Sept. 1912.
12. ibid.
13. ibid. Dec. 1912, p.11.
14. ibid. pp. 11 & 12.

15. ibid. April 1913, p.10.
16. ibid.
17. *The Labour Woman*, 'Poverty in Switzerland', Aug. 1913.

Chapter 8   Grass Roots and Brass Tacks
 1. Williams, Francis *Fifty Years March. The Rise of the Labour Party*, Odhams, 1950, p. 204.
 2. ibid.
 3. Kingston, Beverley *Women at Work*, 'Yours Very Truely, Marion Phillips', Australian Society for the Study of Labour History, ed. A. Curthoys, S. Eade and P. Spearitt, Sydney, 1975.

Chapter 9   The War Years
 1. *The League Leaflet*, early 1913.
 2. *The Labour Woman*, 'The Women's International Council of Socialist and Labour Organisations, British Section', 1914.
 3. Berne Meeting, March 1915.
 4. Longman, M. 'Women and Internationalism', *Women and the Labour Party*, 1918.
 5.*The Book of the Labour Party*, Vol I, 'War Emergency Committee', p.203.
 6. *The Labour Woman*, 'Appeal to Women Workers', 1915, pp.344–5.
 7. Fox, L.E. *Phillips Fox and His Family*, p.123.
 8. *The Labour Woman*, March 1932.
 9. ibid.
10. Kingston, Beverely *Yours Very Truely Marion Phillips*, p.125.
11. *The Book of the Labour Party*, Vol II, p.251–???.
12. *League Leaflets* and *The Labour Woman*, various issues since 1912 re. the National Insurance Act.
13. Cole, M. I. (ed.) *Beatrice Webb Diaries*, Vol I, 1912–24, pp.80–2.
14. Hansard, 9th Nov. 1929.
15. Lloyd George, D. *War Memoirs*, Vol II, p.1160–1.
16. Cole, M. I. (ed.) *Beatrice Webb Diaries*, Vol I, pp.87–92.
17. Owen, Frank *Tempestuous Journey*, p.336, Hutchinson, 1954.
18. Lloyd George, D. *War Memoirs*, Vol I, pp.793 *et seq*.
19. The Consumer Council see 21 Consumer Files M.P.s Labour Party Archives.
20. Lloyd George, D. *War Memoirs*, Vol II, p.1159.
21.Phillips, M. Consumer Files. Papers. Phillips Archive Labour Party Library, cc/ccc.
22. ibid, cc/ccc/39–40.
23. ibid, cc/mil 26.
24. ibid, cc/mil 27–9.
25. ibid, cc/mil 39–41.
26. ibid, cc/mil 83–90.
27. ibid, cc/mil 94–106.
28. ibid, cc/mil 56–66.
29. ibid, c/gen 100.
30. ibid, cc/gen 103–9.

Chapter 10   Chief Woman Officer
 1. *Souvenir, Women's Labour League*, 17t July,1909.
 2. Williams, Francis *Fifty Years March. The Rise of the Labour Party*, p.286.
 3. *The Book of the Labour Party*, p.246.
 4. Manning, Leah *A Life for Education*.
 5. *The Labour Woman*, 'Memorial Tributes', March 1932, p.35.

6. *The Labour Woman*, 'The Policy of the Labour Party', Dec. 1918.

7. *The Book of the Labour Party*, Vol I, p.246.

8. ibid. Vol II, p.250.

9. *The Labour Magazine*, Vol II, May 1923–April 1924.

10. Fox, Len E. *Phillips and His Family*, p.122–3.

11. Cole, M. I. (ed) *Diaries. B. Webb*, Vol I, Longmans, 1952, p.116.

12. *The Labour Woman*, May 1965 'Tributes' and article by M. Gibb.

13. ibid, March 1932.

Chapter 11   Much Work and Little Leisure

1. *The Labour Woman*, Memorial Issue, March 1932.

2. ibid.

3. ibid. Sept. ???

4. ibid. '199 Resolutions re. Women Court Officers', Women's Labour
   Conference, June. 1924.

5. Report of the Annual Labour Women's Conference, June 1924, Labour Party
   Archives, Labour Party Library.

6. S. J. C. Records, Labour Party Archives, 1919–20.

7. Phillips, M. Archives and papers in Labour Party Archives, 1919–20.

8. Fox, L. E. *Phillips Fox and His Family*, p.123.

9. *The Labour Woman*, 'Housing at Home and Abroad', April 1920.

10. International Conferences. M.P. Archives, Labour Party Library. *The Labour Woman*, Nov.
    1922. ibid. Jan. 1923.

11. Fox, L. E. *Phillips Fox and His Family*, p.???. *The Labour Woman*, Memorial Issue, March
    1932.

12. Cole, M. I. (ed.) *Beatrice Webb's Diaries*, Vol II, p.150.

13. Kingston, Beverely *Yours Very Truly Marion Phillips*.

14. Personal information.

Chapter 12   Women and the Labour Party

1. Tuckwell, G. *The National Dictionary of Labour Biography* ed by Bellamy, J. & Savile, J., Vol I
   & VII.

2. Lawrence, S. *The Book of the Labour Party*, Vol III, p.330.

3. Cole, M. I. & Blatchford, R. *Makers of the Labour Movement*, Longman, 1948.

4. *Who's Who*, 1929.

5. Llewelyn-Davies, M. *The National Dictionary of Labour Biography*.

6. Cole, M. I. *Beatrice Webb Diaries*, Vol. I, 1912–24, Longman, 1932.

7. Longman, M. *The National Dictionary of Labour Biography*

8. McMillan, *The National Dictionary of Labour Biography*

9. Hamilton, M. A. *Mary Macarthur — a biographical sketch*, Leonard Parsons, 1925.

10. Lawrence, S. *The Book of the Labour Party*,

11. Bondfield, M. *The Book of the Labour Party*, Vol III, p.259.

12. Conway, K. St J. (Mrs Bruce Glasier) *The Book of the Labour Party*, Vol III, p.106.

13. Smillie, R. *The Book of the Labour Party*, Vol III, p.273.

Chapter 13   Homes for the Future

1. *The League Leaflet*, No. 25, Jan. 1913 'Bathrooms: A First Necessity'.

2. *The Labour Woman*, July 1913, 'Discussion on Houses Utopian etc.'

3. Knevitt, C. *The Times*, 18 Aug. 1988, Architectural correspondent, refers to Coleman,
   Alice, 'Utopia on Trial' and Freeman, Hugh (ed.) *British Journal of Psychiatry*, also to

Murtagh, J. King's College, London; *The Health Implication of Building Design*, see also Hawkes, N. *The Times*, 29 Aug. 1991, Science editor, refers to Prof. Coleman's research on Social-breakdown Estates.
4. Marks, L. *Weekend Observer*, 7 Nov. 19 ??? article on 'Urban Humanity' — the principles of Ralph Erskine, RIBA and 1987 Gold Medallist.

Chapter 14   Open Letter to a Royal Bride

1. Masterman, C. F. G. *England After the War*, London, 1922, p.97.
2. Runciman, W. J. *Relative Deprivation and Social Justice*, Routledge, 1966, pp.58–60.
3. *The Labour Woman*, Feb. 1923, 'An Open Letter to Lady Elizabeth Bowes-Lyon.
4. BBC Radio, A Conversation with Lady Ryder of Warsaw — Sue Ryder, 4th July 1990, BBC Archives.

Chapter 15   Maternity Care and Birth Control

1. Adoption of the Washington Conventions, 1919.
2. Phillips, M. Article in the *Labour Magazine*, 'Socialist Women Meet in Switzerland', Jan. 1930, pp.454–5.
3. Sanderson-Fuyniss, A. 'The Citizenship of Women', *The Book of the Labour Party*, Vol. II, p.250.
4. Phillips, M. *The Labour Woman*, March 1924, and S. J. C. Report ton the June Conference in *The Labour Woman*, JUne 1924, p.85.
5. Hamilton, M. A. *Arthur Henderson*, p.117.
6. ibid, pp.268–70.
7. Report, 1927 Blackpool Labour Party Conference, pp.233–4.
8. Werthwimer, E. *Prophet of the Labour Party, 1929*, Putnam, London, pp.91-2.
9. *The Labour Woman*, Obituary, March 1932, p.26.
10. Reports and Proceedings of the 3rd Women's Socialist and Labour International Conference, Vol. III, Brussels, Aug. 1928, p.24.
11. Phillips, M. Labour Party Archives, 9 Aug. ???

Chapter 16   Women and the Miners' Lockout

1. *The Labour Woman*, Tribute by Ebby Morris, March 1932.
2. ibid. Tribute, March 1932 to her generosity re. expenses of administration.
3. Report from coalfields 1926, Labour Party Archives.
4. BBC's 'Children in Need' annual appeal, BBC Archives.

Chapter 17   Member of Parliament

1. *Bulletin of the N. East Labour History Society*, No. 20, 1986, p.9.
2. ibid.
3. ibid, p.10.
4. *The Labour Magazine*, Vol III, 1929–30, pp.28–30.
5. *The Labour Woman*, May 1931.
6. *Autobiography of D. N. Pritt*, Part I (Lawrence and Wishart), p.29.
7. *The Labour Woman*, Feb. 1932.
8. ibid.
9. Hansard, Vol 229, Col.768–770, 9 July 1929.
10. ibid, Col. 1065, 11 July 1929.
11. Brookes, Pamela *Women at Westminster*,
12. Hansard, Vol. 230, Col 626, 18 July 1929.
13. ibid, Col. 50–51, 16 July 1929.

14. ibid, Col. 920, 22 July 1929.
15. Hansard, 28 Nov. 1930 — 2nd Reading — The Children's (Provision of Footwear) Bill.
16. Hansard, Vol. 231, Col. 1816–1819, 7th Nov. 1929, Children and Young Persons' Bill.
17. ibid, Col. 1651, 21 Nov. 1921, Children Act 1908 Amendment.
18. ibid, Col. 1052–1064, 6 Nov. 1929 & Col 1268–9, Nov. 1929.
19. ibid, Col 2476–9, 15 Nov. 1929, Annual Holiday Bill.
20. ibid, Col. 356–8, Dec. 1929, Unemployment Insurance (No. 2) Bill.
21. ibid, Vol. 237, Col 591, 27 March 1930, Milk for Schoolchildren; Col 894, 31 March 1930, Nursery Schools; Vol. 241, Col. 1103, 15 July 1930; Vol. 241, Col. 615, 10 July 1930, Question of Maternal Morality.
22. ibid, Col.600, 27 March 1930, Disablement Benefit.
23. ibid, Col. 590–1, 27 March 1930, Domestic Science Teaching.
24. ibid, Vol CCXXXVII Col. 2377, 10 April 1930, question on Housing.
25. ibid, Vol. CCXXXVII Col. 2042–4, 8 April 1930, Housing (No. 2) Bill.
26. ibid, Vol. CCXXXVII Col. 2633, 14 April 1930, question on Training Schemes.
27. ibid, Vol. CCXLIV Col. 771–4, 4 Nov. 1930, debate on address — Economic Situation.
28. ibid, Vol CCXLV, Col. 364–7, 18 Nov. 1930, Agricultural Land Utilisation (Money) Bill (Allotments and Smallholdings).
29. ibid, Vol. CCXLV, Col. 1720–3, 28 Nov. 1930, Nationality of Women Act.
30. ibid, Vol. CCXLVII, Col. 734–6, 26 Jan. 1931, India debate — Round Table Conference.
31. Brookes, Pamela *Women at Westminster.*

Chapter 18   Electoral Reform

1. *The British Labour Party,* Vol II, p.203–5.
2. English History Annual Register, 1929, PRO, p.28.
3. HLRO Cmd. 3636. Letter from Lord Ullswater to the Prime Minister, 17 July 1930 and English History Annual Register, p.64.
4. Hansard, Vol. 247, Cols. 1733–40, 3 Feb. 1931, The Representation of the People (No. 2) Bill.

Chapter 19   Gathering Clouds

1. Press reports of the Polish Elections, January 1931: *Daily News* (Perth, Western Australia); *Morning Herald* (Sydney); *The Sun* (Melbourne); various British newspapers.
2. Prague International Committee of Labour and Scoialist Women, 1931. *Labour Party Annual Report*, 1931, p.309. *The Labour Woman, February, 1931.*
3. General situation causing anxiety. *The Labour Woman*, April 1931, p.50; May 1931, p.66, Treatment of Sick O.A.P.s See also note 4.
4. *Hansard.* Vol. CCXLI, Cols. 123–6. Supply Debate 14-4-1931.
5. Inadequate Housing Programmes and Maternity Services. See note 4.
6. See note 5. *Hansard* Vol. CCCCXXIX, Col. 2256. 9 July, 1931.
7. *Hansard*, Vol. CCL, Col. 1024, 17 September 1931.
8. *Hansard*, Suppl. Vol. CCLVI, Col. 1023–4.
9. Questions relating to National Maternity Service: *Hansard* Vol. CCLVI, Col. 1471, 22 September 1931 & *HAnsard*, Vol. CCLVI Col. 1827, 24 September 1931.
10. Second Reading Unemployment Insurance (No. 3) Bill. *Hansard*, Vol. CCLIV, Col. 2130, 2158, 2163, 8 July 1931.
11. Inter-departmental Committee (Marley Committee) P.R.O. Cmd. 3911 HLG, set up 24 November 1930.
12. Report of Marley Committee, HLG 41/35, p.54. Submitted 11 July 1931. Minority Reporty, pp.58–60.
13. The Gorell Depart. Committee 1930-31.

Chapter 20   The Cinderellas

1. *The Labour Woman*, June 1931.
2. *The Labour Party Annual Report, 1931*, p.34.
3. ibid, p.36.
4. Margaret Bonfield, *Women and the Labour Party*, p.66.
5. F. Dawes*Not in Front of the Servants*, p.149.
6. ibid, p.29.
7. ibid, p.139.
8. Parliamentary Paper, 1919, Cmd. 67 xxix.
9. Phillips Archive, Labour Party Library.
10. S. Lewenhak, *Women and Trade Unions*, p.183.
11. ibid, p.184.
12. ibid, p.207.
13. *Manchester Guardian*. Obituary, 25 January 1932.
14. *What's Wrong With Domestic Service?*, pamphlet, S.J. C. Files, Labour Party Library.
15. *The Daily Herald*, Peminist Forum.
16. *The Buenos Aires Journal*.
17. *The Daily Standard*(Brisbane, Australia).
18. The fourteen proposals in 'The Domestic Workers' Charter'.
19. *The Labour Woman*, Adoption of Charter, June 1931.
20. ibid, Vienna Resolution, July 1931.
21. S.J.C. Reports, Labour Party Library, July 1931.
22. ibid.
23. ibid.
24. S. Lewenhal, *Women and Trade Unions*, p.207.
25. *The Daily Herald*, Tributes, 25 January 1932.

Chapter 21   Vienna

1. *The Labour Woman*, August 1931, p.136.
2. ibid.
3. *The Labour Party Annual Report*, 1931, p.317.
4. *The Labour Woman*, August 1931, p.136.
5. *The Labour PArty Annual Report*, 1931, p.318.
6. *The Labour Woman*, August 1931, p.137.
7. *The Labour PArty Annual Report*, 1931, p.318.
8. *The Labour Woman*, AUgust 1931, p.137 & *The Labour Party Annual Report*, 1931, p.320.
9. *The Labour Woman*, August 1931, p.137 & *The Labour Party Annual Report, 1931*, p.319.
10. *Women and Men in britain 1991*, Equal Opportunities Commission.
11. *The Labour PArty Annual Report, 1931* p.320. & *The Labour Woman*, August 1931, p.137.
12. Domestic Workers – *Labour Party Annual Report*, 1931, p.320.
13. *The Labour Woman*, Augsut 1931, p.320. & *The Labour Party Annual Report, 1931* p.320.
14. Phillips's final appeal to the Congress (Vienna) on behalf of women, the 'greatest force'.

Chapter 22   Crisis

1. *Manchester Guardian*, 25 January 1932.
2. R. Skidelsky, *Politicians and the Slump*, p.388–95.
3. Macmillan Committee – Evidence, p.388 and footnote 2502, 2512, 3959, 3987. Memo. Association of Chambers of Commerce p.225, paragraph 15.
4. R. Skidelsky, *Politicians and the Slump*, p.394.
5. ibid, p.395.

6. Reference to Phillips's letter to the Prime Minister.
7. *The Labour Woman*, November 1931, Editor's Letter.
8. ibid, September 1931, Editor's Letter.
9. S.J.C. Records, 17 September 1931, Labour PArty Library.
10. Questions in the House, September 1931. *Hansard:* Vol. CCLVI, Cols. 838–9, 16 September 1931; Vol. CCLVI, Col. 840, 16 September 1931; Vol. CCLVI, Col. 1460, 22 September 1931; Vol CCLVI, Col. 1467, 22 September 1931; Vol. CCLVI, Cols. 1830–1, 24 September 1931; Vol. XXLVII, Col. 196, 29 September 1931.
11. ibid, debate on Budget, Vol. XXLVI, Cols. 358–64, 10 September 1931.
12. ibid, Finance (No. 2) Bill, 1931, Vol. CCLVI, Cols. 1733–40, 23 September 1931.
13. Statement 'Women and Political Situation', drafted for the 1931 Election. S.J.C. Records, Labour Party Library.
14. *The Labour Woman*, Editor's letter, October 1931.

Chapter 23 The last Campaign

1. D. N. Pritt, *From Left to Right*, p.31.
2. ibid, p.32.
3. ibid, p.29.
4. ibid, p.31.
5. *Bulletin of the North East Labour History Society*, No. 20, p.12.
6. Constituency Correspondence, Marion Phillips Archive, Labour Party Library.
7. *The Labour Woman*, February & March, 1931.
8. ibid, November 1931, Editor's letter.
9. ibid, November 1931, Editor's letter.
10. ibid, October 1931, Editor's letter.
11. ibid, December 1931, Editor's letter.
12. ibid.
13. S. J. C. Archives, Labour Party Library.
14. Private Correspondence, letter from M. Gibb.
15. *The Labour Woman*, Tributes, March 1931.
16. ibid, Editorial letter, January 1932.
17. Tributes, March 1932, p.42.
18. ibid, Tributes, March 1932, p.34.
19. Private correspondence.
20. *The Daily Herald*, 25 January 1932.
21. *The Manchester Guardian*, 25 January 1932.
22. *The Labour Woman*, 1969, Socialist Women Pioneers No. 2 — Marion Phillips by L. Middleton.
23. ibid, Tributes, MArch 1932, p.42.
24. *Morning Post*, 25 January 1932, and *Manchester Guardian*, 25 January 1932.
25. *Who's Who*, 1927, Marion Phillips entry.
26. *Daily Herald*, 25 January 1932.
27. *The Labour Woman*, Tributes, March 1932 & editor's letter September 1931, p.39
28. ibid, Tributes, March 1932, p.38.
29. ibid..
30. ibid.
31. ibid.
32. *The Daily Herald*, Hannen Swafer,28 January 1932.
33. *The Labour Woman*, March 1932, p.36.
34. ibid, p.34.

35. ibid, p.35.
36. ibid, p.35.
37. *The Book of the Labour Party*, Vol III, p.263.
38. *The Labour Woman*, March 1932, p.41.
39. Private correspondence.
40. *The Labour Woman*, March 1932, p.42.
41. ibid, p.44.
42. Rebecca West, 'Women as Brainworker's in *Women and the Labour Party*.

Bibliography

Books & booklets

—	*Australian Dictionary of Biography*, pp.216–7, Melbourne, 1966.
Andrews, E.	*A Woman's Work is Never Done*, Cymric Co., Rhondda, 1949.
Bellamy, J. & Saville, J. (eds.)	*National Dictionary of Labour Biography*, Vols I–VII, University of Hull.
Blatchford, R.	*My Eighty Years*, Cassell, London, 1931.
Bondfield, M.	*A Life's Work*, Hutchinson, 1949.
Brookes, P.	*Women at Westminster: an account of women in the British Parliament, 1918–1966, London, 1967.*
—	*Bulletin of the North East Labour History Society*, Vol 20, 1986.
Bunbury, Sir H.N. (ed.)	*Lloyd George's Ambulance Wagon: Memoirs of A. J. Braithwaite*, Methuen, 1957.
Chapman, M.	*The Humanist Jew*, Victoria, Australia, 1981.
Cole, M. I.	*The Diaries of Beatrice Webb*, Vol. I, 1912–24, Longman, 1952.
	Makers of the Labour Movement, Longman, 1948.
	The Story of Fabian Socialism, Heinemann, 1961.
Collette, C.	*For Labour and For Women*, Manchester U.P., 1987.
	The Women's Labour League, 1906–18.
Dawes, F.	*Not in front of the Servants*, Wayland, 1973.
Fox, Len	*E. Phillips Fox and His Family*, Sydney, 1985.
Gregg, P.	*A Social and Economic History of Britain, 1760–1955*, Harrap, 1956.
Hamilton, M. A.	*Arthur Henderson,*
	Margaret Bondfield, London, 1924.
	Mary Macarthur — a Biographical Sketch, L. Parsons, 1925.
Hansard	*Parliamentary Debates, July 1929–end Sept. 1931.*
Henderson, A.	*M. A. Hamilton*, London, 1938.
Hollis, P.	*Ladies Elect: Women in English Local Government, 1865–1914*, Clarendon Press, Oxford, 1987.
—	*Labour's Who's Who, 1924–29*, Labour Party Publishing Co.
Lewenhak, S.	*Women and Trade Unions*, E. Benn, 1977.
Llewelyn Davies, M. (ed.)	*Life As We Have Known It*, Hogarth, 1931.
Lloyd George, D.	*War Memoirs*, Vol. I & II, London, 1934–6.
Longman, M.	*National Dictionary of Labour Biography*, Longman,
MacDonald, R.	*D. Marquand*, Jonathan Cape, 1977.
Manning, L.	*A Life for Education*, 1970.
Masterman, C.F.G.	*England After the War*, London, 1922.
Mowatt, C.C.	*Britain Between the Wars*, Methuen, 1955.
Murtagh, J.	*The Health Implications of Building Design*, London.
Owen, F.	*Tempestuous Journey. Lloyd George His Life and Times*, Hutchinson, 1954.
Phillips, M.	*The Needs of Little Children*, London, 1912.
	The Green-Sprig Party — A Story for Young People, London, 1913.

	The School Doctor and the Home, London, 1913.
	How to do the Work of the League, London, 1914.
(ed. with A.S.	*Women and the Labour Party*, London, 1918.
Lawrence &	
G. Tuckwell)	
	The Organisation of Women Within the Labour Party, London, 1921.
	Women's Work in the Labour Party: Notes for Speakers and Workers' Classes, London, 1923.
	Women and the Miners' Lock-Out: the Story of the Women's Committee for the Relief of the Miners' Wives and Children, London, 1927.
	Socialism and Home, London, 1931.
Pritt, D.N.	*From Left to Right—Autobiography of D. R. Pritt*, Part I, Lawrence & Wishart, London, 1965–6.
Reeves, P.	*Fabian Tract, No. 10*, 'Life on a Pound a Week'.
Reid, M.O.	*The Ladies Came to Stay*,
Runciman, W.J.	*Relative Deprivation and Social Justice*, Routledge & Keegan Paul, 1966.
Skidelsky, R.	*Politicians and the Slump*, Macmillan, 1967.
	Sounvenir, Women's Labour League, 1909.
Tracey, H. (ed.)	*Book of the Labour Party: Its History, Growth, Policy, and Leaders*, Vols I, II, III, Caxton, London, n.d.
	The British Labour Party: Its History, Growth, Policy, and Leaders, Vols I, II, III, Caxton, London, 1948.
Werstheimer, E.	*Portrait of the Labour Party*, Putnam, 1929.
Williams, F.	*Fifty Years March: The Rise of the Labour Party*, Odhams, 1950.

Articles and Journals

Callcott, M.	'Dr Marion Phillips, Labour M.P. for Sunderland, 1929–31', *Bulletin of the North East Labour History Society*, Vol. XX, p.9, 1986.
Coleman, A.	'Utopia on Trial', *British Journal of Psychiatry*.
Drake, B.	'Middle Class Women and Industrial Legislation';
	'New Bills and Old Bogies', *The Labour Woman*, Aug. 1924.
	English History Annual Register, 1929–30, PRO.
Freeman, H.(ed.)	*British Journal of Psychology*,
Gibb, M.	'Diamond Jubilee Gala 1983 — A Memory', Durham County Labour Advisory Council, 1983.
Glasier, K. B.	'The Working Woman's Battle with Dirt', *Women and the Labour Party*, 1918.
Kingston, B.	'Yours Very Truly, Marion Phillips', *Women at Work*, Australian Society for the Study of Labour History, Sydney, 1975.
Llewelyn Davies, M.	'The Claims of Women and Children, *Women and the Labour Party*, 1918.
Longman, M.	'Women and Internationalism', *Women and the Labour Party*, 1918.
Marks, Lawrence	'Urban Humanity', *Weekend Observer*, Aug. 7, 1987.
Middleton, Lucy	'Labour Pioneers (No. 2)', *The Labour Woman*, 1969.
Phillips, Marion	'The Policy of the Labour Party', *The Labour Woman*, Dec. 1918.
	'Birth Control: A Plea for Careful Consideration', *The Labour Woman*, March 1924.
	'Maternity: a Primary Problem of Socialist Policy', *The Labour Magazine*, 7 May, 1928.
(ed.)	'The Cry of the Backwoodswomen', *The Labour Woman*, Jan. 1925.

'Discussion on Houses Utopian and How to Get Them', *The Labour Woman,* July 1913.

Sanderson-Furniss 'The Citizenship of Women', *The Book of the Labour Party,* Vol II, 1925. A.D.

Reports and Journals

Hansard's Parliamentary Debates, July 1929– end Sept. 1931.

10 December, 1929. Unemployment Insurance (No. 2) Bill. Cols. 356–8, 5th Series, Vol. CCXXXIII.

8 April, 1930. Housing (No. 2) Bill, Cols. 2042–4, 5th Series, Vol. CCCCCVII.

10 April, 1930. Questions on Housing, Col. 2377, 5th Series, Vol.CCXXXVII.

14 April, 1930. Question on Training Schemes, Col. 2633, 5th Series, Vol. CCXXXVII.

4 November, 1930. Debate on the Economic Situation, Cols. 771–4, 5th Series, Vol. CCXLIV.

18th November, 1930. Agricultural Land Utilisation (Money) Bill (allotments and small holdings), Cols. 364–7, 5th Series, Vol. CCXLV.

28 November 1930. 2nd Reading The Children's (Provisaion of Footwear) Bill. Moved by Col. Watts Morgan, Cols. 1755–6, 5th Series, Vol. CCXLV.

Debrett (House of Commons), 1930.

I.L.P. Annual Reports.

The Labour Party Conference Reports.

The Women's Labour League Annual Conference Reports.

The Labour Women's Annual Conference Reports.

The Labour and Socialist International Annual Conference Reports.

The League Leaflet (1911 to May 1913).

The Labour Woman, (May 1913–1932, also 1965 and 1969).

The Labour Magazine.

Reports from the Coalfields, 1926.

Report and Proceedings of the Third Women's Labour and Socialist International Conference, Brussels, 1928.

London School of Economics Register, 1934.

Minority Report of the Royal Commission on the Poor Laws and the Relief of Distress, Cmd. 4499, PRO.

Civil War Workers Committee, Cmd 9117, 9192, 9228, 1918.

Ministry of Reconstruction Women's Advisory Committee on the Domestic Service Problem, xxix, 1919.

Evidence before the Departmental Committee on the Employment of Women and Young Persons on the Two Shift System, xix, 1920.

The Speaker's Conference on Electoral Reform, 1929–30, *The British Labour Party,* Vol II, pp.203–5.

Letter from Viscount Ullswater to the Prime Minister, 17/7/30, HLRO, 1930.

Hansard Cols. 1733-1740, Vol CCXLVII, 3 Feb. 1931. The Representation of the People (No. 2) Bill.

Macmillan Report on Finance and Industry. Cmd. 3897. Minutes of Evidence,
    HMSO, 1931.
Inter-Departmental Committee on the Rent Restriction Acts (Marley Committee)
    HLG 41/35, 1930–31, PRO.

Newspapers
Daily Herald
Manchester Guardian
News Chronicle
Morning Post
The Times
Arbeiter Zeitung

Unpublished works
National Museum of Labour History, Manchester:
        Standing Joint Committee Reports and Records. Labour Party Dom. Series.
        File on Domestic Service including Domestic Workers' Charter and
        miscellaneous correspondence addressed to Dr Marion Phillips, especially
            between 1923 and 1930.
        Also Consumer Council files and the Phillips Archive Series — cc–ccc etc.;
            cc–mill etc.; cc–gen etc.
Phillips, M.: A Colonial Autocracy. New South Wales Under Governor Macquarie,
    1810–1821, Phd. Thesis, London School of Economics Library, 1909.

Index